T0374223

GLIMPSE OF GLORY

Understanding Revelation

RON MEACOCK

WESTBOW
PRESS®
A DIVISION OF THOMAS NELSON
& ZONDERVAN

WestBow Press books may be ordered through booksellers or by contacting:

WestBow Press
A Division of Thomas Nelson & Zondervan
1663 Liberty Drive
Bloomington, IN 47403
www.westbowpress.com
844-714-3454

All scripture quotations are taken from the World English Bible. Public domain.

ISBN: 978-1-6642-7418-1 (sc)
ISBN: 978-1-6642-7419-8 (hc)
ISBN: 978-1-6642-7420-4 (e)

Library of Congress Control Number: 2022914077

Print information available on the last page.

WestBow Press rev. date: 08/19/2022

DEDICATION

This commentary is dedicated to Ms. Church and Ms. Butt,
who shared their Christian witness with me as a child and
to George Hoffman of Tear Fund. One day, we shall all
see not just a glimmer but the fulness of God's glory!

"I am deeply impressed with the detailed information provided. Excellent references to Christian and secular history interest the reader to dig deeper for their knowledge and understanding. This book is well worth reading. His unique perspective provides an excellent basis for study, discussion, and internalization."

– Pastor Lionel A. Pye

"Glimpse of Glory" is an insightful, in-depth exploration of the book of Revelation that seeks to shed light on its context and give readers a better understanding of its true meaning."

– WestBow Editing Team

"Glimpse of Glory" offers much that will help locate the complex imagery of Revelation in the life and experience of the early church and its broader historical and narrative context, making its complexities more accessible without diminishing their power. Moreover, it will help the reader understand how this biblical text has shaped, challenged, and envisioned the life of one who is an evangelist at heart.

– The Ven. Peter B Rouch

CONTENTS

REVELATION'S PROPHET JOHN

Revelation's prophet John is writing to us from c90-95 AD. An early part of John's Gospel from c135 AD gives us this date. Papyrus Forty-Six describes Paul's thorn in the flesh (2 Cor. 12:7) and mentions that a man in Christ fourteen years ago went up to the third heaven (2 Cor. 12:2). This reference sounds very much like John of Patmos' revelation. John wrote his Gospel after the other Gospels.

Revelation's contents divide into ten segments.

- Introduction (Rev. 1:1—20).
- Seven Letters (Rev. 2:1—3:22).
- Heavenly Throne Room (Rev. 4:1—5:14).
- Seven Seals (Rev. 6:1—8:1).
- Seven Trumpets (Rev. 8:2—11:19).
- Seven Signs (Rev. 12:1—14:20).
- Seven Bowls (Rev. 15:1—19:5).
- Coming Again (Rev. 19:6—20:15).
- New Jerusalem (21:1—22:5)
- Conclusion (Rev. 22:6—21).

These writings were on papyrus, a material similar to brown paper as a writing surface. Workers produced it from the pith of a wetland grass-like plant, *Cyperus papyrus*. Tomb paintings on it are trendy today as tourist keepsakes from Egypt, and my wife and I have four of them on the walls of our home.

Many Biblical Scholars identify Revelation's writer as John, the son of Zebedee, one of the disciples of Jesus. The early church leaders, Justin Martyr,[1] Irenaeus,[2] Melito of Sardis,[3] and Clement of Alexandria,[4] also believed the author to be John the Evangelist, a close friend of Jesus.

Scholars confirm John of Patmos was also the author of John's Gospel and John's Epistles. He called himself "the disciple whom Jesus loved" and spoke fondly of his Lord and Savior. Communicating to us through his scribe Prochorus from his cave on the Greek prison Isle of Patmos, he reveals divine truths to us today and our destiny tomorrow.

Students know John by many titles and sometimes refer to him as John the Evangelist, John the Divine, John the Elder, John the Presbyter, or the apostle John. In this study of Revelation, I will use "John of Patmos" in "Glimpse of Glory" to refer to John. He was a prophet and visionary and bound by an oath in Revelation to write down only what he saw, nothing more and nothing less. He was faithful in that task, even though he did not always understand what he was describing.

John of Patmos gives us a clue in Revelation about why we are born and our eternal destiny! We are shown the radiant Jesus in all his glory in the heavenly realms speaking to his church through graphic word pictures. We all need to seek the Lord's glory in our lives. We are reminded of the Battle Hymn of the Republic by the American poet, author, and abolitionist Julia Ward Howe.

> "Mine eyes have seen the glory of the coming of
> the Lord;
> He is trampling out the vintage where the grapes
> of wrath are stored;

---

[1] (100—165 AD).
[2] (130—202 AD).
[3] Melito of Sardis coined the phrase "Old Testament." (?—180 AD).
[4] (150—215 AD).

He hath loosed the fateful lightning of His terrible
swift sword;
His truth is marching on."[5]

"In the beauty of the lilies, Christ was born across
the sea,
With a glory in His bosom that transfigures you
and me.
As He died to make men holy, let us die to make
men free,
While God is marching on."

This magnificent song was one of Winston Churchill's favorites
and was sung at his funeral in 1965. Manchester United and other
soccer fans still sing it as an anthem during their matches.

Warren Carroll[6] writes that church leaders worldwide at the
Council of Nicaea in 325 AD confirmed that John, the disciple
Jesus loved, was Revelation's author. The Christian Emperor
Constantine financed and arranged the council meeting and
made a ceremonial entrance at its opening in early June 325 AD.
Eusebius described Constantine as "proceeding through the
assembly like some heavenly messenger, clothed in glittering
raiment with rays of light, reflecting the glowing radiance of his
purple robe, and adorned with the brilliant splendor of gold and
precious stones."[7]

John of Patmos' name means "God has been gracious." After
being plunged into a vat of boiling oil and miraculously surviving,
the authorities banished him to the Island of Patmos! To this day,
icons bearing his image show a scar down one side of his head
and face. He was the only one of the apostles of Jesus who lived
a long life and died a natural death. Kings, church leaders, and
public officials visited Patmos to seek his godly advice towards
the end of his life.

---

[5] Lyrics by Julia Ward Howe (1819-1910). Music by William Steffe (1830-1890).
[6] Of Thornhill, Ontario, Canada (1933-2015).
[7] The Building of Christendom, (Christendom College Press) (1987).

God showed beautiful things to John of Patmos in a spectacular and mysterious vision. He was not attempting to predict the future here but to faithfully record and obediently describe the wonders shown to him. We make a grave mistake if we reconstruct a definitive calendar of future events from these chapters. He is told not to write down on certain occasions what he saw. Only Christ himself will fill in the blanks when he comes!

Unfortunately, many commentators unfairly present Revelation as sensational and incomprehensible. On the contrary, it is a beautiful biblical book. John of Patmos frames it in Roman customs and the ethos of the last part of the first century AD. No commentator, in my estimation, has contributed more to its study and understanding than Dr. William Barclay.[8] He was enormously popular in his lifetime and wrote Bible study commentaries on most Bible books through the St Andrew Press in Scotland. He spoke daily to ordinary folk in his radio broadcasts about Revelation and other Bible books in simple terms to encourage and educate workers.

Barclay concluded a distinguished ministry as a Glasgow University professor and passed away in 1968. Two years later, I started my ministry in Glasgow as a young man at the Bible Training Institute, which later became the International Christian College. Though we never crossed paths physically, he left a deep spiritual impression on me from his writings. More than anyone else, he brought the scriptures alive. He drew on scholarship but also wrote in a universally accessible style.

I love the story that when asked to read a lesson in the Presbyterian church he attended, Barclay pulled out the Hebrew and Greek originals from his pocket and translated them on the fly. In his book, "The Mind of Christ," Dr. Barclay stated his aim to make the figure of Jesus more vividly alive so that we may know him better and love him more. I pray this little book on Revelation will do the same for you!

---

[8] He was a distinguished Scottish author, radio and television presenter, Church of Scotland minister, and Professor of Divinity and Biblical Criticism at Glasgow University (1907-1978 AD).

I owe a debt of gratitude to the many scholarly works I have consulted over many years of study. Revelation has absorbed my energies as I have discovered more about it and its context. It may be a splendor-filled vision, but it is also written for ordinary folk, like you and I, to build us up and bless us. "Glimpse of Glory" takes the same approach as Dr. Barclay. Like those early Christians, I am confident we will grow in the Christian Faith as we study the Word of God. We will see Jesus of Nazareth as the eternal wondrous one in a new light. He may be our savior now, but we will see him, one day, as our glorious Lord.

Like John of Patmos, Habakkuk was a biblical prophet and the eighth of twelve minor prophets. Of the three chapters in his book, the first two are dialogues between God and himself. Habakkuk's prophecy came to us three thousand years ago as a precursor to Revelation's apocalypse. Before John of Patmos came on the scene, the prophet Habakkuk spoke and wrote of the end times in the seventh century BC. He related that the Lord told him to write the revelation.[9] He said, "Write the vision, and make it plain on tablets, that he who runs may read it. For the vision is yet for the appointed time, and it hurries toward the end and won't prove false. Though it takes time, wait for it; it will surely come; it won't delay" (Hab. 2:2—3).

Habakkuk's apocalypse brings us a fascinating forecast of future things. The Lord is the speaker, telling him to write down the revelation to encourage subsequent listeners. Today, we have his words authenticated by John of Patmos. We can be sure of the story's completion, whether for Habakkuk's listeners from three or four thousand years ago or other Christians a thousand years from now. Though we do not know the date or time, it is a certainty we should await. The end may appear at any time!

Question: "How would the fabulous scenes in Revelation have affected the practical disciple whom Jesus loved?"

---

[9] Perhaps indicating clay tablets

REVELATION'S
SYMBOLIC COLORS

Revelation's unfamiliar language and symbolic colors purposefully dot the pages of this biblical book. R. H. Charles wrote about apocalyptic texts, "This supernatural coloring will often strike the reader of this literature as fantastic, and at times bizarre; but this should not be permitted to obscure the reality which often lies behind these weird shadows."[10]

Colors symbolize various emotions impacting society. Using tints and numbers, John of Patmos purposely hides his intent and meaning from the ancient Roman authorities, but Christians and Jews understood to what he was inferring! They are of immense importance to understanding the text's meaning and subtleties as they were to John's readers.

We can begin with "white," which symbolizes purity, perfection, and innocence and explains why brides usually wear white dresses. It is the most popular car color in America, followed by black, with a twenty-four percent poll share. It is technically a "color without a hue" or an "achromatic color." Sir Isaac Newton[11] discovered that it was not a single color, for when a glass prism separated sunlight, it produced a rainbow color blend.[12] He wrote, "The most surprising and wonderful composition was whiteness. All the prism colors converge and are mixed, reproducing light,

---

[10] "The Book of Enoch" (300-200 BC) Introduction, ix. *Global Grey Publishing 2021*
[11] English mathematician, physicist, theologian, and author (1643—1727).
[12] The 1672 AD Royal Society's minutes refer to the color white.

entirely and perfectly white." There are endless variations of white, but top designers pick out "Cloud Nine" as the best of the top thirty-five or more alternatives.

Black, in contrast, often indicates darkness, death, and distress in the Bible. In society, it means mystery, elegance, and evil. However, black is also not considered a color. In times of mourning, people wear black clothing. Today, it has become standard attire for any ceremonial or formal occasion. The Bible also associates it with violence and evil, particularly the absence of God's presence.

The "Black Death," also known as the "Great Plague," occurred in Europe and Asia between 1347 and 1351 AD and resulted in an estimated seventy-five to two hundred million deaths. It killed thirty to sixty percent of Europe's population. In Revelation, the "black horse" is an example of its symbolic reference to death and destruction (Rev. 6:5). Covid-19 is another type of plague that has devastated communities worldwide, especially their most fragile, elderly and young members. Unsurprisingly, people try to play down the negatives of a pandemic even by calling the present outbreak "Covid-19" rather than an epidemic or a plague! When a death occurs on a cruise ship, the intercom announces "Operation Rising Star" to alert the crew but not spook the other passengers!

The color purple describes the deep rich shades between crimson and violet. It is symbolic of creativity, royalty, and wealth in society. It was costly to produce in biblical times because of the rarity of natural dyes! Luxurious purple and red silk clothing were rare, limited to royalty and nobility, and more valuable than gold. Israeli Antiques Authority expert Dr. Naama Sukenik[13] discovered purple cloth from the time of King David in 1000 BC and noted that the gorgeous color had not faded! We also read about purple in the wilderness tabernacle, "They shall take away the ashes from the altar, and spread a purple cloth on it" (Num. 4:13). Over time, purple became a symbol of wealth and authority

---

[13] The Slaves' Hill archeological dig 137 miles south of Jerusalem.

worn by Roman emperors, kings, and princes. Bishops still wear purple in modern times.

The color "red" in the Bible is a blood indicator and warns of "danger, murder, rage, and anger." In society, it means "passion, love, and anger." Highway stop signs are colored red to catch our attention and alert us to danger. In earlier times, the word "red" in English represented any color between purple and orange.[14] The fiery red horse is another excellent example. "Another came out: a red horse. To him who sat on it was given power to take peace from the earth, and that they should kill one another. There was given to him a great sword" (Rev. 6:4).

Wearing red in sixteenth-century England was a great privilege and honor because of its scarcity. Queen Elizabeth the First[15] was so impressed with the plays of William Shakespeare[16] that she permitted him the honor of wearing scarlet silk. King James the First[17] followed Elizabeth on the throne and recorded Shakespeare as one of his servants in the Grand Accounts Book, for which he received four and a half yards of red cloth, "a color befitting his status as a Royal Court member."

On the other hand, blue means holiness. In society, it means calm, responsibility, and sadness. Aaron's blue robes are significant for the Lord God commanded, "You shall make the robe of the ephod all of blue" (Ex. 28:31). He ordered, "You shall make a plate of pure gold, and engrave on it, like the engravings of a signet, 'HOLY TO YAHWEH.' You shall put it on a lace of blue, and it shall be on the sash" (Ex. 28:36—37). Blue cloth also covered the curtain in the Holy of Holies. "When the camp moves forward, Aaron shall go in with his sons; and they shall take down the veil of the screen, cover the ark of the Testimony with it, put a covering of sealskin on it, spread a blue cloth over it, and put in its poles" (Num. 4:5—6).

---

[14] The word *Orange* was first recorded in 1380 AD, describing any color between red and yellow, like fire and carrots!

[15] (1558-1603)

[16] (1564-1616)

[17] (1603-1625)

The ancients produced blue color from the crushed semi-precious stone "lapis lazuli," which was more precious than gold. This blue was as "bright blue as the sky" and "like the skies for clearness" (Ex. 24:10). These semi-precious stones were mined in Afghanistan and ground up to make the pigment "ultramarine." Artists today still favor its intensity and brightness.

Blue carpeting in many church sanctuaries signifies a special and holy place. Another blue color, "turquoise," was selected by Muslims in Constantinople and used widely to decorate their mosques. It became known as "the color of the Turks" or "turquoise!" The two horizontal bands of blue and yellow on the Ukrainian flag were adopted in 1848 and hoisted over Kyiv Town Hall. Blue represents peace and the sky's appearance, and yellow is the symbol of prosperity depicting its vast golden wheat fields.

Yellow in nature describes the color of gold, butter, and ripe lemons. In society, it indicates happiness, hope, and deceit. Pale yellow in Revelation points to one's end as it is often the skin color as life ebbs away. An example of this is the Pale Horse. "And behold a pale horse, and the name of he who sat on it was Death. Hades followed with him" (Rev. 6:8). "Hades" also may be translated as "Hell."

Revelation's colors may be fascinating to us, but they should not halt us in our studies. Instead, try to look beyond them to their context's subtle meanings. Let them affect your experience of the scriptural text, and you will get the greatest blessing from the Word of God.

Question: "What colors are most important to you? What do they mean?"

REVELATION'S DEVOTIONAL NUMBERS

Numbers in the biblical text have significant symbolic meaning for Jewish and Christian readers. Assigning a numerical value to a word or phrase is technically known as *gematria* from the Greek word meaning "geometry." So, MMXIV in Roman numerals gives us the date 2014. The M equals one thousand, the X equals ten, and the IV means four. Similarly, Greek numerals also each bear values in which "alpha" equals one, beta is two, iota means ten and omega indicates eight hundred. So one can turn a word into a series of numbers that add to a value. Mathematicians adapted the Hebrew equivalent in which aleph is one, and tau means four hundred, from the Greek numerals system in the second century BC.

The number "seven" indicates a conclusion and implies that this process, number, or act is fulfilled. The seventh day of creation is when God finished. "God blessed the seventh day and made it holy because he rested in it from all his work of creation which he had done" (Gen. 2:2—3). Notice the emphasis here on the words "the seventh day" and "the work he had done" in the Genesis scripture.

The book of Revelation has thirteen thematic groups of seven

- Spirits of God (Rev. 1:4, 4:5, 5:6),
- Churches or assemblies (Rev. 1:11),
- Golden lamp stands (Rev. 1:12),

- Stars (Rev. 1:16),
- Lamps of fire (Rev. 4:5),
- Seals (Rev. 5:1),
- Horns and eyes (Rev. 5:6),
- Angels and trumpets (Rev. 8:2),
- Thunders (Rev. 10:3),
- Crowns (Rev. 12:3),
- Last plagues (Rev. 15:1),
- Golden bowls (Rev. 15:7),
- Kings (Rev. 17:10).

In other New Testament places, seven is a prominent number. We find seven Holy Spirit gifts for our encouragement and support (Rom 12:6—8).

- Prophecy (Rom. 12:6),
- Service (Rom. 12:7),
- Teaching (Rom. 12:7),
- Encouragement (Rom. 12:8),
- Giving (Rom. 12:8),
- Leadership (Rom. 12:8),
- Showing Mercy (Rom. 12:8).

There are seven deadly sins comprising lust, gluttony, greed, laziness, anger, envy, and pride though the Bible does not mention them as a group.

Surprisingly, J. L. Meredith[18] also lists seven suicides

- Abimelech (Judg. 9:54),
- Sampson (Judg. 16:30),
- Saul (1 Sam. 31:4),
- Saul's armor-bearer (1 Sam. 31:5),
- Ahithophel (2 Sam. 17:23),
- Zimri (1 Kgs. 16:18),
- Judas (Matt. 27:5).

---

[18] "Meredith's Big Book of Bible Lists" (Inspirational Press NY; 1980) pp.143-144.

There are many other references to seven in the Old Testament, including seven of every clean animal entering Noah's ark. Yahweh said to Noah, "You shall take seven pairs of every clean animal with you, the male and his female. Of the animals that are not clean, take two, the male and his female. Also of the birds of the sky, seven and seven, male and female" (Gen. 7:2—3). We even find a child who sneezed seven times and opened his eyes after Elisha raised him from the dead! (2 Kgs. 4:32—35).

The number "seven" also features in the Gospels.

- Seven loaves (Matt. 15:32—37),
- Seventy-seven times or seventy times seven times to forgive (Matt. 18:21—23),
- Seven demons driven out of Mary Magdalene (Luke 8:2),
- Seven last sayings or words of Jesus from the cross.

The "Seventh Heaven,"[19] or the highest of the celestial spheres in cosmology, is a biblical concept with deep Jewish and Christian roots related to the Muslim idea of Paradise. The "Seventh Heaven" has come to mean a state of extreme joy or ecstasy!

The number "three and a half" seems odd because it characterizes an imperfect or incomplete time or an unfulfilled event. It is the opposite of the number seven, which indicates completeness. For example, "Elijah was a man with a nature like ours, and he earnestly prayed that it might not rain, and it didn't rain on the earth for three years and six months" (James 5:17). The phrase "time, times, and half a time" is another way of saying "three and a half." It is present elsewhere as "forty-two months" or "one thousand two hundred and sixty days."[20] God nourished the woman "for a time, and times, and half a time from the face of the serpent" (Rev. 12:14). The woman fled into the wilderness, where God might "nourish her 'one thousand two hundred

---

[19] also an American family drama television series
[20] To be mathematically accurate, the Jewish equivalent to one thousand two hundred sixty days would be one thousand two hundred and seventy-seven days, as their calendar is not the same length as today's Western solar calendar.

sixty days" (Rev. 12:6). "Forty-two months" was the duration of Antiochus IV Epiphanes'[21] vicious persecution

"Ten" is the symbolic number used for eternity, like a gold wedding band that goes on endlessly or the infinity symbol. This point is not lost on a bride and groom when they commit themselves "till death do us part" at their wedding ceremony.

"Twelve" indicates the "kingdom of God," with "three," being God's signature number multiplied by the human number "four" to equal "twelve." The number "twelve" in the Gregorian calendar defines the time in watches, computers, clocks today, and even some currencies, such as the old British Imperial System of pounds, shillings, and pence. Similarly, our sixty seconds in a minute, sixty minutes in an hour, and three hundred and sixty degrees in a circle originate in a cuneiform writing system in ancient Mesopotamian society from BC 5,000!

A fourth-century soldier who worshiped the emperor's image might have a forearm tattoo mark of "six hundred and sixty-six." If this number connects to the beast, those who worship the beast from the sea are his devoted followers. John writes that the beast number is the number of a man. "His number is six hundred sixty-six" (Rev. 13:18). The beast brands adherents with this number in this passage, which points to the Greek form of Nero's name.

A few early manuscripts have the number "six hundred and sixteen" [22] in place of "six hundred sixty-six." Interestingly, this also points to Emperor Nero, for the Latin form also adds to Nero's name.[23] Another early writing has the number written out in full as "six hundred and sixteen," as if the writer wanted to emphasize and make a particular point by it!

Whatever the specific application of "six hundred sixty-six" or

---

[21] (BC 215—164). His detractors disparagingly called him Antiochus *Epimanes* or "the Mad One," a wordplay on his name *Epiphanes* in BC 167. The Greek king Antiochus ruthlessly persecuted Judean and Samarian followers and the Jewish Maccabees.

[22] like Codex Ephraemi Rescriptus

[23] Papyrus 115. Revelation's oldest preserved manuscript from c317 AD.

"six hundred sixteen," whether to President Putin, Adolf Hitler, the world's unified governments, communism, Napoleon, or Emperor Nero, this number symbolizes worldwide dominion and an unholy force's evil. His design is to undo Christ's work and overthrow his followers.

Interestingly, the name "Jesus," when added up in the same way, gives us the Greek number "eight hundred and eighty-eight." The Jesus number is more significant and outdoes them all! Watch for these Revelation numbers as you read, understand their intended interpretation, and view them in their context to illuminate your reading!

Question: "Discuss the symbolism of numbers. How do they affect your view of the book of Revelation?"

1

REVELATION WORDS
OF JESUS

1:1 "This is the **Revelation of Jesus Christ,**
which God gave him to **show to his servants**
the **things which must happen soon.**"
(Rev. 1:1 emphases added).

1:1 | The **revelation of Jesus Christ** is sometimes called the Revelation "from Jesus Christ" or "the Apocalypse." It contains words from Jesus, not John, as might be the case in an ordinary book authored by an average person. Here Jesus is dictating directly to John of Patmos, through his angel servants, what to write.

1:1 | The opening phrase of the **Revelation** scroll's first page gives the biblical book its name. In the same way, "Genesis" in the Old Testament is named from its scroll's opening Hebrew word *Bereshit*, meaning "in the beginning." The Greek for Genesis is *gena*, meaning "birth," and its roots mean "origin, source, beginning, nativity, generation, production, and creation."

1:1 | Dr. William Barclay"[24] explains that the Greek word for "**Revelation**" is *apokalupsis*. This word combines *apo*, meaning "away from," and *kalupsis*, meaning "a veiling." "Revelation"

---

[24] "The Daily Study Bible" rev. ed. (Toronto G.R. Welch).

therefore means "an unveiling." Veils are common in many cultures, including Judaism, Islam, and Christianity. Veiled head coverings are traditional Muslim women's apparel. There are five types of veil. A "Burka" covers the eyes with a mesh screen, but a "Niqab," meaning "full veil," is open across the eyes. A "Hijab" is a head scarf covering the hair and neck but not the face, and the "Chador" is a full-length cloak. The "Dupatta" is a long scarf loosely draped around the head and shoulders. This biblical book unveils God's truths and makes them known to us.

1:1 | John of Patmos presents **Revelation**'s message in terms and picture language that the people of his day would understand. "Revelation" means disclosing and revealing the future Jesus. We see him not as a preacher from Galilee or the Savior on the cross but as the universal Lord, the "Great I am." Revelation is "an unveiling" of God's truth.

1:1 | Jewish scholars included many books in their canon called "Apocalypses," unveiling the end-times and the blessedness to come. These biblical pictures are to show his servants what will soon take place. **Revelation** has Old Testament parallels in Ezekiel, Habakkuk, and Daniel and is a development of these books in that it focuses on the words and actions of Jesus. "Revelation," meaning "disclosing a fact, uncovering a secret, or even interpreting dreams," was not originally a religious term.

1:1 | "Apocalypse" is a unique name for a particular literature type. Genuine apocalyptic literature unveils details of the unseen spiritual realm and indicates its impact on history. It refers to the end of the world, where the Greek phrase *apokalupsis eschaton* means the "**revelation** at the end of the age." Interestingly, apocalyptic literature was popular in the apostle John's day and in our own time in literary works such as Margaret Atwood's "Oryx and Crake."

1:1 | Many apocalyptic books are wild and incomprehensible, attempting to describe the indefinable. The subject matter with which **Revelation** deals is why it is sometimes hard to understand. The revelation from Jesus begins with God, the fountain of all truth. Whether scientific, medical, or otherwise, every discovered truth is God's gift. People do not create truthfulness but receive it from God whether they realize it or not. This reception comes from diligently seeking and reverently waiting for it.

1:1 | Many other apocalyptic documents were circulating about the time when John of Patmos was recording this **revelation** vision, such as the "Apocalypse of Baruch."[25] Later, authors wrote the Gospels of Peter[26] and Thomas[27]and, in more recent days, the Gospel of Abraham.[28] It became popular to attribute writings to famous biblical people. Early church leaders rejected all these as fake and did not include them in the biblical canon. It was crystal clear to the apostolic fathers, as it is to us today, that many apocalyptic books are not of the same quality or authenticity as the biblical ones. God's inspired Word has the distinctive mark of being genuine, which these other secondary readings do not have.

1:1 | Paul later used **Revelation's** phrase "apocalypse" differently and explained that he traveled to Jerusalem by *apokalupsis*. He went because God revealed that he wanted him to go there. He wrote, "for I didn't receive it from man, nor was I taught it, but it came to me through revelation of Jesus Christ" (Gal. 1:12). Paul received the gospel through the *apokalupsis* of Jesus Christ.

1:1 | Today, the preacher's message is also "apocalyptic." God reveals to his ministering servants his mysteries, especially concerning the coming of Jesus Christ. *Apokalupsis* is Jesus Christ's **revelation** of God's power and holiness. It will mean judgment and justice for some, but it will be an unveiling of praise, glory, grace, and joy for others.

1:1 | God gives us this **Revelation** teaching directly from the Lord Jesus. The Bible stresses his utter dependence on his heavenly Father. Jesus said, "My teaching is not mine but his who sent me" (John 7:16). He added later, "For I spoke not from myself, but the Father who sent me, he gave me a commandment, what I

---

[25] (100—200 AD).
[26] (200 AD).
[27] (60—200 AD).
[28] around 1835 AD.

should say, and what I should speak" (John 12:49). Jesus Christ's revelation from God highlights their reliance on one another. Therefore, Jesus said to them, "When you have lifted up the Son of Man, then you will know that I am he, and I do nothing of myself, but as my Father taught me, I say these things" (John 8:28). The words of Jesus are valid, so they are unique and final.

1:1 | The Holy Spirit's work has been intricately connected with **Revelation** from the earliest times. The vision God gave John of Patmos came through him, showing us what will soon occur and conveying insight as we read this intriguing document. God reveals Revelation through the Holy Spirit to all who want to understand.

1:1 | The term **servant** in this verse is from the Greek *doulos*, meaning "enslaved person." John is a Roman prisoner on Patmos Isle, but he is, more importantly, Jesus Christ's servant. "His servants" in this verse may mean "you, men or women of God." Sometimes John and his scribe, Prochorus, are told not to write down something he sees but to leave it hidden. Some of Revelation must remain concealed for the time being for reasons known only to God, who will reveal all when Jesus comes back.

1:1 | John of Patmos further emphasizes the need **to show his servants** how to read Christ's revelation carefully and not reconstruct it according to their ideas. Prophecy is more than telling the future; God's essential characteristics are behind the predictions. He frames prophecy and reflects his qualities. As we read of Jesus in Revelation, he intends us to get to know him personally, copy his attributes, and receive his reader blessings.

1:1 | Revelation is also the "unveiling" of **the things which must happen soon**. History is not haphazard, but it has a purpose. It is wrong to use it as a theological timetable for what might happen in the future, thousands of years from now or even next week. Jewish scholars anticipate that what must soon occur will follow the present evil age. Between the two end times, there will be a trial. Many Christians understand from the scriptures that this will last seven years before Christ's final victory.

1:1 | As you read about these end-times, allow their vivid word pictures to flow over you. Try to open yourself up to the Holy Spirit to help you understand the words of Jesus and what **will happen** in the near and distant future in the heavenly realm. God has created humans with thinking minds and caring hearts and speaks to us through our intellects and emotions. He does not usually convey the truth to someone too lazy to think but gives it to the one who waits in prayerful devotion. Devotional prayer and faith mean active, dedicated listening to God's voice in the scriptures.

Question: "Describe what an unveiling means to you. What have you already glimpsed that is new?"

2

ULTIMATE PURPOSE OF JESUS

1:1 "Which he sent and made known by
his angel to his **servant, John**."
(Rev. 1:1 emphases added).

1:1 | An "angel" is a supernatural being who is a messenger
or a ministering servant of God. We read of **his angel** addressing
John of Patmos in this first verse of Revelation. They look like
ordinary people though we don't generally recognize them if they
walk among us. We might think of a muscular man with wings,
such as in the painting "Angel of the Revelation" by William
Blake[29] or "The Wounded Angel" by Hugo Simberg, showing two
sullen boys carrying an injured one on a stretcher.[30] The movie
"Archangel Michael," played by John Travolta, gives us another
memorable and amusing impression of one who dropped little
white feathers from his wings wherever he went!

1:1 | Here, in Revelation, **angels** make known the words of
Jesus to John of Patmos. We read in the Acts of the Apostles that
angels "ordained the law." Stephen tells the High Priest, "You
received the law as it was ordained by angels, and didn't keep it!"
(Acts 7:53). Paul writes that the law "was ordained through angels

---

[29] (1757—1827).The painting shows a colossal figure with a tiny book in his hand.
[30] (1873-1917), voted Finland's national painting in 2006.

by the hand of a mediator" (Gal. 3:19). To "ordain" in this context is to "order" or "decree officially."

1:1 | Interestingly, there is a "wheel of **angels**," known as the "seventy-two names." This idea originates in Exodus, where 'The angel of God, who went before the camp of Israel, moved and went behind them" (Ex. 14:19). G. Lloyd Jones explains that Jewish mystics sought to overcome the doctrinal problems posed by God's transcendence and existence beyond the ordinary or physical level. His transcendence is an aspect of his nature and power wholly independent of the material universe and beyond all known physical laws. The word comes from the Latin meaning "going beyond." The question is, "how could God be present simultaneously in multiple places?" Strangely, "Transcendence" is also the name of a 2014 science fiction movie starring Johnny Depp and a familiar face, Morgan Freeman.

1:1 | To overcome this transcendence challenge, specific qualities, symbols, and prayers are assigned to seventy-two angels.[31] Jewish mystics[32] called this an emanation theory meaning something that flows from or originates in a source. The alphabet played an essential part in this concept. The seventy-two names were developed and made pronounceable by introducing the Hebrew *El* (merciful God) and *Ya* (strong God) to the four consonants of the name YHWH, which we write as Yahweh.

1:1 | Who was this **John** mentioned in the first verse of Revelation? The Council of Nicaea, in 325 AD, confirmed that John of Patmos authored Revelation, the Gospel of John, and John's Epistles in the church's approved Biblical canon. He is named the fourth of the Gospel writers with Matthew, Mark, and Luke. The letters' tone indicates his authority as a respected Christian leader in Ephesus in the First Century AD. John was known for his wisdom as a close disciple of Jesus.

1:1 | Revelation encourages Christians today, as in every century, to stand firm in their faith. **John** of Patmos, the disciple

---

[31] G. Lloyd Jones *"The Discovery of Hebrew in Tudor England: a third Language"* (New Hampshire, Manchester University Press).
[32] Between 1150 and 1200 AD.

of Jesus, is described as "his servant John" and Justin Martyr referred to him as Zebedee's son in the second century.[33] God entrusted Revelation's ultimate purpose and vision to him. Like angels, humans play an essential role in Jesus Christ's revelation and God's ultimate purpose in his coming. He seeks today to find people, like John, to whom he can entrust his truth and use as his mouthpiece. Your destiny might be as one he charges with a message for others.

1.1 | We don't have to understand every detail when seeing these scenes from God's **servant John** in our minds. We only need to allow the word pictures to flow over us. Everything points us to Christ, the apocalyptic Lord, for he is the glorious, victorious one who will burst onto the world stage at the appointed time. The message of "Revelation" is of the tremendous love, power, and justice of Jesus so that everyone will know that he is the great God! Those who love him will greet him with songs of praise but those who don't would rather not be there!

Question: "Does the Jesus of Revelation appear to be a different person than the Jesus of Nazareth?"

---

[33] Matthew lists the names of the twelve apostles with the son of Zebedee and his brother John amongst them (Matt. 10:2).

3

READER BLESSINGS

1:2 "Who **testified to God's word** and of the testimony of Jesus Christ, about everything that he saw. ³ **Blessed** is he who **reads** and those who **hear the words of the prophecy,** and keep the things that are written in it, for the **time is at hand."** (Rev. 1:2—3 emphases added).

1:2 | John was an eyewitness of the ministry of Jesus, a member of his inner circle, and his friend in Palestine as a young man. He **testified to God's word** and, as an elder statesman, received a remarkable vision of the same Jesus, but this time in heavenly glory. He urged his followers to read Christ's revelation and added that the one who reads this prophecy's[34] words and takes heart from it is blessed.

1:3 | In time, the "**reader**" became a significant official in the early church, more important even than a Priest or Deacon! One of Tertullian's[35] complaints against heretical sects was how a man speedily attained a reader's office without training. He wrote, "and so it comes to pass that today one man is their bishop and tomorrow another. Today, he is a deacon who tomorrow is a

---

[34] A "prophecy" is "a God-given vision of what lies ahead in both the immediate and long-term future."

[35] "On Prescription against Heretics 41." Tertullian was a respected church leader, apologist, and the earliest writer to use the word "Trinity." (160—220 AD).

reader." To be a reader was to play a vital and prominent role in the early church, unlike today, when anyone reads the lessons. It reflects how meaningful the Bible was to early Christians and should be to us today.

1:3 | Justin Martyr[36] gives us the oldest known account of a Christian worship service, including the **words of the prophecy.** It includes reading "the apostles' memoirs" or Gospels and the "prophets' writings" from the Old Testament."

1:3 | Those who read this biblical book's words are **blessed.** Acts describes an early church service when Paul and his companions "went into the synagogue on the Sabbath day and sat down. After reading the law and the prophets, the synagogue rulers asked them, "Brothers, if you have any word of exhortation for the people, speak" (Acts 13:14—15). In the Jewish synagogue, seven ordinary members read the scriptures to the congregation, although a Priest or Levite took precedence if they were in attendance. Paul may have been regarded as an honored teacher and asked to explain the scriptures they had heard. Later, the Christian church took much of its service order from the synagogue with scripture at its core.

1:3 | We should read the Bible aloud and in the quietness of our hearts. Interestingly, we encounter Hannah's silent prayer in the temple. She prayed in her heart, and her lips moved, but Eli did not hear her voice. He thought she was intoxicated and rebuked her, saying, "How long will you be drunk? Get rid of your wine!" (1 Sam. 1:14). Hannah explained that she was distraught and was pouring her soul out to the Lord. He then gave her his blessing.

1:3 | There are great **blessings** for those who read the scriptures. Revelation is the only biblical book that promises such benefits. Studying the Bible in our language is a great privilege, for, in past generations, men and women died and were tortured because they sought to pass on this beautiful Word of God. Today, translating the scriptures into other languages continues

---

[36] an early Christian apologist. (100—160 AD).

in remote and dangerous places. I recently read about a Bible translation into the Inuktitut language in the Canadian Arctic.

1:3 | Those who hear the Bible in English, French, Cree, or another tongue and who keep it know God's **blessing**. Reading God's word today is our blessing and duty, but receiving a personal gift for reading it is icing on the cake. There can be no benefit for the one who hears, forgets, or deliberately disregards scripture's message. Some critics today argue that only certain parts, like the sayings of Jesus, are God's word. However, the Bible reassures us that "every Scripture is God-breathed and profitable for teaching, for reproof, for correction, and for instruction in righteousness, that each person who belongs to God may be complete, thoroughly equipped for every good work." (2 Tim. 3:16-17).

1:3 | I still clearly remember the day I gave my life to the Lord and received a great **blessing**. I was on a long journey on a motorbike from Liverpool to Birmingham to work there. The weather was so bad that I had to break my journey in Wolverhampton at a hotel. Heavy rain and the road were challenging, but I believe God spoke to me that night. A voice in my head asked me, "Why did Jesus die on the cross? I realized there and then that he died for me! I asked him, "If you are real, come into my life." I distinctly remember opening a copy of Gideon's bible later in the room and being not just blessed but astonished by what I read. Instead of cold stories, it was now alive and speaking to my heart. This gift was the greatest blessing ever.

1:3 | As you read Revelation, I pray that God will bring this special blessing and unique insights into the person and work of Jesus into your life. John of Patmos lifts his eyes to you and me and other third millennium readers and announces that those who **hear the words** of the prophecy and take to heart what God has written are blessed.

1:3 | First and second-century household assemblies copied Revelation and sent it to other churches. Their message would encourage Christians everywhere in the Roman empire, especially those enduring persecution, as they **hear the words**.

To be "blessed" means "to be made holy or consecrated" and "to live with God in heaven." The Revelation blessings are like the "Beatitudes" or, as Robert Schuyler[37] called them, the "Be-Happy Attitudes!"

1.3 | Here is a new set of seven Revelation beatitudes, each beginning with the Latin *beauti*, meaning "happy, rich, or blessed."

- "Blessed is he who reads and those who hear the words of the prophecy, and keep the things that are written in it, for the time is at hand." (Rev. 1:3).
- "Blessed are the dead who die in the Lord from now on" (Rev. 14:13).
- "Blessed is he who watches" (Rev. 16:15).
- "Blessed are those who are invited to the wedding supper of the Lamb" (Rev. 19:9).
- "Blessed and holy is he who has part in the first resurrection" (Rev. 20:6).
- "Blessed is he who keeps the words of the prophecy of this book" (Rev. 22:7).
- "Blessed are those who do his commandments, that they may have the right to the tree of life, and may enter in by the gates into the city" (Rev. 22:14).

1:3 | Jesus pronounces a benediction on a group of people In each Revelation blessing. Then, as if to emphasize the urgency of the matter, he adds **the time is at hand!** In the "Sermon on the Mount," the poor in spirit, mourners, the meek, those who hunger and thirst for righteousness, the merciful, pure in heart, and peacemakers are made holy. "Blessed are you when people reproach you, persecute you, and falsely say all kinds of evil against you, for my sake. Rejoice, and be exceedingly glad, for great is your reward in heaven." (Matt. 5:11—12).

1:3 | Jewish people hoped when the **time is at hand,** which they called the *eschaton*, for God's direct intervention in history. The word "eschatology" comes from this root meaning "study of

---

[37] the tele-evangelist (1926—2015).

the last days." In Jewish belief, God will gather the Israeli nation, the *diaspora,* from around the world back to the Holy Land for the Messiah's coming and a glorious afterlife. Jewish people also believe in the return of the *Tsadikim,* thirty-six righteous persons in each generation who will welcome the Messiah's divine presence.

1:3 | When Revelation says that the **time is at hand,** we note that the Jewish concept of time is new. The Gregorian calendar is widely used today except by some Jewish religious groups. To the Jewish person, two ages divide all time. The first age begins with the creation and ends with the Jerusalem Temple's destruction in seventy AD. In the Jewish calendar, "BC," meaning "before Christ," is referred to as "BCE" or "before the common era." "AD" or "anno domini" in medieval Latin means "in the year of the Lord." Israeli scholars transcribe this as "CE" or "the common era." In Jewish terms, this year, "2022 AD," coincides with "5782 CE" and lasts until September the second, 2022, when "5783 CE" in the Jewish calendar begins. The Jewish year 5783 CE is read in years from creation's first day to today in this calendar.

1:3 | When we think of **the time at hand,** we need to remember that the concept of time has also changed from the Julian Calendar in 46 AD to the Gregorian one of 1582 AD. Because of this, Britain and the British Empire lost eleven days in September 1752 when they brought their time into line with Europe. Before 1752 AD, Britain followed the Julian calendar. Unfortunately, this calendar had an inbuilt error of one day every one hundred and twenty-eight years due to a miscalculation of the solar year by eleven minutes. This error affected the date of Easter, traditionally observed on March 21st, and moved further away with each passing year. Gregory based his calendar on three hundred and sixty-five days divided into twelve months with thirty or thirty-one days per month, twenty-eight in February, and a leap year every fourth year in February. Though France, Italy, Poland, Spain, and Portugal adopted it in 1582 AD, Turkey did not come into line until 1927! This change created problems. 1751 AD was a short year of two hundred and eighty-two days, lasting from March 25th to December 31st! The new year then began on January 1st on the new system.

1:3 | **The time at hand** was emphasized in 1752 AD when Britain lost eleven days on Thursday, September 14th, followed by Wednesday, September 2nd! Civil unrest resulted upon the announcement of the calendar change, and rioters wanted their eleven days back! Many people mistakenly believed that it would shorten their lives by eleven days! Not everyone was unhappy about the new time. William Willett,[38] always enthusiastic for a bet and a joke, wagered he could dance non-stop for twelve days and 12 nights. On September 2nd, 1752, he started dancing in triple rhythm around the village and continued throughout the night. On September 14th, William stopped dancing and claimed his winnings! According to the new calendar, he had danced for 11 days nonstop!

Question: "Count the blessings you have received from Jesus"

---

[38] William Willett of Endon. According to W.M. Jamieson, in "Murders Myths and Monuments of North Staffordshire."

4

THE ETERNAL GOD

1:4 "John, to the seven assemblies that are in Asia: Grace to you and peace from God, **who is and who was and who is to come;** and from the **seven Spirits who are before his throne;** [5] and from Jesus Christ, the faithful witness, the **firstborn of the dead,** and the **ruler of the kings of the earth.** To him who loves us, and washed us from our sins by his blood—[6] and he made us to be a Kingdom, to his God and Father—to him be the glory and the dominion forever and ever. Amen." Rev. 1:4—6 emphases added).

1:4 | In this passage, the eternal God greets John of Patmos with "grace and peace from God **who is, and who was and who is to come."** Later, he repeats this statement when the four living creatures continually address the Lord God Almighty, using the exact phrase.[39] It describes the eternal nature of God and is related to the "Alpha and the Omega."

1:4 | **Seven spirits before his throne** indicate "the Holy Spirit" or may also refer to the Revelation churches' seven leaders in Asia. Under the Holy Spirit's guidance, John of Patmos sent letters to these churches situated on a crescent-shaped line in present-day Turkey. Each one commends their strengths and warns them

---

[39] (Rev. 4:8).

of their failures. They are appropriate for today's assemblies and our personal lives also. Christians today can become loveless, immoral, or compromising in their faith, and our Lord clarifies how he feels about these faults in the seven letters.

1:5 | Jesus is called **the firstborn from the dead**. John of Patmos uses the Greek word *prototokos* for "firstborn," referring to the birth order in a traditional family where the first male child inherits the bulk of the inheritance from his birth father. Jesus inherits everything from his Father. The concept of the "firstborn" or "divine providence" is at odds with the "divine right of kings" or "God's mandate" introduced by King Henry VIII.[40]

1:5 | The divine right of the **firstborn** is a religious doctrine of political legitimacy in a monarchy and is often expressed in the phrase "by the Grace of God," attached to the reigning monarch's titles. Interestingly, my Admitting Certificate to the Office of Evangelist[41] is signed, "Donald, by Divine Providence, Lord Archbishop of Canterbury, and Primate of All England." "Divine providence" is similar to "divine right" as a claim of special favor. I remember Lord Coggan as a caring, kind, humble, and godly gentleman when I met him in the interview process for Church Army, who would never ask for any personal favors or special power.

1:5 | Jesus Christ is also called the **ruler of the kings of the earth**, for he governs and regulates all earthly kings and leaders, sometimes keeping them from doing evil or frustrating their plans, sometimes using them to serve his purposes. Jesus always has the last say!

Question: "What difference does it make to your life knowing that God is eternal?"

---

[40] (1491—1547) when he declared himself supreme head of the Church of England at the Reformation in 1531.
[41] 16th December 1975

5

ETERNAL LORD JESUS

1:7 "Behold, he is coming with the clouds, and every eye
will see him, including those who pierced him. All the tribes
of the earth will mourn over him. Even so, Amen. [8] "I am
the **Alpha and the Omega**," says the **Lord God, "who is
and who was and who is to come**, the Almighty." [9] **I John,
your brother and partner with you in the oppression**,
Kingdom, and perseverance in Christ Jesus, was on the
isle that is called Patmos because of God's Word and the
testimony of Jesus Christ. [10] I was in the Spirit on **the Lord's
day**, and I heard behind me a loud voice, like a trumpet
[11] saying, "**What you see, write in a book** and send to
the seven assemblies: to Ephesus, Smyrna, Pergamum,
Thyatira, Sardis, Philadelphia, and to Laodicea."
(Rev. 1:7—11 emphases added).

1:8 | God employs the first letter in the classical Greek
alphabet, *Alpha*, and the last letter, *Omega*, as titles for Jesus.
This pair of letters, **Alpha and Omega**, are used as Christian
symbols and often combined with the Cross, the *Chi-Rho* sign,
and other Christian characters to indicate God's eternal nature.
The *Chi-Rho* sign is one of the earliest forms of Christogram,
formed by superimposing the first two capital letters, *Chi* and
Rho, of the Greek word *Christos* so that the vertical stroke of the

Rho intersects the center of the *Chi*. A Christogram is, therefore, a combination of letters that form an abbreviation for the name of Jesus Christ.

1:8 | Interestingly, the *Chi-Rho* sign or the Latin, *Labarum* appeared on Emperor Constantine's military standards. To say Jesus is "first and last" emphasizes his existence for all eternity, from before the creation to after the last moment in time. Jesus is the constant one, the past, and present **Alpha,** and the future **Omega.** He controls all time and our lives from beginning to end.

1:8 | The fascinating Hebrew term *emet,* meaning "truth," comprises the Greek alphabet's first, middle, and last letters. *Emet* is called the "Seal of God" and encompasses everything between the **Alpha and Omega**. The Talmud says that "the seal of the Holy One is truth." Israel's King and Redeemer claims, "I am the first, and I am the last, and besides me, there is no God" (Isa. 44:6).

1:8 | Surprisingly, **Alpha Omega** was the name of two albums issued and sold on television as the Beatles' "Blue and Red" long-playing records.[42] The two recordings were declared "the only authorized Beatles collection." They contained songs composed only by John Lennon[43] and Paul McCartney[44] and were a nod to their talents as the originators, the *Alpha* of the band until the *Omega* at the Beatles' breakup. John Lennon's last words to Paul McCartney were, "Think of me now and then, old friend."

1:8 | The phrase **the Lord God who is and who was and who is to come** is one of only two places in Revelation where God speaks directly about his eternal nature. The second place is at the end of the book. The Lord God told John that it was done. " He said to me, 'I am the Alpha and the Omega, the Beginning and the End'" (Rev. 21:6). The Lord Jesus is the eternal Lord God.

1:9 | According to tradition, John of Patmos was the only apostle not martyred for his faith who died a natural death. **I, John,**

---

[42] The two albums were also known as the "Red Album" (1962--1966) and the "Blue Album" (1967--1970.)

[43] (1940-1980)

[44] (1942—Present)

your brother, and partner with you in the oppression, describes how he suffered during Emperor Domitian's persecution.[45] Legend has it that the Romans tried to poison John's wine goblet on one occasion, but a snake-like head arose out of it and alerted him. He and many other Christian believers suffered, and large numbers died during this empire-wide persecution. John sought to encourage survivors to persevere. He saw the Lord, whom he knew as a friend, return as a triumphant King. Towards his life's end, the Romans imprisoned John[46] on Patmos Island, one of three Greek coastal islands situated fifty miles offshore from Ephesus in the Aegean Sea. Banishment there was a regular punishment for many offenses, including magic and astrology.[47] The Romans viewed Pagan, Jewish, or Christian prophecy similarly and perceived John as threatening political power and order.

1:10 | John of Patmos sees his savior in a **Lord's Day** vision. The early church marked "the Lord's Day," or the resurrection day of Jesus, on the first day of the week or Sunday. The seventh day, Saturday, was the Jewish sabbath day and commemorated the creation's completion. As crucial as the sabbath was, the resurrection day of Jesus was considered more meaningful and essential to Christians. They replaced the Jewish sabbath on the seventh day with "the Lord's Day" on the first day of the week. The resurrection of Jesus is responsible for a significant change in our weekly calendar.

1:11 | Under the Holy Spirit's direction, John dictated Revelation to his scribe, Prochorus. God told him **what you see, write in a book,** and send it to the seven assemblies. Prochorus has some history before coming to Patmos. He was one of seven deacons[48] chosen to care for Jerusalem's poor. He was one of the seventy disciples dispatched by Jesus, who consigned them two by two ahead of him (literally "before his face") "into every city

---

[45] (51—96 AD).

[46] (6—c100 AD)

[47] Pliny the Elder, the secular author In his book, "Natural History," (23—79 AD).

[48] The seven deacons were Stephen, Philip, Prochorus, Nicanor, Timon, Parmenas, and Nicolas (Acts 6:5).

and place where he was about to come" (Luke 10:1). In Orthodox iconography, he appears as John of Patmos' scribe. Tradition adds that he was the nephew of Stephen, the first Christian martyr.

1:11 | Prochorus, whose task was to **write in a book** for John of Patmos, accompanied Peter in Nicomedia. Tradition says he returned to Antioch and was martyred there at the end of the first century AD. John's dwelling place, the "Cave of the Apocalypse," is still a sought-out destination for many Christian pilgrims today.

Question: "What difference does knowing Jesus, the Alpha, and the Omega, make in your life?

6

SON OF MAN

1:12 "**I turned** to **see the voice** that spoke with me. Having turned, I saw **seven golden lamp stands**. [13] And among the lamp stands was one like **a son of man**, clothed with a **robe reaching down to his feet**, and with a **golden sash** around his chest. [14] His head and his hair were **white as white wool**, like snow. His eyes were like a flame of fire. [15] His **feet were like burnished brass**, as if it had been refined in a furnace. His voice was like the **voice of many waters**. [16] He had seven stars in his right hand. Out of his mouth proceeded a **sharp two-edged sword**. His face was like the sun shining at its brightest." (Rev. 1:12—16 emphases added).

1:12 | In his Revelation vision, John of Patmos recognized the voice of his friend Jesus whom he had known for three years, and **turned** around immediately. He walked and talked with him in Galilee and saw the radiant Son of God at the Transfiguration. He even stood at the foot of his cross, watched him die, and described himself touchingly as "the disciple whom Jesus loved." However, Jesus is not just a humble earthly teacher but God's Lamb and the glorious King here. John sees Jesus in all his honor, glory, and power!

1:12 | John of Patmos turned expecting to see the speaker and observed instead **seven golden lamp stands** representing the seven churches.[49] God called each assembly to shine the Gospel light in their area, like a lamp stand in the Temple. Moses described the seven Temple or Tabernacle lamp stands called *Menorah*, made from solid gold with seven branches to light the Holy Tabernacle. (Ex. 25:31—37).

1:13 | Jesus stands among the golden lamps in a long white **robe reaching down to his feet** and a golden sash around his chest. The prophet Daniel tells us, "There came with the clouds of the sky one like a son of man" (Dan. 7:13).

1:13 | Interestingly, Jesus adopted the title of the **son of man** during his earthly ministry. "He began to teach them that the Son of Man must suffer many things, and be rejected by the elders, the chief priests, and the scribes, and die, and after three days rise again" (Mark 8:31). Jesus also said, "whoever will be ashamed of me and of my words in this adulterous and sinful generation, the Son of Man also will be ashamed of him, when he comes in his Father's glory, with the holy angels" (Mark 8:38).

1:13 | John of Patmos points out that Revelation originates from the Lord Jesus Christ. He walked and talked with Jesus in Galilee many years before. The "**son of man**" title in "koine" New Testament Greek is *ho huios tou anthropou* and refers to his humanity during his time on earth. It occurs eighty-one times in the Greek text of the four gospels and is used only in the sayings of Jesus. The Hebrew expression "son of man" is *ben-'adam* and appears in the Torah over a hundred times. Jesus injects new meaning in heaven into this Old Testament phrase. He allows all humans like himself to enter Almighty God's presence. He is God, but he is also a man.

1:13 | Jesus' **robe reaches down to his feet.** John of Patmos uses the same Greek words in Revelation to describe the High Priest's robes in the Tabernacle and Temple. These garments included "a breastpiece, an ephod, a robe, a fitted tunic, a turban, and a sash" (Ex. 28:4). Imagine Jesus dressed this way! He is the High Priest "par excellence." Many influential people, priests,

---

[49] Ephesus, Smyrna, Pergamum, Thyatira, Sardis, Philadelphia, and Laodicea. (Rev. 1:11)

princes, and kings in both Testaments wore long white robes and golden sashes like the High Priest.

1:13 | King Saul and his son Jonathan's long robes are similar to the High Priest's. The ascension robes of Jesus were also "royal garments." In Revelation, people no longer view Jesus as a criminal on a cross but as an elegantly dressed victorious king and pre-eminent High Priest. Other Bible passages describe the **long white robe** of Jesus in heaven. Daniel's vision saw a divine figure as "a man clothed in linen, whose thighs were adorned with pure gold of Uphaz" (Dan 10:5). The risen Lord's robe indicated his three-fold ministry on earth as a king, a priest, and a prophet.

1:13 | Jesus commenced his priestly work with a **golden sash** around his chest. The historian Josephus[50] described the High Priest's clothing he had witnessed and recorded in the Jerusalem Temple. He wrote, "The vestment reaches down to the feet, sits close to the body, and has sleeves tied to the arms. It is girded to the breast a little above the elbows, by a girdle often going round, four fingers broad, but so loosely woven that you would think it was a serpent's skin." The girdle or golden sash was "embroidered with flowers of scarlet, purple, blue, and fine twined linen." The white robe hung loosely down to the ankles.

1:14 | Almighty God acknowledges the power and authority of Jesus by describing him with hair, **white like wool**. "His clothing was white as snow, and the hair of his head like pure wool" (Dan. 7:9). Eastern 6th century Christian art portrayed Jesus as a white-haired older man with a long beard. The Ancient of Days title symbolically indicated that he existed for all eternity. White hair was the mark of a superior wise person with pure motives, and his eyes, like blazing fire, pointed to his all-knowing nature.

1:15 | The feet of Jesus were described as **burnished brass** glowing in a furnace. This picture may seem strange, but it amplifies the precious metal's color and glow. The metal *Electrum* is one such silver and gold combination. The description may

---

[50] The Roman Jewish historian was a gifted scholar from a priestly family in Jerusalem. (37—100 AD). Description of the high priests robes comes from "The Antiquities of the Jews 3.7.2,4."

also reference bronze soldier's shoes, the latest technology in the ancient Roman world. They protected a soldier's feet in battle and on the march. They "were not like other shoes but made of bronze or brass and leather." They comprised two parts, the upper part from the foot's top extending upwards across the shin to below the knee. The shoe was like a boot crafted of finely tooled brass and formed to the soldier's calf. It had two metal pieces on top and bottom. Thin brass parts covered the foot. The sides were held together by multiple leather pieces. The shoes had dangerous spikes, sometimes up to three inches long which were a deadly weapon in close combat. Bronze was commonplace, and Romans used it for coins, ornaments, and even toiletry items like nail cleaners, tweezers, and toothpicks!

1:15 | Jesus speaks with divine authority, and his voice sounds to John of Patmos, like the **voice of many waters.** What springs to mind is the roar of a magnificent waterfall like Niagara Falls. This sound would have been one of the loudest noises of the day, like a jet plane flying overhead today. Surprisingly, the loudest animal sound recorded in nature is from the whale. An even greater noise was generated in 1883 when the Krakatoa volcano erupted.[51] The sound from a Saturn Five rocket at takeoff at one hundred and eighty-five decibels melts concrete! Compare that to a thunderstorm at one hundred and twenty-five decibels, but the voice of Jesus here is no doubt louder!

1:16 |The appearance of Jesus was like the sun shining in all its brilliance. His face's brightness indicated his divine majesty, like his glowing appearance at the Transfiguration. The **sharp two-edged sword** or *gladius* in his mouth intends us to realize that his message contains power and judgment. It may also refer to the Roman foot soldiers' primary weapon in close combat or the arena.

Question: "How can Jesus, the Son of Man, be a real human being and God simultaneously?"

---

[51] It ejected twenty-five cubic kilometers of rock, ash, and pumice with a 180 decibels explosion and carried it as far as Perth in Australia! It ruptured sailors' eardrums forty miles away!

7

DEATH AND HADES' KEYS

1:17 "When I saw him, I fell at his feet like a dead man. He laid his right hand on me, saying, "**Don't be afraid.** I am the **first and the last,** [18] and the Living one. I was dead, and behold, I am alive forever and ever. Amen. I have the **keys of Death and of Hades.** [19] Write therefore the things which you have seen, and the things which are, and the things which will happen hereafter. [20] The mystery of the seven stars which you saw in my right hand, and the seven golden lamp stands is this: The seven stars are the angels of the seven assemblies. The seven lamp stands are seven assemblies." (Rev 1:17—20 emphases added).

1:17 | As the Roman government stepped up its persecution of Christians, John of Patmos must have wondered if the church would die out altogether or whether it could survive. When Jesus appeared, he reassured John, **don't be afraid,** for God will give you and your fellow believers strength to face these trials.

1:17 | There were numerous other occasions when Jesus told his disciples, **"don't be afraid."** On the Galilee Sea, when strong winds blew through the surrounding valleys and fierce storms resulted, Jesus told them, "Cheer up! It is I! Don't be afraid" (Matt. 14:27). In this verse, "It is I" may be translated as "I am," which is God's name from the Old Testament. It's as if Jesus is saying,

"Don't be afraid, for the God of our fathers, the "I am" is with you!" At the Transfiguration of Jesus, John was frightened by Moses and Elijah's appearance in an eerie cloud. In the Garden of Gethsemane, the soldiers fell fearfully to their knees when Jesus uttered the holy "I am" name. He reassured his disciples on both occasions, "don't be afraid."

1:17 | Jesus elaborates here on an earlier title he had used, the **first and the last**. He says that he is the living one who was dead. But now he is alive forever.

1:18 | **Death and Hades** are interesting terms. The Greek word *Hades* means "unseen" and translates the Hebrew *Sheol* to describe the "dead's resting place in an unseen location" or "the place of departed spirits." *Hades* is also the name of an ancient Greek underworld god emphasizing the dread of that awful place in the afterlife. On the other hand, "Death" translates *Sheol* and describes "the home of the righteous and the wicked," where all went after death before Christ's resurrection.

1:18 | Believers do not have to fear death because Jesus of Nazareth holds the "**keys of Death and Hades**." Those who face premature death from Cancer, Covid-19, AIDS, heart attack, or some other terminal illness need to remember that the power of Jesus was available to John and the early church in their second-century persecutions and is accessible to us today. He will lead Christians facing the end through the shadow of death into eternal life. Jesus Christ holds the keys of Death and Hades, and he alone can open or close these two compartments in the underworld, and they are under his sole power. Death and Hades' keys keep people in or let them out. Interestingly, "Hades" is also the name of a successful action video game developed and published by Supergiant Games.[52] It has sold over a million copies and was named 2020's game of the year.

1:18 | The Psalmist explains, "even though I walk through the valley of the shadow of **death**, I will fear no evil, for you are with

---

[52] Hades publicity material explains, "Players control Zagreus, the son of Hades, as he attempts to escape from the Underworld to reach Mount Olympus, at times aided by gifts bestowed on him from the other Olympians." Released in 2020."

me. Your rod and your staff, they comfort me" (Ps. 23:4). There is no more incredible promise than "you are with me." I remember being at a youth conference at Scargill House in Yorkshire. One day we studied the twenty-third Psalm, but the teacher wouldn't answer my question about what the rod and staff were! Later, I learned that the rod was a club for defense, and the staff was a long stick with a hook, called a "crook," to rescue a lamb. I then realized that the Lord Jesus, the good shepherd, defends and rescues his sheep!.

1:18 | Charles Haddon Spurgeon[53] wrote, "God removes **death**'s substance, and only its shadow remains." Nobody fears a shadow, for it cannot block a person's pathway. The dog's shadow cannot bite, and the sword's shadow cannot kill. Jesus, the light of the world, removes all shadows. The American speaker and author Roger von Oech[54] writes, "Life is like a maze in which you try to avoid the exit." Christians do not have to avoid the exit, but can look forward to it, for they know the blessings beyond.

1:18 | The biblical story of Lazarus and Dives speaks clearly about **Death and Hades**. It describes how a rich man, Dives, lived in luxury, and a beggar named Lazarus lay at his gate covered in sores. Both died. Dives went to torment in hell, and Lazarus "was carried away by angels to Paradise with Abraham" (Luke 16:22). Jesus controlled these two compartments in the afterlife.

1:18 | The body's life may ebb away, but the Spirit lives on in a Christian, for Jesus said, "I have the keys of **Death and Hades**." The soul and personality continue in a new incorruptible body. Jesus said to Mary in her bitter grief over the death of Lazarus that the one who believed in him would still live, even if he died. Whoever lives and believes in Jesus will never die. Jesus then asks, "Do you believe this?"

Question: "How have Jesus' words, "Do not be afraid," encouraged you when you were down?"

---

[53] Renowned preacher who authored a devotional book called "Mornings and Evenings." (1834—1892).
[54] (1948—present).

8

FIRST LOVE JESUS

2:1 "To the angel of the **assembly in Ephesus** write: "He who holds the seven stars in his right hand, he who walks among the seven golden lamp stands says these things: ² "I know your works, and your toil and perseverance, and that you can't tolerate evil men, and have tested those who call themselves apostles, and they are not, and found them false. ³ You have perseverance and have endured for my name's sake, and have not grown weary. ⁴ But I have this against you, that you **left your first love**." (Rev. 2.1—4 emphases added).

2:1 | The angel tells John of Patmos to write a letter to the church or **assembly in Ephesus**. In it, he explains the mystery of the seven stars in the right hand of Jesus and the seven golden lamp stands. The seven "stars" mean the "seven assembly or church leaders," and the "seven lamp stands" are the "seven churches themselves" (Rev.1:20). If Ephesian Christians failed to shine the light of Jesus, God could remove their lamp stand. Just as the Temple candlesticks give light both day and night, the assembly is to provide a continual witness to its surrounding community. Jesus warns them that he may extinguish their lamps if they do not change.

2:1 | John of Patmos also sends epistles to the other six churches on an arc. The first letter addresses Ephesus, a Greek city with a quarter-million people on Turkey's western coast.[55] It was Asia Minor's capital and a significant trade center.

2:1 | Along with Alexandria and Syrian Antioch, **Ephesus** was one of the three most influential eastern Roman cities and where John wrote his Gospel. Artemis was the most revered Greek god in Ephesus. Its magnificent Temple was one of the seven wonders of the ancient world. A flood destroyed the original temple in the 8th Century BC.[56] Still, Croesus, who founded Lydia's empire, sponsored the new Greek temple[57] built of marble with an imposing double row of columns reaching forty feet high. Excavated deposits from the site contain some of the earliest inscribed coins. The only other wonder of the world remaining today is Giza's Great Pyramid in Egypt at an imposing four hundred and eighty-one feet high. John of Patmos spent most of his ministry in Ephesus and knew its shortcomings. He realized their first love was not Jesus but the pagan goddess Artemis!

2:4 | Ephesian Christians were in grave danger of losing the foundation of their Christian faith, **their first love**. It was a silver manufacturing center for metal images of the goddess Artemis.[58] The ordinary people described her as "Ephesus' first love," and no doubt the sellers of the trinkets loved her too! The Ephesians worshipped her as one of the goddesses of midwifery which the Romans identified with their deity Diana. Among the rural populace, Artemis was their favorite. She was considered the goddess of nature, who danced, usually accompanied by nymphs, in mountains, forests, and marshes. She embodied the sportsman's ideal, killing game, and protecting it, especially the

---

[55] Ephesus was founded in the 10th century BC and built on earlier ruins mentioned in 14th century BC Hittite sources.

[56] The flood deposited over three feet of sand and debris over the original clay floor.

[57] It was designed and constructed around 550 BC and was three hundred and seventy-seven feet long and one hundred and fifty one feet wide.

[58] Artemis was the goddess of wild animals, the hunt, vegetation, chastity, and childbirth. She was the patron and protector of young children and women. She brought disease upon women and children and also relieved them of it.

young. She was described as "the mistress of animals." Artists and sculptors often showed her with a stag or hunting dog.

2:4 | A man and a woman's **first love** is precious. There is a delightful poem called "First Love" by John Clare.[59]

> I ne'er was struck before that hour
> With love so sudden and so sweet,
> Her face it bloomed like a sweet flower,
> And stole my heart away complete.
>
> I never saw so sweet a face,
> As that I stood before.
> My heart has left its dwelling-place
> And can return no more.

John Clare wrote it about his first love, Mary Joyce. Like his father, he was a farm laborer in England and was commonly known as "the Northamptonshire Peasant Poet." He wrote "Childe Harold's Pilgrimage," which became a lament for past lost love.

Captain Alan Price, a Church Army colleague, wrote a lovely children's chorus describing this same closeness to Jesus.

> "Be the centre of my life, Lord Jesus,
> Be the centre of my life I pray.
> Be my Saviour to forgive me,
> Be my friend to be with me,
> Be the centre of my life today."[60]

The Ephesians initially prayed that the Lord Jesus would be their life center, but somehow their first love waned. Jesus said, "But I have this against you, that you left your first love."

2:4 | A large and proud church had developed in **Ephesus**. Jesus reminded them that he alone still headed the assembly

---

[59] (1793-1864)
[60] Copyright Alan Price © Daybreak Music 1990

there. He jogged their memory of his words, "where your treasure is, there your heart will also be" (Matt. 6:21).

Question: "Is your first love, Jesus, and is he the center of your life today?"

9

PARADISE TREE OF LIFE

2:5 "Remember therefore from where you have fallen, and repent and do the first works; or else I am coming to you swiftly, and will move your lamp stand out of its place, unless you repent. [6] But this you have, that you hate the works of the **Nicolaitans**, which I also hate. [7] He who has an ear, let him hear what the Spirit says to the assemblies. To him who overcomes I will give **to eat** from **the tree of life**, which is in the **Paradise** of my God." (Rev. 2:5—7 emphases added).

2:6 | We do not precisely know who the **Nicolaitans** were, except for their sexually immoral ways. God hated these heretics for encouraging participation in pagan practices. Samuel Taylor Marshall[61] believed that *Nicolaitan* meant "peoples' conqueror." David Chilton[62] added, "the Greek term for 'Balaam' means 'people destroyer.'" The Old Testament presented him as a diviner but condemned him as a "wicked man." His followers went astray, but he was rebuked for his disobedience.

2:6 | A mute donkey spoke with a man's voice and stopped the prophet Balaam's madness (2 Pet. 2:15—16). However, he refused

---

[61] Miami University (1812—1895)
[62] the American reformed scholar (1951—1997).

to curse Israel but blessed them even though an angry King Balak pressured him with a bribe! The **Nicolaitans** and those who held to his teaching seem the same, for they set out to destroy God's people and tolerated Jezebel, who called herself a prophetess. John writes, "she teaches and seduces my servants to commit sexual immorality and eat things sacrificed to idols" (Rev. 2:20). These heretical sects mixed Christianity and pagan practices, so God and the Ephesian church hated them!

2:7 | Those who overcome enjoy the right to eat from the **tree of life,** an archetype of paradise in many of the world's mythologies. It is closely related to the "sacred tree" concept. We find the roots of these myths in writings from Ancient Mesopotamia.[63] People at the Revelation tree of life will be free from need, hunger, corruption, or pain and have their longings fulfilled. "Hope deferred makes the heart sick, but when longing is fulfilled, it is a tree of life" (Prov. 13:12).

2:7 | There are two trunks to the **tree of life,** for it grew "in the middle of its street on this side of the river and on that" (Rev. 22:2). It bears twelve kinds of fruits every month, and its leaves are for the healing of the nations. The pure water flows from God and the Lamb's throne in the middle of its street, and many types of fruit grow on them for the faithful.

2:7 | The **tree of life** first appears in the Garden of Eden (Gen. 2:9) as the source of nourishment for Adam and Eve. God takes access to it away when he drives humans from the garden because they disobeyed him. It reappears as an essential part of the new paradise. God welcomes entry, for "Blessed are those who do his commandments, that they may have the right to the tree of life, and may enter in by the gates into the city" (Rev. 22:14). He promises that the overcomer will eat from it in his paradise. In Jewish thought, it meant human fulfillment and will grow in heaven alongside the "tree of the knowledge of good and evil." Many Jewish people believed that when the Messiah, the "expected anointed one," comes from God and the new age

---

[63] in BC 230.

dawns, the paradise tree of life will grow in their midst, and the faithful will eat from it. The Rabbis said, "the tree of life's boughs overshadow paradise." It has five hundred thousand fragrances, and its fruit has many pleasant tastes, each different.

2:7 | Other early Christian leaders interpreted the meaning of the **tree of life** differently. Augustine of Hippo[64] and Bonaventure[65] taught Christ himself is the fruit of the tree of life. Augustine suggests, "God did not wish the man to live in Paradise without the mysteries of spiritual things being presented to him in bodily form. So in the other trees, he was provided with nourishment, in this one with a sacrament." [66]

2:7 | The Persian word *paradaijah,* meaning **Paradise,** pictures "a walled enclosure" or "a beautiful garden with pleasant meadows, stately trees, and many flowers." It reminds me of the walled enclosures on the grounds of many stately homes in England. The walls had chimneys and were heated with fireplaces to grow vegetables and fresh produce in the winter.

2:7 | Revelation's garden **Paradise** has direct links to Genesis. Archibald Geikie Brown[67] wrote eloquently about this connection.

"In Genesis, we see the earth created.
In Revelation, we see it passing away.
In Genesis, there is a garden home for human beings.
In Revelation, there is a city, the nation's home.
In Genesis, we see humans driven from the garden and away from the "tree of life."
In Revelation, we see them welcomed back, with the "tree of life" at their disposal."

How wonderful that will be!

Question: "What do you think Paradise will be like?"

---

[64] (354—430 AD).
[65] (1221—1274 AD).
[66] "The Literal Meaning of Genesis, VIII, 4, 8" ("On Genesis," New City Press, p. 351-353).
[67] (1844—1922)

10

FAITHFUL SMYRNA CHURCH

2:8 "To the angel of the assembly in **Smyrna** write: "The first and the last, who was dead, and has come to life says these things: ⁹ "I know your works, oppression, and your poverty (but **you are rich**), and the blasphemy of those who say **they are Jews**, and they are not, but are a synagogue of Satan. ¹⁰ Don't be afraid of the things **which you are about to suffer**. Behold, the devil is about to throw some of you into prison, that you may be tested; and **you will have oppression for ten days.** Be faithful to death, and I will give you the **crown of life.** ¹¹ He who has an ear, let him hear what the Spirit says to the assemblies. He who **overcomes** won't be harmed by the **second death."** (Rev 2.8—11 emphases added).

2:8 | **Smyrna,** now called Izmir in Turkey, is a Greek city on the Aegean Coast. Strabo's[68] "Geographica" mapped out most of Europe during Caesar Augustus' time[69] and described Smyrna as "the most beautiful of all cities." In ancient times, Smyrna and Rome were close allies. Its name means "bitterness" from *myrrh*, the city's chief export in ancient times. This faithful church was twenty-five miles north of Ephesus on the Mediterranean Coast.

---

[68] A Greek philosopher and historian famous as a geographer (BC 63--24 AD).
[69] (BC 27--14 AD).

Known as the "Port of Asia," it had a deep harbor for Aegean ships. It was materially poor but spiritually rich. It struggled against two hostile forces, a Jewish population that strongly opposed Christianity and a group that supported worship of the female deity "Roma," personifying the city of Rome.

2:8 | Polycarp was one of **Smyrna's** most eminent leaders and a second-century martyr.[70] As he entered the stadium, a voice from heaven said, "Be strong, Polycarp, and play the man." No one saw the speaker, but believers who were present heard it. On entering, a great roar arose, "they have taken Polycarp!" Under pressure to renounce his faith, he uttered the memorable words, "Eighty and six years have I served him, and he did me no wrong. How can I blaspheme my king, who saved me?" When the flames miraculously failed to burn him, his persecutors stabbed him to death.

2:8 | Polycarp's name meant "much fruit." His death in **Smyrna** produced abundant blessings in those who witnessed his martyrdom. Persecution and suffering seemed inevitable there, and the church stood up well, but Jesus reminded them that he was the "First and the Last" and the *Alpha and Omega*. He was the only one they should worship, not the imperial cult or the goddess Roma.

2:9 | This letter to the faithful Smyrna church encouraged Christians as they suffered persecution. John of Patmos wrote that **you are rich** despite your afflictions and poverty. Christians may suffer, even to death, but their pain will be minor compared to their eternal reward. The Smyrna persecutions lasted ten days and had a specific beginning and end.

2:9 | Translating the word "**Jews**" is difficult in our modern, politically correct environment. We are urged to substitute "Jewish person," "Israeli," "Israelite," or "Israeli Citizen" for this word. The Orthodox Jewish Bible[71] renders Revelation 2:9 in part

---

[70] (69--155 AD).

[71] The Orthodox Jewish Bible, completed by Phillip Goble in 2002, is an English language version that applies Yiddish and Hasidic cultural expressions to the Messianic Bible. The Orthodox Jewish Bible fourth edition, OJB. Copyright 2002,2003,2008,2010, 2011 by Artists for Israel International. All rights reserved.

as "the ones making a claim and declaring themselves to be Bnei Brit and are not."

2:9 | Researching this section, I discovered to my surprise, that Judaism is not a faith-based religion like Christianity, as I supposed, but "orthopraxy," meaning displaying an "ethically and liturgically correct conduct." This realization brought back memories of ministry in the East End of London, England, with a community of Orthodox **Jewish** believers. As a colleague, Tom Heriot, and I walked along the main street on the Sabbath day, a Jewish shopkeeper called Tom over and asked him a favor. He agreed and unlocked the tailor's shop door, picked up his mail, opened the letters, and carefully laid them out on the counter for him to view. Because he was a tailor, even carrying a needle in his lapel was forbidden as it was considered work! Proper behavior is more important to a Jewish person than the faith or grace of the Christian belief system.

2:9 | **Jewish** culture covers many aspects of religion, traditional dress, gender attitudes, marriage and family, social customs and lifestyles, music, and dance. Jewish persons authored the Bible, founded early Christianity, and profoundly influenced Islam. "Despite their small percentage of the world's population, they have significantly influenced and contributed to human progress in many fields, both historically and in modern times."[72]

2:10 | **You will have oppression for ten days** may refer to the pagan persecution under Emperor Diocletian. Jesus commended the faithful Smyrna church and encouraged them not to fear the future if they remained loyal. Interestingly, after a devastating fire in 303 AD, Diocletian blamed the Christians for starting it and began a persecution lasting ten years, like Emperor Nero before him.

2:10 | Smyrna was widely known as "the crown city" because of her beautiful setting between the sea and the mountains. Jesus will reward faithful Christians with a **crown of life**. This Olympic award comprised interlocking laurel tree twigs and

---

[72] from Wikipedia.

leaves, producing an aromatic evergreen fragrance. For this reason, the "victor's crown" was sometimes called a "laurel wreath." Later, "cherry" was also woven into them and named a "spineless butcher's broom." Interestingly, the name originated from butchers tying a bundle of laurel branches together to clean off their chopping blocks.

2:10 | Organizers placed circular or horseshoe-shaped crowns upon the victors' heads or shoulders in the Smyrna, and Greek Olympic Games, much like modern athletes receive gold, silver, or bronze medals and sometimes a representation of a crown on their heads, as at the Beijing Olympic Games 2022. Smyrna was famous for its athletic games in ancient times. It was a smaller version of the Olympic Games in Greece, from BC 700 to 500 AD. The Greeks held the first modern Games in Athens[73] and then in different locations every four years. In Revelation, those faithful under persecution will receive a **crown of life** as a triumph sign symbolizing eternal life. We must keep our eyes on Christ to receive our victor's crown.

2:11 | The **second death** is part of the Christian belief system. The Rabbis used this term in New Testament times for the wicked's death in the next world. Although the Hebrew Bible does not mention it, the Targums[74] do. "But for the cowardly, unbelieving, abominable, murderers, sexually immoral, sorcerers, idolaters, their part is in the lake that burns with fire and sulfur which is the second death" (Rev. 21:8).

2:11 | R. H. Charles described some types of sorcery that Christians must resist and **overcome**. "Semjaza taught enchantments, root-cuttings, Armaros the resolving of enchantments, Baraqijal, (taught) astrology, Kokabel the constellations, Ezeqeel the knowledge of the clouds, Araqiel the signs of the earth, Shamsiel the signs of the sun, and Sariel the course of the moon."[75] Jesus doesn't say Christians can avoid

---

[73] in 1896 AD.

[74] An ancient, paraphrased Aramaic Bible from about 100 AD when Hebrew was declining as a spoken language.

[75] The Book of Enoch: SPCK Classic

temptations, suffering, troubles, or persecution. Instead, faith will be genuine when they overcome and remain loyal to him.

Question: "How is your church or assembly like or unlike the Smyrna church?"

11

ROMAN EMPEROR AUGUSTUS

2.12 "To the angel of the assembly in **Pergamum** write: "He who has the **sharp two-edged sword** says these things: ¹³ "I know your works and where you dwell, **where Satan's throne is.** You hold firmly to my name, and didn't deny my faith in the days of **Antipas** my witness, my faithful one, who was killed among you, where Satan dwells. ¹⁴ But I have a few things against you, because you have there some who hold the teaching of Balaam, who taught Balak to throw a stumbling block before the children of Israel, to eat things sacrificed to idols, and to commit sexual immorality. ¹⁵ So you also have some who hold to the teaching of the Nicolaitans likewise. ¹⁶ Repent therefore, or else I am coming to you quickly, and I will make war against them with the sword of my mouth." (Rev. 2:12—16 emphases added).

2:12 | Rome was Satan's capital, and **Pergamum** was his throne. "Pergamum," sometimes spelled as "Pergamon," became the official emperor worship center in Asia, with temples to Augustus[76] and Trajan[77] and the pagan sky and thunder god Zeus. It looked like a giant throne on top of an eight-hundred-foot-high

---

[76] (BC 63--14 AD)
[77] (53--117 AD)

cliff perched on an impressive forty-foot-high projecting rock ledge. It was a natural fortress above the surrounding countryside, which the Christian community hated and feared because it always smoked with animal sacrifices.

2:12 | Pergamum boasted a medical healing center dedicated to "Asclepion,"[78] called the "Savior." Interestingly, the Pergamum Asclepion symbol of the serpent wrapped around the "Rod of Asclepius" still appears as the medical profession's emblem.[79] The modern logo has a Moses connection, who "made a serpent of bronze and set it on the pole. If a serpent had bitten any man when he looked at the serpent of bronze, he lived" (Num. 21:9). Adherents traveled from around the world to seek healing from Asclepion.

2:12 | Pergamum became a sophisticated Greek cultural and educational center with a two hundred thousand volume library. The scrolls were made from the parchment of smooth, polished, and sewn-together animal skins and were unique.

2:12 | Pergamum was the center of four cults and rivaled Ephesus in idol worship. The Pergamum letter praises Christians for persevering even in this pagan setting despite the threat of martyrdom. This letter admonishes those who followed the Nicolaitans' teaching[80] and advocated immorality. Clement of Alexandria[81] wrote that Deacon Nicholas' views encouraged lacking legal or moral restraints and sexual immorality.

2:12 | The saying that the Lord will fight against them with the **sharp, two-edged sword** references the twenty-four to thirty-three inch long "Roman short sword," called the *gladius* or "Hispanic sword." It was used effectively by Roman soldiers in close combat.[82] A soldier led with the shield and thrust with the

---

[78] An *Asclepion* meant literally "a healing temple."

[79] The Medical Corps symbol was adopted in 1902 in the United States, and was called the *Caduceus*, featuring two snakes winding around a winged staff.

[80] According to the Church Fathers Irenaeus, Hippolytus, Epiphanes, and Theodoret, the Nicolaitans taught Deacon Nicolas' heretical beliefs.

[81] (150--215 AD)

[82] The armaments of a fully equipped Roman Legion soldier were a shield (*scutum*), one or two javelin weapons (*pila*), a sword (*gladius*), often a dagger (*pugio*), and, in the later empire period, darts (*plumbatae*).

sword. It came to represent the Christian sword of faith. It also symbolized the Roman proconsul's power when he controlled the justice system, having every accused person's life and death in his hands.

2:13 | Early Roman emperors like Augustus declined to be called **gods** by their people. Later, some emperors who realized this could be politically useful started believing they were gods and expected it everywhere. Citizens were required to burn a pinch of incense to the emperor's bust in the public square to show their loyalty and say, "Caesar is Lord." This act became a unifying principle in the Roman empire as it was a simple and easy way to identify disloyalty to the emperor. Christians who believed that "Jesus is Lord" and to burn incense to any other God, even the emperor's image, was wrong[83] now stood out. Paul writes, "no one can say, 'Jesus is Lord,' but by the Holy Spirit" (1 Cor. 12:3). This oath countered the emperor's pledge of allegiance of "Caesar is Lord." This loyalty oath is a backdrop to Revelation.

2:13 | **Satan's throne** may refer to the white marble altar in Pergamum City dedicated by Eumenes II,[84] surnamed *soter* or "savior," who was Pergamum's ruler. This imposing altar was dismantled and moved by the German engineer Carl Humann[85] to the Pergamum Museum in Berlin, where it is today. The museum has several original full-sized monumental buildings transported from present-day Turkey and meticulously reconstructed stone by stone. It is an imposing edifice.

2:13 | **Satan's throne** was where the Roman gods were honored. In BC 43, Julius Caesar was assassinated, and Augustus named his successor. The Roman Senate conferred the title "Augustus," meaning "the Exalted One." He replaced the Roman republic with a monarchy, brought stability and peace during his long reign, and became known as Rome's greatest Emperor. In 8 B.C., he had the month of Sextilius renamed August after himself.

---

[83] In those days, "pagan" described anyone who was not a Christian and worshipped any other god or none.

[84] (BC 221—159)..

[85] (1839-1896).

His great-uncle and predecessor Julius Caesar had previously done the same with July. He also renamed his homeland "Italy."

2:13 | The Pergamum letter states that **Antipas**, a faithful witness, died in the city where Satan lives. Tradition has it that he lived in Pergamum during Emperor Nero's reign and was martyred in c92 AD. He was roasted to death over a fire in a copper bull-shaped altar because he cast out demons worshiped by the local people. Later, oil seeped from his bones which early Christians called "the saint's manna." They used it to relieve toothache and other ailments!

Question: "How is your assembly or church like or unlike the Pergamum church?"

12

THE WHITE STONE

2:17 "He who has an ear, let him hear what the Spirit
says to the assemblies. To him who overcomes, to him
I will give of the **hidden manna**, and I will give him
a **white stone**, and on the stone a **new name** written,
which no one knows but he who receives it."
(Rev. 2:17 emphases added).

2:17 | We all need spiritual food in our lives. Jesus says that he
will give **hidden manna** for our inner beings. "Hidden " implies
that our divine food is known only to God and us and concealed
from others. As we pray, worship, and study the Word of God, we
receive personalized interior nourishment for our daily Christian
activities.

2:17 | The Hebrew word for *manna* sounds like "What is it?"
The people were confused as they had not seen anything like this
before. Moses described it as "a small round thing, small as the
frost on the ground," which appeared when the dew disappeared.
It looked white like aromatic coriander seed, and its taste was like
wafers with honey.

2:17 | **Manna** also looked like the tiny white peas used as a
spicy meal flavoring. It could be baked or boiled, and surprisingly,
the people of Israel lived on it for forty years until they arrived at
the borders of Canaan (Ex. 16:4—35). Not many modern people

would stick with such a rigid diet! Israelis were to gather enough *manna* for each day, but any kept over "bred worms and became foul." They collected twice as much on the sixth day for the sabbath. Moses explained that the hidden manna was the bread of life the Lord had given them to eat.

2:17 | Every Christian who overcomes receives a **white stone** inscribed with a new name. In Greek, the word "stone" is *kainos*. There are, however, two words for "new." There is *neos*, which means "new in time." A thing could be *neos*, yet precisely like any other stone. The other word for "new," *kainos*, means "new not only in time but also in quality for nothing like it has existed before." This new "kainos" name is written on Revelation's white stone and indicates the fresh bond of Jesus with Christians like nothing before it.

2:17 | Every morning, the great houses in Rome presented food and money to their dependents, who received a **white stone**. It was a ticket, giving free entry into the arena or to a complimentary banquet. Revelation's white stone indicates that Christ grants unique spiritual rewards to his own.

2:17 | Upon retiring, a victorious swordsman or swordswoman gladiator received a **white stone** with "S.P." inscribed. These letters celebrated faithful service and stood for the Latin *spectatus*, meaning "a man or woman of proven valor beyond a doubt, tested and esteemed." Most gladiators were enslaved people or captives from wars, but some volunteers enlisted for the notoriety. They repeatedly fought until either killed or allowed to retire in case of a draw! When they grew old, those with a specially illustrious career were permitted an honorable retirement and a parting gift by the game's master. A victorious gladiator was the most admired hero in ancient Roman society. Similarly, Revelation's white stone confirms that the victorious believer will share in the reign and future glory of Jesus.

2:17 | As in Roman times, a gladiatorial arena still stands at Verona in Italy. While on holiday near Lake Garda, the famous tenor Andrea Bocelli[86] performed at the restored colosseum. It

---

[86] a very gifted singer, a kind and generous Christian family man.

provided entertainment, concerts, and other events as it did in ancient times. Like the movie gladiator Russell Crowe, Christ calls Christians to be his warriors, for they will rest with honor when they have proved their bravery in life's battles. The Christian **white stone** bears a new name, possibly "Jesus" or the phrase "Devout Christian." It grants admission to messianic banquets and is a mark of faithfulness and a job well done. What an honor that will be!

2:17 | A **white stone** marked with a Roman general's name was considered a lucky thing to carry into battle.[87] This talisman could be in remembrance of someone special. It was inscribed with the giver's name and made of wood, stone, or bone in ancient Rome and Greece. A white stone was also sometimes split in two as a friendship token. After that, the two halves guaranteed a warm welcome and safety when visiting the other's home or territory. William Barclay writes, "In the ancient world, a pleasant day was called a 'white day.'" A white stone was a delightful gift to receive!

2:17 | Jesus will give each believer a unique **white** stone. The word "white" describes how it glistens like fresh snow in the sunshine, and "new" is another characteristic word in Revelation. R. H. Charles[88] writes that white is "the color and livery of heaven." The "white stone" had other uses in that age. A Greek court used a white pebble to indicate acquittal or innocence and a black tessera determining guilt in court trials.

2:17 | Artisans utilized **a** small square-colored piece of stone or glass called a *tessera* on wall and floor mosaics. Unearthed Pompeii and Herculaneum buildings reveal many fine examples of *tesserae* in mosaics.

2:17 | In the shadow of the iconic pointed "Shard Building" in London, England, archeologists in 2022 discovered a brightly colored mosaic floor of tiny **stones** from a second-century AD Roman mansion. Houses and churches used mosaics widely across the empire. Tesserae mosaics also appeared as murals,

---

[87] An "amulet" in the ancient Roman world was a "talisman" or *"good luck charm."*
[88] (1855—1931)

especially where candles were burning. The tiny colored glass or pottery pieces were easy to clean and kept their bright colors in churches despite smoke and candle soot, which soon darkened and discolored ordinary paintings.

2:17 | Elections historically used small stones as lots. **White stones** referred back to the blessings or curses of the black and white Urim and Thummim, embedded in the high priest's breastplate or *hoshen* and employed to cast lots. They were used to make decisions by sewing embroidered linen into a square two layers thick with four rows of three engraved gems in a golden setting. The Lord ordered it to be made "of gold, of blue, and purple, and scarlet, and fine twined linen" (Ex. 28:15). The breastplate was placed over Aaron's heart whenever he entered the Lord's presence. In this way, he "shall bear the judgment of the children of Israel on his heart before Yahweh continually." (Ex. 28:30).

2:17 | Revelation's **white stone** was both an emblem of sin's forgiveness and a reminder that God chooses Christians and loves them individually. It signifies that he acquits a person and declares them worthy of eternal life. "A new stone name" may refer to the Christian's spiritual rebirth or the practice of giving a person a fresh name.

2:17 | I remember meeting a disheveled young man outside the Drawbridge Christian Club in Birkenhead in the early sixties. It was in a church basement reached by a bridge. He told me his name was Russell Parker, and for no real reason, I said, "No, your name is now Russell, but I am going to call you Russ!" He was later converted and admitted to having drink and drug abuse problems. The Lord wonderfully changed him, but not the new name I gave him. He proved to have a powerful testimony and several years later was ordained into full-time ministry as director of the Acorn Trust in Britain. He excelled in University and, at the last count, had more than fifteen books published.[89] What's in a name when the Lord makes it new?

---

[89] See for example "Free to Fail" Triangle Books SPCK London, England ISBN 0-281-04527-2 by Russ Parker © 1992.

2:17 | On the other hand, Revelation's **white stone** may be an actual person! The risen Christ is given to his faithful ones with a new self, cleansed of all earthly stains and glistening with heavenly purity!

2:17 | The **white stone** also provided a pension for a victor for the rest of their lives. They often had a sacred or new name carved or written on them. Some people believed that knowing a god's identification gave the bearer certain special powers. The deity's identity came with the ability to summon it to one's aid in difficult times. Here Jesus gives his faithful followers a white stone with a new name upon it, not as a good luck charm but bearing the secret and unique identity of Jesus himself. John of Patmos says that you carried an 'object that protected you from trouble' with supernatural power, even with superstitious inscriptions like your heathen friends. Now, you need nothing like that, for you are safe in life and death because you know 'the new name,' that of Jesus Christ.

Question: "How do hidden manna and a white stone support your Christian life?"

13

YOUR WOMAN JEZEBEL

2:18 "To the angel of the assembly in **Thyatira** write: "The Son of God, who has his eyes like a flame of fire, and his feet are like burnished brass, says these things: [19] "I know your works, your love, faith, service, patient endurance, and that your last works are more than the first. [20] But I have this against you, that you tolerate **your woman, Jezebel**, who calls herself a prophetess. She teaches and seduces my servants to commit sexual immorality, and to eat things sacrificed to idols. [21] I gave her time to repent, but she refuses to repent of her sexual immorality. [22] Behold, I will throw her and those who commit adultery with her into a bed of great oppression, unless they repent of her works. [23] I will kill her children with Death, and all the assemblies will know I am he who **searches the minds and hearts**. I will give to each one of you according to your deeds." (Rev. 2:18—23 emphases added).

2:18 | **Thyatira**, which meant "daughter" from the Greek *thuatira*, was a frontier city famous for its trade guilds, including the Guild of Dyers of purple cloth. Many there participated in the Saturnalia festival, with a sacrifice in the Temple of Saturn, a public banquet, continual partying, gift-giving, and gambling that overturned Roman social norms. Masters provided table service for their enslaved persons in the festival on 17th December and expanded through to 23rd December. Christians eventually absorbed this festival into what we now call "Christmas" on 25th December. The priests offered meat to images in the temples and then sold what remained. Thus arose the criticism of "eating meat sacrificed to idols." Consuming food bought from the temple market may not have been wrong, but it was unwise as it could upset sensitive Christian brothers and sisters.

2:20 | In Thyatira, **Jezebel** forced her evil influence on her followers and encouraged sexual immorality. Its many trade guilds controlled the cloth-making, dyeing, and pottery industries. Interestingly, Paul's first Philippian convert was "Lydia, a seller of purple, of the city of Thyatira, one who worshiped God. The Lord opened her heart to listen to the things which were spoken by Paul" (Acts 16:14).

2:20 | John of Patmos may have used the name **Jezebel** to symbolize the evil she promoted, like the historical queen.[90] We read that King Ahab married her and began to serve and worship the pagan god Baal at an altar in Samaria. "Ahab did more yet to provoke Yahweh, the God of Israel, to anger than all the kings of Israel who were before him" (1 Kgs. 16:31-33). She tried to kill the worship leaders but met a final gruesome death when her servants threw her from a window, and wild dogs ate her flesh! God called upon the Thyatira Christian community to repent for tolerating and allowing her to lead them astray.

2:20 | The label "a **Jezebel**" is offensive to any woman. Her name meant, "Where is the prince," referring to a ritual summoning of the god Baal. She introduced pagan customs from Sidon into Israel's pure religion. This new Jezebel in Revelation does the same to the Thyatira Christian community. She is more concerned about her selfish pleasures than the Christian believers' needs, concerns, and spiritual purity.

2:23 | Jesus reminded Thyatira that he was "truly God's son" rather than Apollo or the Emperor.[91] The letter praises this small

---

[90] In Israel, the original Jezebel was Ithobaal I of Sidon's daughter and wicked King Ahab's wife (BC c871--c852).

[91] "Sons of God" under the influence of "Jezebel" were considered "Idols."

Christian community's virtuous growth but admonishes them for accepting the false prophetess. Jesus knows Satan's deep secrets and the people's intentions, for he **searches minds and hearts**.

2:23 | A fascinating translation of the phrase "**minds and hearts**" in the King James Version reads instead "reigns and hearts." "Reigns" were literally "kidneys," which people believed in ancient times to be a human's emotional seat. God knows every feeling and thought, and all are open to him. He explores the innermost thoughts of our minds and the most tender feelings of our hearts.

Question: "How do you feel about God knowing your innermost thoughts and emotions?"

14

THE MORNING STAR

2:24 "But to you I say, to the rest who are in Thyatira, as many as don't have this teaching, who don't know what some call 'the **deep things of Satan**,' to you I say, I am not putting any other burden on you. [25] Nevertheless, hold that which you have firmly until I come. [26] He who overcomes, and he who keeps my works to the end, to him I will give authority over the nations. [27] He will rule them with **a rod of iron**, shattering them like clay pots as I also have received of my Father: [28] and I will give him **the morning star**. [29] He who has an ear, let him hear what **the Spirit** says to the assemblies." (Rev. 2:24—29 emphases added).

2:24 The "**deep things of Satan**" has two meanings: advocating false teachings or offering secret personal insights claiming to guarantee deeper spiritual life. We need to hold tightly to our Christian faith and cautiously view any new teaching that turns us away from belief in our Lord, the Bible, or our faith. This scathing criticism may refer to "Nicolaism" or the Nicolaitan sect's perverse teaching. The phrase "her children" used about Jezebel describes those she led astray into pagan immorality and worship.

2:27 | "Break them with **a rod of iron**" may be translated as "rule them with an iron scepter." In Jewish belief, the end times envisaged a conquering Messiah who destroyed the heathen and extended Israel's rule. The Morning Star will rise with the iron scepter of a ruling monarch in his hand. The use of the morning star title by Jesus places him above all other Bible heroes.

2:27 | In Esther, one of its leading lights, Mordecai, was also called the "**Morning Star**" by rabbis. This name recalls the tremendous messianic prophecy that "a star will come out of Jacob. A scepter will rise out of Israel, and shall strike through the corners of Moab, and crush all the sons of Sheth" (Num. 24:17).

2:28 | The **morning star** is also a resurrection promise. The Christian will rise after death as the morning star appears after the night's darkness. When life ends, those who possess Christ will never lose him again, for "those who are wise will shine as the brightness of the expanse. Those who turn many to righteousness will shine as the stars forever and ever" (Dan.12:3). "Wise" here refers to the one "who imparts wisdom."

2:28 | A bright **morning star** comes to all who are righteous and helps others walk in righteousness. The morning star finds those who endure, overcome, and are faithful, for they will rule over Christ's enemies and reign with Jesus. He says that the person who "does my will" is the one "who keeps my works." He is given authority over the nations and says, "I will give the nations for your inheritance, the uttermost parts of the earth for your possession. You shall break them with a rod of iron. You shall dash them in pieces like a potter's vessel" (Ps. 2:8—9).

2:28 | Interestingly, "Lucifer," another name for Satan, was also called the **Morning Star** before falling from grace. *Lucifer* means "bearer of light" or "shining one." Many believe that Satan was a senior angel before his disobedience. Jesus takes over the title of the once pre-eminent angel Lucifer.

2:28 | Other "**Morning Star**" references appear elsewhere in scripture, describing Christ's advent in a person's life. Peter writes that prophecy is like a light shining in a dark place "until the day dawns, and the morning star arises in your hearts" (2 Pet. 1:19). Each Christian must allow the morning star to transform their minds and radiate from their hearts!

2.28 | Morning Star also describes the planet "Venus," the "Light Bringer," when it appears before sunrise in the east. It is a name given to Venus with Mercury when they show up together before dawn. This most brilliant light in the night sky is described as the "bright morning star" in the star system "Sirius,"[92] one of the earth's nearest neighbors.

2.28 | The **Morning Star** Ceremony is significant among indigenous peoples in North American history. This rite performed up to 1838 by the Skiri Pawnees of Central Nebraska included the human sacrifice of a 14-year-old Oglala Lakota girl named Haxti.[93] The ceremony was to provide success in war and fertility and was performed with a ceremonial bow and arrow. Then, the entire village, including children, lodged dozens of arrows in the victim's back. It reasserted devotion to the power of the rising Eastern Star. The Skiris believed that this ceremony allowed the victim's spirit to ascend to the sky to become a star while her body returned to the earth. The United States Government suppressed the ritual, and it has disappeared from tribal traditions.

2:29 | The **Spirit** says that Christ, the morning star, will come to those who overcome and will give them victory over death. Christians who persevere in the faith will share the messiah's authority. When the world is at its bleakest point, the bright morning star bursts onto the scene, exposing evil with its light of truth and bringing the promised reward of Jesus, symbolizing his resurrection victory over death. Later in Revelation, we find a similar reference, " I, Jesus, have sent my angel to testify these things to you for the assemblies. I am the root and the offspring of David, the Bright and Morning Star" (Rev. 22:16).

2:29 | I am reminded of the words of a beautiful chorus, "The Lily of the Valley" ("I've found a friend in Jesus"), written

---

[92] The name "Sirius" comes from the Greek word meaning *"glowing."* It is also named "the dog star" for its place in the constellation "Canis Major" or "Greater Dog."

[93] Human sacrifice was performed by the Skidi band of the Pawnee tribe in North America on April 22, 1838. Material from the University of Nebraska–Lincoln.

by William Charles Fry[94] for the Salvation Army[95] in London, England. Mr. Fry acted as one of four bodyguards to William Booth, its founder. The chorus goes,

> "He's the lily of the valley. He's the **bright and morning star,**
> He's the fairest of ten thousand. Everybody ought to know."

Everybody should know that Jesus, the morning star, will come to us and dwell in our hearts by faith!

Question: "What does the Morning Star mean to you?"

---

[94] (1837—1882).
[95] He founded the first Salvation Army brass band. The music was by William Shakespeare Hays' (1837--1907) for a minstrel show in 1871.

15

DEGENERATE SARDIS CITY

3:1 "And to the **angel of the assembly in Sardis** write: "He who has the seven Spirits of God and the seven stars says these things: "I know your works, that you have a reputation of being alive, but **you are dead**. ² **Wake up** and keep the things that remain, which you were about to throw away, for I have found **no works of yours perfected** before my God. ³ Remember therefore how you have received and heard. Keep it and repent. If therefore you won't watch, I will come as a thief, and you won't know what hour I will come upon you. ⁴ Nevertheless you have **a few names** in Sardis that didn't defile their garments. They will walk with me in white, for they are worthy. ⁵ He who overcomes will be arrayed in white garments, and I will in no way blot his name out of the book of life, and I will confess his name before my Father, and before his angels. ⁶ He who has an ear, let him hear what the Spirit says to the assemblies." (Rev. 3:1—6 emphases added).

3:1 | The **angel of the assembly in Sardis** means the "messenger or leader of the Sardis church." "He who has the seven spirits," the Holy Spirit or "God's sevenfold Spirit," communicates to the church leader. The "seven stars" are leaders of the churches in Asia to whom John of Patmos, under the guidance of the Holy Spirit, wrote his letters. Sardis was the capital city in the ancient

Lydian Empire and was prominent in the Roman world. A leader in it received this letter and undoubtedly would have read John's words to the congregation there.

3:1 | Sardis, also called "Sardes," is the site of the modern city of Sart in Turkey. In John of Patmos' day, it was important and of great wealth but then declined. William Mitchell Ramsay[96] wrote, "there was no greater example of the contrast between past splendor and present decay as in the degenerate Sardis City." Seven hundred years before John of Patmos wrote, the King of Lydia ruled in Asian splendor over his empire until Its citizens eventually abandoned it around 1402 AD.

3:1 | Sardis stood as an impregnable fortress in the middle of the River Hermus valley. To the north rose the long ridge of Mount Tmolus. Several hills went out like spurs from that ridge, forming a narrow plateau. The original city sat fifteen hundred feet up on one of these outcrops. Despite its unassailable position, Jesus Christ gave this nominal, sleepy, degenerate church a wake-up call. The sides of the Sardis City ridge were smooth and steep, and only where the spur met Mount Tmolus was there any approach, and even that wasn't easy. Sardis City stood like a massive watchtower guarding the Hermus valley. The Greek name for "Sardis" is *Sardeis*, a plural noun, for there were two Sardis cities, one on the high plateau and one in the valley. The narrow space at the top was too small for the expanding population, so the town developed below.

3:1 | The legendary King Croesus once ruled the city of **Sardis.**[97] He was immensely wealthy like Bill Gates or Warren Buffett in his day and reigned over Lydia for fourteen years[98] until his defeat by King Cyrus of Persia. The River Pactolus, which flowed through the lower town, was reputed to have gold-bearing waters. However, it was *electrum*, a naturally occurring amalgam of silver and gold found on the riverbed. Much of the king's wealth came from these deposits. The gold was also the source of

---

[96] (1851—1939).

[97] (BC 595-546).

[98] from BC 560 to BC 546.

the "Midas touch" legends. Anything that Midas touched turned to gold, but his real identity and its mythology are unclear. A fascinating side story is that his daughter supposedly turned to gold when he touched her!

3:1 | King Croesus was considered the wealthiest **Sardis** king, and his name is commemorated in the modern saying, "as rich as Croesus." He was the first to issue gold coins with standardized purity and weight, but he had one critical flaw. With wealth, Sardis degenerated and plunged into disaster.

3:1 | The so-called "wisest of the Greeks," Solon,[99] visited **Sardis** and warned Croesus where he was heading. He considered himself the happiest man alive, but Solon advised him, "Count no man happy until he is dead."[100] With incredible arrogance, he showed Solon all the magnificence and wealth of Sardis. Solon saw his blind confidence that nothing could end his rule and that the seeds of softness and degeneration were in him. He then embarked upon a foolish war with King Cyrus the Great.[101]

3:1 | To attack Cyrus' armies, Croesus of **Sardis** had to cross the Halys River. Before he advanced, he sought counsel and was told, "If you cross the river Halys, you will destroy a great empire."[102] He assumed his campaign would cement his power and Cyrus' destruction but this victory brought about his ultimate defeat at the Battle of Pteria. He crossed the river, engaged in battle, and Cyrus routed his army. However, he was not worried, for he thought that all he had to do was retreat to Sardis' impregnable citadel, recuperate, and fight again. The victory of King Cyrus initiated the siege of Sardis. Cyrus waited for fourteen days, then offered a reward to anyone who could find a weakness in the city's defenses. Sardis' "Achilles Heel" turned out to be its crumbling rock. It was like close-packed dried mud!

---

[99] (BC 638—558).

[100] Herodotus 1.30.

[101] (BC 576--530).

[102] The river Halys is known today as the Kizilirmak River, the longest river in Turkey.

3:1 | In BC 546, a Persian Mardian soldier called Hyeroeades, from Iran, where Cyrus the Great originated, saw a serviceman accidentally drop his helmet over the battlements and then go down the precipice of **Sardis** to retrieve it. Hyeroeades figured there must be a pathway by which a troop of agile men could climb up and attack the city. That night, he led a squad up along the fault, and when they reached the top, they found, to their surprise, that the battlements were completely unguarded. The Sardians considered themselves too impregnable to even post a guard, so Sardis fell. A city with a history like that knows what the risen Christ means when he says, "If you don't watch, I will come like a thief, and you won't know what hour I will come upon you" (Rev. 3:3).

3:1 | John of Patmos wrote this letter to Sardis. which was in his day a wealthy but unfortunately spiritually **dead** city for there was no life or Spirit there. The once-great Sardians had become soft, and twice they lost their city because they were too lazy to keep watch. It is a warning to Christian communities of the death trap of lethargy. Though once a magnificent citadel, Sardis is only a pile of rubble on a hilltop today.

3:2 | The Sardis church is a picture of nominal Christianity, busily being religious but lacking spiritual life. The angel to the Sardian church writes, "I have found no works of yours perfected before my God." He calls them to **wake up**.

3:2 | Douglas Wilson argues with the "nominal Christian" notion.[103] He believes all Christians enter into a covenant with God at conversion and are obligated to serve him. Therefore, there is "no such thing as a nominal Christian any more than we can find a man who is a nominal husband!" God orders the Sardis church to **wake up**, and with this call comes the possibility of recovery and new life. The Sardis church should be able to regain its power, but it fails.

3:4 | Several dedicated Sardis Christians received a special robe because they were deserving. "You have a **few names** that

---

[103] in "Reformed is Not Enough."

didn't defile their garments. They will walk with me in white, for they are worthy." Jesus said, "Be watchful, or I will come like a thief, and you will not know at what time I will come to you." A faithful few will wear holy shining attire rather than soiled clothing in this cloth-making city.

Question: "How can we wake up ourselves, our families, our churches, and communities to the importance of the Christian faith?"

16

PHILADELPHIA
BROTHERLY LOVE

3:7 "To the angel of the assembly in **Philadelphia** write:
"**He who is holy, he who is true**, he who has the **key
of David,** he who opens and no one can shut, and who
shuts and no one opens, says these things: ⁸ "I know
your works (behold, I have set before you an **open door,**
which no one can shut), that you have a little power,
and kept my word, and didn't deny my name."
(Rev. 3:7—8 emphases added).

3:7 | Philadelphia has long had the title of the city of "Brotherly
Love." The name comes from the Greek words *phileo*, meaning
"love," and *adelphos*, for "brother." Revelation's "Philadelphia"[104]
is now called "Alasehir" on Turkey's western side. It was the
youngest of seven cities founded by Pergamum colonists under
Attalus the Second.[105] His affection for his brother "Eumenes"
was such that he renamed him "Philadelphos" and labeled the
city after him.

3:7 | A Quaker pioneer, William Penn,[106] founded

---

[104] also spelled "Philadelphus," or "Philadelphos,"
[105] (BC 159-138).
[106] (1644-1718).

Philadelphia, the largest city in the US state of Pennsylvania,[107] in 1682. Penn notably said, "God must govern men, or tyrants will rule them," and "Right is right, even if everyone is against it, and wrong is wrong, even if everyone is for it." He established the colony's democratic principles, which inspired the United States Constitution. He was ahead of his time and envisioned a federation of countries in Europe in his essay, "European Dyet, Parliament or Estates."

3:7 | Revelation's **Philadelphia** became an open door for Greek culture and language into Lydia and Phrygia. So well did it work that by 19 AD, the Lydians spoke only Greek and had forgotten their native tongue. According to William Mitchell Ramsey,[108] it became "the center for the diffusion of Greek language and letters in a peaceful land." It was a wealthy trade hub in the Roman empire. The Risen Christ spoke of the "open door" set before it as a marvelous opportunity to spread the message of Jesus Christ's *phileo.*

3:7 | Earthquakes left their mark on **Philadelphia** more than on most cities. Strabo's "Geography" chronicled all of Europe and recorded that in 17 AD, it was a "city full of earthquakes," which continued for years. People met them with courage when they happened, but recurring shocks drove them to panic. In Philadelphia, aftershocks occurred daily, with gaping cracks appearing in walls and roads. One part of the city was in ruins, then another. Most people dwelt on the streets outside their homes in temporary shelters. They feared to enter the town lest its walls should fall on them. This situation challenged the church, but Jesus encouraged them. Tremors terrified Christians, and others considered them mad, for they spent their time shoring up shaky buildings and fleeing for safety to open spaces.

3:7 | **Philadelphia** sat on a fault line on the edge of a broad flat valley called "The Burned Land." It was naturally fertile and

---

[107] Philadelphia's name undoubtedly came from an English Gloucestershire village and the biblical "Philadelphia."
[108] (1851--1939).

benefitted by becoming a grape-growing region and a famous wine hub.

3:7 | In the introduction to this letter to Philadelphia, the writer gives us two titles for Christ, each of which carries an extraordinary claim. Jesus says he is "**he who is holy, he who is true.**" God calls himself "Holy, holy, holy, the Lord Almighty" (Isa. 6:3). He is also "the Holy One" (Isa. 40:25). "Holy" from the Greek word *hagios* means "separate from." Now Jesus receives the title, "he who is holy."

3:7 | Christ is also described as **he who is true.** He is a completely authentic person. He said, "I am the way, the truth, and the life. no one comes to the Father except through me" (John 14:6). An old chorus reflects this truth,

> "Without the Way, there is no going.
> Without the Truth, there is no knowing.
> Without the Life, there is no living.
> I am the Way, the Truth, and the Life.
> That's what Jesus said."[109]

3:7 | The holy and true Jesus Christ also holds the **Key of David,** which opens the door to eternal life. David's key, or David's house key, refers to the New Jerusalem and signifies the power of Jesus to unlock this future kingdom. David's keyset gives him final unquestionable authority.

3:7 | Behind these words is an interesting Old Testament picture from the Prophet Isaiah. King Hezekiah of Judah gave his faithful steward Eliakim the right to admit others to his presence and the key holder or doorkeeper to the royal court. God said, "I will lay the **key of David's house** on his shoulder. He will open, and no one will shut. He will shut, and no one will open" (Isa. 22:22). This may have been in John of Patmos' mind as he wrote about Jesus authorizing others to enter David's city.

3:7 | The "Te Deum," a selection of verses from the Psalms

---

[109] Music traditional arr. D.J.Cradshaw. Music arrangement Copyright 1971 Scripture Union, from *Sing to God.*

composed by Ambrose,[110] says, "Thou didst open the kingdom of heaven to all believers." The Latin *Te Deum* means "To you be glory, O God," and is important to me as this was the name of a Gospel rhythm group I sang with on Merseyside for four years in the sixties. We aimed to open a **door** for young people to God through word and song. Five hundred young adults, teenagers, and probably more committed their lives to Christ through this ministry. Jesus is the believers' open door into God's presence!

3:8 | King Eumenes[111] established Philadelphia as a border town for the Greek language and culture to the barbarous peoples beyond because of its vital position on the imperial postal service road from Troas.[112] Caesar's armies and merchants' caravans rode it! As Philadelphia was the society's open way, so Jesus Christ is the missionary **door**, and he beckons Christian missionaries.

3:8 | The Apostle Paul wrote, "a great and effective **door** had opened to me" (1 Cor. 16:9). When he returned to Antioch, he reported that God "had opened a door of faith to the nations" (Acts 14:27). Before every Christian, there is a doorway of ministry opportunity. To be a missionary is to be called to share the Good News, teach, educate, and engage in healing ministries. However, a person does not need to leave their country or neighborhood to do this. There are those to be won for Christ within our homes, schools, friends, cell phone bubbles, and workplaces. To use this window of opportunity is at once our privilege and responsibility. Philadelphia's church proved faithful, but the reward for her loyalty was, surprisingly, to receive more work from him! In his way, the bonus of successful labor is more to do!

3:8 | The Philadelphia **door** could also be Jesus himself. He said, "Most certainly, I tell you, I am the sheep's door" (John 10:7). Just as a Middle Eastern shepherd slept across the sheepfold's opening to prevent a predator from entering and attacking the sheep, Jesus protects his flock with his own body. The Jesus entrance is there to admit only willing, contrite persons to God's

---

[110] (340—397 AD).

[111] (BC 221—160).

[112] via Pergamum, Thyatira, Sardis, and Phrygia.

kingdom and bar the way to all others. He said, "no one comes to the Father except through me" (John 14:6).

Question: "How can we win for Christ those within our home, school, circle of friends, cell phone bubble, or work associates?"

17

PHILADELPHIA
ENDURES PATIENTLY

3:9 "Behold, I give some of the synagogue of Satan, of those who say they are Jews, and they are not, but lie—behold, I will make them to come and worship before your feet, and to know that I have loved you. [10] Because you kept **my command to endure**, I also will keep you from the hour of testing which is to come on the whole world, to test those who dwell on the earth. [11] I am coming quickly! Hold firmly that which you have, so that no one **takes your crown.** [12] He who overcomes, I will make him a **pillar in the temple** of my God, and **he will go out from there no more.** I will write on him the **name of my God** and the name of the city of my God, the New Jerusalem, which comes down out of heaven from my God, and my own **new name.** [13] He who has an ear, let him hear what the Spirit says to the assemblies." (Rev. 3:9—13 emphases added).

3:10 | Up to this point, Philadelphia had kept God's **command to endure** patiently, implying the church had triumphantly emerged from a trial. "My command to endure patiently" may not refer to their perseverance but the gritty determination of Jesus on the cross. Like him, he requires us to maintain what we have and persevere, for loyalty has its sure reward.

3:10 | When Jesus calls us to **endure** patiently, he supplies us with his example, inspiration, and fortitude. Let us look to Jesus, the author and perfector of our faith, who "endured the cross, despising its shame, and has sat down at the right hand of the throne of God" (Heb. 12:2). We can last to the end with his example, vision, and grit.

3:10 | The ancient Philadelphians were encouraged to **endure** and not allow anyone to take their crown, the reward for their faithfulness when Christ returns. "Coming soon" is repeated three times at the end of Revelation![113] Until Christ comes again, God warns the Philadelphia church to be patient in adversity, and the risen Christ tells them that he is approaching quickly. His words warn the heedless and comfort the oppressed. The Letter of James also encourages us, "you also be patient. Establish your hearts, for the coming of the Lord is at hand" (James 5:8).

3:11 | The risen Christ asks the Philadelphians to hold on to what they have so that no one **takes their crown.** It is not a question of someone stealing it but of God taking it and giving it to someone else because they are not worthy to wear it.

3:12 | In Philadelphia, the earth's tremors were always on people's minds. The promise that **he would go out from there no more** gave Christians great security after the insecurity of having to leave one's home quickly each time an earthquake struck.

3:12 | In later days, **Philadelphia**'s brotherly love would make it great. When the Turks and Muslims flooded Asia Minor and every other town capitulated, Philadelphia stood firm against the invaders. For centuries, it was a free Christian city among Muslim peoples and the Asian Christian faith's last bastion. It was not until midway through the fourteenth century that Philadelphia eventually fell. But there are still a bishop and a thousand or so Christians today. Except for Smyrna, the other churches addressed in the seven Revelation letters are now in

---

[113] (Rev. 22:7, 22:12 and 22:20).

ruins. However, Philadelphia, the city of brotherly love, still holds the Christian faith banner aloft.

3:12 | Abraham said Jewish Rabbis "were the world's pillars." Each of Jesus Christ's faithful followers will also become a dedicated member, a **pillar in the temple**. Paul wrote that "James and Cephas and John" (Gal. 2:9) were pillars in Jerusalem's early church. Solomon's temple originally had two decorated copper brass or bronze freestanding pillars named "Boaz" and "Jachin." They were six feet in diameter and twenty-seven feet tall, but the Chaldeans destroyed them at the fall of the First Temple in Jerusalem in BC 587.

3:12 | In Asia Minor cities, when a Jewish priest died after a lifetime of faithful service, he was honored with a new pillar erected in the synagogue inscribed with the **name of my God,** his name, and his father's name. In the same way, Christ endows lasting honor on his faithful ones by giving them the chosen name of Jesus. God will write their Christian name and city name on each one. When he told Moses about Aaron and the priests' blessing over the people, he said, "So they shall put my name on the children of Israel, and I will bless them" (Num. 6:27). Jesus himself is to write Christian names upon Israel so that all may know that they are now his people.

3:12 | Faithful Jewish people have a special place in the New Jerusalem. The victorious ones will become pillars in God's temple. "I will write on him the **name of my God** and the name of the city of my God, the New Jerusalem."

3:12 | When it comes to monikers, some Bible students have counted as many as thirty-eight **new names** for Jesus in the book of Revelation. Here is the full list,

1. Jesus Christ (Rev. 1:1)
2. Faithful witness (Rev. 1:5)
3. Firstborn of the dead (Rev. 1:5)
4. Ruler of the kings of the earth (Rev. 1:5)
5. Alpha and the Omega (Rev. 1:8)
6. Who Is, who was, and who Is to come (Rev. 1:8)
7. The Almighty (Rev. 1:8)

8. Son of Man (Rev. 1:13)
9. First and the last (Rev. 1:17)
10. Living one (Rev. 1:18)
11. Have the keys of Death and of Hades (Rev. 1:18)
12. Who holds the seven stars (Rev. 2:1, 3:1)
13. Who walks among the seven golden lamp stands (Rev. 2:1)
14. Who has the sharp two-edged sword (Rev. 2:12)
15. Son of God (Rev. 2:18)
16. Searches minds and hearts (Rev. 2:23)
17. Has the seven Spirits of God (Rev. 3:1)
18. Holy and true one (Rev. 3:7)
19. Has the key of David (Rev. 3:7)
20. Opens and none can shut (Rev. 3:7)
21. Shuts and none can open (Rev. 3:7)
22. Amen (Rev. 3:14)
23. Faithful and True Witness (Rev. 3:14)
24. Beginning of God's creation (Rev. 3:14)
25. Lord and God (Rev. 4:11)
26. Holy One (Rev. 4:11)
27. Lion of the tribe of Judah (Rev. 5:5)
28. Root of David (Rev. 5:5; 22:15)
29. Lamb (Rev. 5:6,8,12; 17:14)
30. Lord of lords (Rev. 17:14; 19:16)
31. King of kings (Rev. 17:14; 19:16)
32. Rider of the white horse (Rev. 19:11)
33. Faithful and True (Rev. 19:11)
34. Word of God (Rev. 19:13)
35. Christ (Rev. 20:4)
36. Beginning and the End (Rev. 21:6)
37. Lord God of the spirits of the prophets (Rev. 22:6)
38. Bright and Morning Star (Rev. 22:16).

Jesus says we will have his "new name written" upon us, but I don't know which of the thirty-eight he means! All will then see that we belong to him, for we are citizens and pillars of the New Jerusalem.

3:12 | The **new name** of my God's city stands for citizenship in his eternal city. Philadelphians knew all about taking a new identity. In 17 AD, a terrible earthquake devastated their city, but Emperor Tiberius dealt kindly with them, remitted their taxes, and offered a generous gift to rebuild. The people of Philadelphia then named their community "Neo-Caesarea" or "Caesar's New City" after their benefactor. Later Philadelphia, in gratitude, renamed it "Flavia" in honor of the family of Emperor Vespasian, who was also helpful to them.

3:12 | Tiberias was honored by the emperor and gave their community a **new name** on the Sea of Galilee's western shore. Tourists still come to Tiberias, the largest town in Galilee, to enjoy its hot springs and mineral baths. After a busy day sailing across the sea of Galilee and visiting Capernaum, I remember lounging in the warm mineral bath water at sunset on my trip there. Generations of people down the ages had no doubt done the same.

3:12 | Cities **named** buildings and streets after those who had endowed them in some unique way. The same thing has happened elsewhere and in other generations. Up the street from my home is a road called "Carnegie Avenue" after the famous American philanthropist Andrew Carnegie.[114] He endowed numerous towns, cities, and organizations with gifts to develop their communities, including building many town halls and libraries. He gifted newly invented pipe organs to churches. Like the recipients of Carnegie grants who named streets after him, Jesus Christ's name also marks his faithful ones. When Christ conquers all, his faithful ones will bear his name as their benefactor. What a great privilege that will be. It will show that we are his and share his triumph!

Question: "Which of the thirty-eight names of Jesus in Revelation is most important to you?"

---

[114] (1835--1919.)

18

LAODICEA'S LUKEWARM FAITH

3:14 "To the angel of the assembly in **Laodicea** write: "**The Amen**, the Faithful and True Witness, the **Beginning of God's creation**, says these things: [15] "I know your works, that you are neither cold nor hot. I wish you were cold or hot. [16] So, because you are **lukewarm**, and neither hot nor cold, I will vomit you out of my mouth." (Rev. 3:14—16 emphases added).

3:14 | This epistle is one of seven Revelation letters addressed to the ancient city of **Laodicea**.[115] It was founded in BC 262 by the Greek King Antiochus Theos of Syria[116] on the River Lycos and named after his wife, Laodice. It is mentioned six times in the New Testament and was Asia's most southerly church. Now called "Denizli," in Turkey, it had the grim distinction of being the only assembly that had nothing good to commend it.

3:14 | Interestingly, the founder of **Laodicea**, Antiochus, appears in the "Edicts of Ashoka," about the Emperor of India who received Buddhist proselytes and prescribed herbal medicine

---

[115] Laodicea was originally called "Diospolis" or "City of Zeus" commemorating the ancient Greek deity of sky and thunder.
[116] (BC 286--246) During the second Syrian war, Antiochus 11 received the title of "theos" by one of his liberated peoples.

to treat humans and animals. Although with no evident and particular faults, this Revelation letter reprimanded Laodicea. The Lord says he will vomit them out of his mouth for being lukewarm and neither hot nor cold.

3:14 | Paul criticized Archippus, the assembly leader in **Laodicea,** for his negligence. When writing to neighboring Colossae, he ordered them, "Tell Archippus, 'take heed to the ministry which you have received in the Lord, that you fulfill it'" (Col. 4:17). Archippus[117] was one of the seventy-two disciples sent out by Jesus. Still, he failed to fulfill his appointed ministry.[118]

3:14 | In **Laodicea,** an aqueduct provided water for the city's woolen clothing manufacturers. These violet-black tunics and salve ointment remedies were the sources of the city's wealth. Buyers prized the sheep's soft, glossy wool as outer garments, but this black clothing compared poorly to baptism's pure white robes. The Christians' material prosperity contrasted with their spiritual poverty. The risen Christ's words spoke directly against this reliance on wealth. In their minds, their riches eliminated the need for God when they had the "stuff." It is not unlike our materialistic society today.

3:14 | The **Laodicean** medical center generated incredible wealth for the city. Their coins symbolized this acquired affluence from producing a healing ointment for various eye problems. Physical sight and perception contrasted with spiritual blindness, for it did not take a stand for anything, and indifference led to idleness. They had vision loss, for they could not see the real needs around them. As my mother-in-law would say, "A blind man would be happy to see it."

3:14 The church at **Laodicea** needed eye salve itself but in a radically different spiritual sense. It was now hard-hearted and self-satisfied because it failed to do anything for Christ. He said, "I came into this world for judgment, that those who don't see may see; and that those who see may become blind" (John 9:39).

---

[117] Archippus was Greek for the "master of the horse" in the First Century AD.
[118] "The Apostolic Constitutions 8:46"

3:14 | **Laodicea** was on Asia's most strategically important highway and connected Ephesus in the west to Syria in the east. It was a critical hub in this part of the Roman empire. The road through Laodicea began at the coast and climbed to an eight thousand five hundred feet high central plateau. It followed the River Meander valley, which wandered about until it reached what was known as the Gates of Phrygia. It was symbolic of the directionless and lethargic church led by Archippus.

3:14 | This letter begins with a series of titles for Jesus Christ, including the most prestigious, **The Amen.** The English phrase comes from Hebrew, indicating "certainty and truth." "Amen" affirms "it is so" or "so be it" and is commonly used after a prayer, hymn, or sometimes by a congregation member to show agreement. "Amen" indicates concurrence with the prayer and recognizes the "God of Amen" and the "Jesus Amen." Hence the phrase "Amen to that!" Experts tell us that the UK English pronunciation would be "ah-men" and the US English "ay-men!" It affirms the deity of Jesus as "the God of Amen," "the Amen," or "the God of truth." Rabbinic scholars from medieval France believed that the root word "amen" was derived from the Hebrew word *emuna* for "faith."

3:14 | If Jesus is "the God of **Amen**," then his words can be utterly relied upon to be entirely accurate and faithful. His promises are authentic, honest, trustworthy, and genuine.

3:14 | The Son of God and the creation interconnect in the New Testament. John of Patmos writes that the Amen is **the Beginning of God's Creation.** "All things were made through him. Without him, nothing was made that has been made" (John 1:3). Paul adds, "For by him all things were created in the heavens and on the earth, visible things and invisible things, whether thrones or dominions or principalities or powers. All things have been created through him and for him" (Col.1:16). As Christians see it, the "Creation God" and the "Redemption God" are the same.

3:14 | **The firstborn of all creation** emphasizes that Jesus is the *arche* or "archetype." He is the original pattern or model for all things. Jesus, who created the water and the land, can speak of God because he coexisted with his Father from the beginning. His witness is faithful because he is "God's creation ruler" who began and organized the creation process.

3:16 | Ancient Laodicea always had water supply problems. It traveled so far by viaduct from the Hierapolis springs that it was **lukewarm** when it arrived. Its neighbors' hot springs at Hierapolis were famous for their abundant hot water. Travelers journeyed great distances to bathe there, believing they had medicinal powers, and to the hot spring baths in Colosse. In Roman times, raised structures and tunnels carried water long distances to supply outlying communities. The Laodicea aqueduct[119] transported it six miles from Baspinar across valleys on tall brick columns and arches then through mountain tunnels. The waterway was an impressive construction feat, and some brick and stone aqueducts survive today because of the excellence of Roman engineering skills two thousand years ago. By the time water reached its destination, it was not only lukewarm, but it had developed a sickening, nauseating taste!

3:16 | Like **Laodicea's** aqueduct, King Hezekiah of Israel built a water channel underground beneath Jerusalem, enabling the city to resist a Babylonian siege in the eighth century BC for over a year. Known as "Hezekiah's" or "Siloam's Tunnel," it was carved in the rock within the City of David in ancient times. It was a curving tunnel one thousand seven hundred feet long, falling twelve inches and connecting the Gihon Spring outside the city to the Pool of Siloam inside. It was designed to ensure a besieging force would not have access to any water. A team dug from both ends and managed to link up! The Bible talks about it as a "conduit." "Now the rest of the acts of Hezekiah, and all his might, and how he made the pool, and the conduit, and brought water into the city, aren't they written in the book of the chronicles of the kings of Judah?" (2 Kgs. 20:20)

3:16 | Interestingly, in many of Rome's squares today, you

---

[119] An "aqueduct" was a large stone or brick engineered structure built to transport water over vast distances. The word "aqueduct" comes from the Latin *aqua* for "water" and *ducere* meaning "to lead."

can still see fountains where the Roman bathhouses and brothels used to be. The statement of Jesus to the Laodicea church is that their spirituality had faded and was about as useless as their tepid, **lukewarm** water. The church's angel writes that he knows their deeds and that they are neither cold nor hot. The ancient ruins of Laodicea are sadly all that remains today.

Question: "How was Jesus the firstborn of all creation?"

19

RICH LAODICEA CITY

3:17 "Because you say, 'I am **rich**, and have gotten riches, and have need of nothing;' and don't know that you are the wretched one, miserable, poor, **blind**, and **naked**; [18] I counsel you to buy from me **gold** refined by fire, that you may become rich; and white garments, that you may clothe yourself, and that the shame of your nakedness may not be revealed; and eye salve to anoint your eyes, that you may see. [19] As many as I love, I **reprove and chasten**. Be zealous therefore, and repent. [20] Behold, **I stand at the door and knock.** If anyone hears my voice and opens the door, then I will come in to him, and will dine with him, and he with me. [21] He who overcomes, I will give to him to sit down with me on my throne, as I also overcame, and sat down with my Father on his throne. [22] He who has an ear, let him hear what the Spirit says to the assemblies." (Rev. 3:17—22 emphases added).

3:17 | In the first century AD, the Laodicean banking center was well-known and **rich**. It was a vital hub about one hundred miles east of Ephesus and was the wealthiest of the seven cities in the "Ephesus Crescent." It was so prosperous that the Romans permitted it to mint silver and gold coins. When Cicero[120] traveled

---

[120] (BC 106--43), a Greek philosopher and one of Rome's most exceptional speakers.

in Asia Minor, it was at the banking center there that he cashed his credit letters. In 61 AD, it was devastated by an earthquake, but the wealthy and independent citizens refused any government help to rebuild but financed it from their resources. It benefitted from its position on an important trade route on the Lycus River. Like Sardis, they were also free of persecution. Because they were rich, what they could buy became more valuable than their unseen and eternal spiritual assets. They boasted of their wealth from the eye treatments and the clothing trade, but Jesus criticized them for being wretched, pitiful, poor, blind, and naked.

3:17 | The Greeks called their "eye salve" *collyrium*, meaning a "course bread roll." These little cylinders contained medication, crushed Phrygian stone, and amber-colored essential oil spice nard or spikenard.[121] Healers used this fragrant oil as a traditional medicine across Europe. They believed the eye treatment drew out "evil humor," which caused visual impairment or hearing loss. Laodicea was so proud of its medical skills in caring for people's eyes and ears that it did not see itself as spiritually **blind** and deaf. Jesus tells them they need spiritual eye medicine from him for their blindness.

3:17 | Despite being famous for its purple woolen cloth, Jesus accused Laodicea of its shameful **nakedness**. It was proud of its clothing and dyeing industries, but he told them to purchase gleaming white, spotless garments from him, symbolic of righteousness. Its sheep produced beautiful black woolen fabric, but only the gleaming white clothing of the pure in heart would satisfy God. It appeared richly dressed, but it was still spiritually naked.

3:18 | Laodicea was also well known for its **gold** and silver coins. Gold refined in a fire referred to God's grace, for it involved mining the ore, crushing, and heating it intensely until the dross separated from the metal and only pure gold was left. Laodicea would receive the same harsh spiritual treatment at God's hand.

3:19 | Jesus told the Laodiceans, **"As many as I love, I reprove**

---

[121] from a Himalayan flowering plant in Nepal, China, and India.

and chasten." He loved them, but they were distracted by their wealth. Its medical center was significant, as attested by the massive columns[122] discovered in the city's northern district. A bustling trade route brought crowds of visitors seeking cures, making it very wealthy. So renowned were its doctors that some of their names, such as Zeuxis, an ophthalmologist specializing in eye diseases, and Alexander Philalethes, another doctor, survived on gold coins.

3:20 | The famous verse, **"Behold, I stand at the door and knock,"** brings to mind the striking painting, "The Light of the World" by William Holman Hunt,[123] showing Jesus knocking on a garden door. Hunt was an English artist who co-founded the London Pre-Raphaelite Brotherhood[124] and sought a return to the abundant detail and intense colors of Italian art compositions. He believed the world should be read as a visual sign system and incorporated these ideas into his paintings. Paul Kuritz[125] elaborated, "He painted the entire canvas out of doors whenever the moon was full, from nine o'clock in the evening until five o'clock the next morning." Some have suggested that he found the perfect dawn light he longed for outside Bethlehem on his Holy Land visits. His oil painting on canvas was celebrated and became so popular that crowds of people paid a fee to view it at Keble College, Oxford. Hunt also completed a smaller version between 1851 and 1856 and later a life-sized one. However, his eyesight was failing, and he needed the help of another artist, Edward Robert Hughes,[126] to finish it. The painting drew large crowds on a world tour between 1905 and 1907. Robert Fulford[127] claimed in 2007 that four-fifths of Australia's population viewed it.

3:20 | In his picture, Hunt attempted to show how much Jesus wanted to share personal fellowship and friendship with

---

[122] from c100 BC

[123] (1827--1910).

[124] with John Everett Millais (1829--1896) and Dante Gabriel Rossetti (1828--1882) in 1848.

[125] the American theatre and film critic

[126] (1851-1914)

[127] (1932--present).

us. He wrote, "One can only open the human heart's **door** from the inside." The door handle does not appear on the outside of the door in the painting. He wanted us to unlock our lives, minds, and emotions to him like opening a latch inside a door. Interestingly, Joel Osteen, the American pastor of Lakewood Church in Houston, Texas, televangelist, and author, spoke of his father, John Osteen. He went to a church meeting as a young man with a friend and gave his life to Christ. Returning home in the dark, he tried not to wake his parents. On the table was one of those large bibles for display. Joel's father opened it to the Holman Hunt paining, "The Light of the World." Immediately, Joel's father knew that God had called him into a unique ministry.

3.20 | Jesus graciously allows us to decide whether or not to respond to him. He persists in knocking and not breaking in but gently tapping. The question is, "Do you hear Jesus knocking on your heart's door, and will you open the handle on your side to him?

Question: "Did Jesus ever knock at the door of your life? Did you let him in?"

20

HEAVEN'S OPEN DOOR

4.1 "After these things I looked and saw a **door opened** in heaven, and the first voice that I heard, like a trumpet speaking with me, was one saying, "**Come up here**, and I will show you the things which must happen after this." ² Immediately I was **in the Spirit**. Behold, there was a **throne set in heaven**, and **one sitting** on the throne ³ that looked like a **jasper stone and a sardius**. There was a **rainbow** around the throne, like an emerald to look at." (Rev. 4:1—3 emphases added).

4:1 | In his vision, John of Patmos saw a **door opened** into the heavenly court where God sat on his throne surrounded by angel multitudes. The ancients believed heaven had doors into a vast vaulted roof on a square flat earth.

4:1 | John heard a trumpet blast at Christ's voice and an angel saying, "**come up here**." He saw God's magnificent throne room through the open door and approached. This vision reminds us of the prophet Ezekiel's summons into ministry and his sight of God's heavenly throne. "As I was among the captives by the river Chebar, the heavens opened, and I saw visions of God." "Over their heads was the likeness of a throne, appearing like a sapphire stone" (Ezek. 1:1,26).

4:2 | John of Patmos wrote that the Spirit showed him

situations and events not visible to human eyes. A celestial sky blue-colored **throne of lapis lazuli**[128] was before him in heaven. Its color was a universal symbol of wisdom and truth. The semi-precious stone, "lapis lazuli," was made into "ultramarine blue," the most desired and expensive of all color pigments. Some very famous Renaissance artists, including Vermeer and Titian, favored it. John of Patmos saw God's throne with "someone" sitting on it, surrounded by an emerald rainbow's shimmering colors emphasizing the scene's otherworldliness. After describing heaven's wonder, he reassures us that future events will not frighten us.

4:2 | The golden sarcophagus of King Tut Ankh Amun was also richly inlaid with **lapis lazuli** when discovered in 1923 by Howard Carter. Wikipedia reported that Carter made a hole in the door and used a candle to check for foul gases before looking inside. "At first, I could see nothing," he wrote, "the hot air escaping from the chamber causing the candle flame to flicker, but presently, as my eyes grew accustomed to the light, details of the room within emerged slowly from the mist, strange animals, statues, and gold – everywhere the glint of gold." After a pause, his companion Lord Carnarvon asked, "Can you see anything?" he replied, "Yes, wonderful things." The throne in heaven also revealed beautiful things to John of Patmos, expressing Almighty God's royalty, honor, and power.

4:2 | Overcome by the awe-inspiring sight of someone seated on the throne, John avoided naming or describing God. He saw **one sitting** on the heavenly throne glistening like a jasper stone and a sardius. The focal point of heaven was not empty as many in our generation would wish but occupied. The deity there had a human being's appearance hence the personal descriptive phrase "someone" or "one." We must remember that God is not a giant super-computer or a frightening space alien but like ourselves. He cares for us because he is one with us. But as the Almighty Creator who formed the universe out of nothing, he is different

---

[128] Mined in Egypt from 4000 BC to today.

from us. He orchestrates all that John of Patmos records. Some assert that the world is spinning out of control, but God directs everything from his high place.

4:3 | Shining, precious gems appear as a rainbow of crystalline **jasper,** fiery red **sardius,** and green emerald around God. These three gems represent wrath, blood, and mercy, essential elements in his relationship with us through the Lord Jesus Christ. Jasper is sometimes called *carnelian*, a transparent crystal found in Sardis and a symbol of avenging wrath. The green emerald symbolizes soothing mercy and expresses God's majesty. These gems are especially significant because jasper, carnelian, and emerald decorated the High Priest's breastplate and the New Jerusalem's foundations.

4:3 | The sight of a fantastic glimmering **rainbow** around God's throne spontaneously brings forth a praise song within us. The lovely Christian hymn by Carl Gustav Boberg[129] beautifully conveys this wonder.

> "O, Lord my God. When I in awesome wonder,
> Consider all the works thy hands have made.
> I see the sun. I hear the rolling thunder,
> Thy power through all the universe portrayed.
> Then sings my soul, my savior God to thee.
> How great thou art, how great thou art.
> In all the World, there is no God like Thee.
> How great thou art, how great thou art!

Question: "Imagine looking through heaven's open door. Close your eyes to picture God's throne and everything around it. Describe what you see?"

---

[129] (1859--1940)

21

TWENTY-FOUR ELDERS

> **4:4** "Around the throne were twenty-four thrones. On the thrones were **twenty-four elders** sitting, dressed in white garments, with crowns of gold on their heads. [5] Out of the throne proceed **lightnings, sounds, and thunders.** There were seven lamps of fire burning before his throne, which are the **seven Spirits of God**."
> (Rev. 4:4—5 emphases added).

4:4 | The **twenty-four elders** represent God's redeemed people of all ages before Christ's Resurrection and after it. Some scholars try to name the elders individually, but they represent the whole faith community. Twelve is a multiple of three times four. Three is God's number, four is a human being's number, and twelve represents God's Kingdom. Multiplying twelve times two indicates God's entire Kingdom. The city's gates bear the twelve patriarchs' names, and its foundation stones show the twelve apostles. These symbolize faithful Jewish and Gentile peoples as God's heavenly family.

4:4 | The **twenty-four elders** in white robes have golden crowns on their heads. Wearing white garments or "glowing white robes" represents their purity, and "crowns of gold" portray their victory.

4:4 | There are other indications of **twenty-four elders** in a heavenly council. At the creation, the Lord God said, "Behold, the man has become like one of us, knowing good and evil" (Gen. 3:22). "Like one of us" suggests a council speaking with God, a Trinity reference, or even an angels' gathering. Isaiah further fuels this intriguing concept when he writes that the Lord Almighty will reign on "Mount Zion, and in Jerusalem; and glory will be before his elders" (Isa. 24:23).

4:4 | Who are these **twenty-four elders** seated on thrones? An answer might be that they are twelve faithful tribal leaders from the Old Testament and twelve New Testament apostles. They are not angels, and their crowns are not kingly crowns but victory garlands, indicating they were victorious in life and death.

4:5 | **Lightnings, sounds, and thunders** evoke fear and terror at events in heaven. In the account of the giving of the Law, or "the Torah" on Mount Sinai, on the third morning, "there were thunders and lightnings, and a thick cloud on the mountain, and the sound of an exceedingly loud trumpet, and all the people who were in the camp trembled" (Ex. 19:16).

4:5 | There are seven Revelation lamps representing God's seven spirits. The **seven Spirits of God** translates as "the sevenfold Spirit," indicating the Holy Spirit's presence.

Question: "Would you be encouraged or afraid of the lightnings, sounds, and thunders in heaven?"

22

FOUR LIVING CREATURES

4:6 "Before the throne was something like **a sea of glass**, similar to crystal. In the middle of the throne, and around the throne were **four living creatures** full of eyes before and behind. [7] The first creature was like a **lion, and the second creature like a calf, and the third creature had a face like a man, and the fourth was like a flying eagle**.[8] The four living creatures, each one of them having six wings, are full of eyes around and within. They have no rest day and night, saying, "**Holy, holy, holy** is the Lord God, the Almighty, **who was and who is and who is to come!**" [9] When the living creatures give glory, honor, and thanks to him who sits on the throne, to him who lives **forever and ever**, [10] the twenty-four elders fall down before him who sits on the throne, and worship him who lives forever and ever, and throw their crowns before the throne, saying, [11] "Worthy are you, our Lord and God, the Holy One, to receive the glory, the honor, and the power, for you created all things, and because of your desire they existed, and were created!" (Rev. 4:6—11 emphases added).

4:6 | Before God's throne was a **sea of glass.** We can trace glass back to the library of King Assurbanipal[130] in the sixth century

---

[130] (BC 668-627)

BC in Mesopotamia in present-day Syria and Iraq. Glassmakers discovered how to mix sand, soda, and lime to make the raw product. Cuneiform script on clay tablets in Mesopotamia gave instructions for forming it. The earliest glass vessels are core-formed and created by gathering molten glass around a solid core. It was scarce and precious in Old and New Testament times. Glassmakers learned to color the ingots by mixing metallic oxides into the ingredients. Artisans made it into jewelry and tableware of popular colors, including royal blue and turquoise. Glassmakers sought to imitate the semi-precious lapis lazuli, which early cultures valued. Glass beads from BC 3,000 appeared as jewelry on Egyptian and Mesopotamian mummies. The Arab poet al-Buhturi[131] described the clarity of such glass, "Its color hides the glass as if it is standing in it without a container."

4:6 | One ancient concept pictures a glass sea above heaven's dome on which God's throne rests. It is awe-inspiring and magnificent, highlighting God's beauty and holiness. The glass sea described in Revelation looked "like an awesome crystal" (Ezek. 1:22). John of Patmos says it was "a sea of glass mixed with fire" (Rev. 15:2).

4:6 | There is a fascinating tradition of a **glass** floor in King Solomon's[132] palace. It was so shiny that the visiting Queen of Sheba from South Arabia[133] thought it was water and picked up her skirts to walk across it! Her name, according to legend, was *Makeda* in Ethiopian or *Bilqis* in Arabic. We read, "She came to Jerusalem with a great caravan, with camels that bore spices, very much gold, and precious stones; and when she came to Solomon, she talked with him about all that was in her heart" (1 Kgs. 10:2). The Queen of Sheba had heard of Solomon's God-given wisdom even in a faraway land.

4:6 | According to the historian Josephus, Sheba was also the home of Princess Tharbis, Moses' first wife, whom he married to break the siege on a city in Ethiopia. She had watched him lead

---

[131] (820–897 AD)

[132] who reigned BC c961--922.

[133] or modern-day Sudan.

the Egyptian army and had fallen in love with him. After some bickering, he left for Egypt. Interestingly, there is strong biblical support for this marriage: "Miriam and Aaron spoke against Moses because of the Cushite woman whom he had married; for he had married a Cushite woman" (Num. 12:1).

4:6 | In the Genesis account, **four living creatures** guarded the way to the Garden of Eden after God expelled Adam and Eve. Revelation's "living creature" or "living being" translates from the Hebrew *hayyoth*. The prophet Ezekiel writes, "Out of its center came the likeness of four living creatures. This was their appearance: They had the likeness of a man. Everyone had four faces, and each one of them had four wings. Their feet were straight. The sole of their feet was like the sole of a calf's foot, and they sparkled like burnished bronze. They had the hands of a man under their wings on their four sides. The four of them had their faces and wings like this: Their wings joined to one another. They didn't turn when they went. Each one went straight forward" (Ezek. 1:5—9). Ezekiel continued to explain that they appeared "like burning coals of fire, like the appearance of torches. The fire went up and down among the living creatures. The fire was bright, and lightning went out of the fire" (Ezek. 1:13). The four living creatures represented all forms of amazing beings described in both Ezekiel and Revelation.

4:6 | The Greek for "**living creatures**" is *tessera zoia. Tessera* is an individual tile usually formed in a cube or a square shape on a mosaic floor or wall. *Zoia* is a name or surname meaning "life." Hence, the heavenly court's guards are like "a four-sided living cube!" The four living creatures are "covered with eyes all around" even under their wings, emphasizing their all-seeing "knowledge and alertness." Each created being was "in the throne's center" in God's court. "Eyes" may refer to "stars" or describe mirror-like reflectors or fish scales. Living creatures incorporate wild beasts, domesticated animals, human beings, and flying creatures. It must have been a remarkable sight for John of Patmos to behold!

4:6 | Some people ask whether animals are capable of praising God. Here in Revelation, on eight occasions, the **four living**

creatures give glory, honor, and thanks to him, who sits on the throne. Irenaeus[134] held that these four creatures represented four aspects of Christ's work and the four Gospel writers - Matthew, Mark, Luke, and John.

4:7 | God's attributes appear in the **lion, calf, man, and flying eagle** of each living creature. The lion has majesty and power, the ox is faithful, the man is intelligent, and the eagle is swift. Traditionally translated as "ox," the "calf" refers to a "heifer" or a "young bull." Ezekiel also saw four similar creatures called *tetramorphs* in one of his visions.[135] *Tetra* means "four," and *morph* means "shape." The four living creatures are a symbolic representation of four parts that move as one. The lion, calf, human being, and eagle symbolize all that is noblest, strongest, wisest, and swiftest in creation.

4:8 | Around the throne, the four living creatures cry out continuously, "**holy, holy, holy** is the Lord." The Greek phrase *Trisagion* translates as "three times holy" or "thrice holy" and refers to the three persons of the Trinity, the Father, the Son, and the Holy Spirit, and their holiness.

4:8 | **Holy, holy, holy** infers the "Trinity" and appears In several other places, such as at the Baptism and Transfiguration of Jesus, where the three persons of the Godhead are linked together. The Latin word *Trinitas* gives rise to other English words like "tripod" or three-legged stand, "triangle" with three sides, "tricycle" or a cycle with three wheels, and "trimaran," a boat with three hulls. This threefold greeting has curious similarities to the "Celtic Trinity symbol" or "Triquetra," meaning "triangle" or "three-cornered," and the "Trinity Knot" or a "triangular Celtic figure composed of three interlaced arcs." The word "Trinity" initially appeared in the writings of the theologian Tertullian in the second century AD, who explained that it meant "three persons, one in essence - not one in person."

4:8 | Another intriguing symbol for **holy, holy, holy** as the

---

[134] Irenaeus (130--202 AD) was a Christian leader in France in 180 AD.

[135] The technical theological term *tetramorph* is "a symbolic arrangement of four different elements in one unit."

trinity exists as the "three hares" or the "Tinners' Rabbits." The circular three hares motif appears in sacred sites from Middle and East Asia to medieval Devon churches. The three hares are carved, chasing each other in a circle. Each of their ears is shared by two rabbits so that only three appear. Similar appearances occurred in Chinese Buddhist cave temples from the 6th to 7th Centuries AD.

4:8 | The Celtic leader Patrick[136] used the **holy, holy, holy** trinity symbol and became famous for the three-leaved shamrock to explain the concept to Irish clan leaders. He also gave us a Trinity blessing. Patrick held his arm with a finger pointing straight ahead and then turned around three hundred and sixty degrees. This blessing acknowledged God's supreme control over all life and creation everywhere. Irish Celtic Christians believed that this Trinity blessing applied everywhere, in every way, and for all time.

4:8 | Interestingly, Patrick's grave in Downpatrick, Northern Ireland, also contains three prominent Christian leaders from that era. The remains of Patrick, Columba,[137] and Brigid[138] are all in one place. These three are disciples of the threefold **holy, holy, holy.** A kind of saintly trio! One heavy uncut stone covers all three. Some years ago, my wife and I visited this interesting graveyard on an Irish sightseeing holiday. An enormous rock lies at the top of the hill in the Holy and Undivided Trinity Cathedral Church cemetery in Downpatrick. We were naturally curious why such a large stone rested on the remains of three renowned Christian leaders. Apparently, it was necessary to prevent local people and visitors from removing gravesite soil to treat sick people and heal them!

4:8 | On the other side of the world, almost a millennium later, an Italian mystic called Catherine of Sienna[139] wrote a masterful poem and meditation on the **holy, holy, holy** Trinity God,

---

[136] (385--461 AD)
[137] (521--597 AD)
[138] (451--525 AD)
[139] (1347--1380 AD)

"You, O eternal Trinity, are a deep sea,
Into which the more I enter, the more I find,
And the more I see, the more I seek.
I cannot satisfy my soul in your abyss,
For she continually hungers after you, the eternal
Trinity.
I desire to see you with the light of your light.
As my heart desires the springs of living water,
So my soul longs to leave the prison of this dark
body and see you in truth."

Thomas Ken[140] adds a special Holy Trinity blessing of his own,

"Blessing and honor, thanksgiving and praise
More than we can utter be unto thee,
O most adorable Trinity, Father, Son, and Holy Ghost,
By all angels, men, and creatures forever and ever,
Amen and Amen.
To God, the Father, who first loved us and made us
accepted in the Beloved.
To God, the Son who loved us and washed us from
our sins in his blood.
To God, the Holy Ghost, who sheds the love of God
abroad in our hearts,
All love and all glory for time and eternity. Amen."

4:10 | Forever and ever indicates constant eternal praise of God from the living creatures. The twenty-four elders lay their crowns before the throne as a mark of submission like conquered kings to a more powerful ruler in ancient cultures. All living creatures give God glory in heaven and on earth because he is the creator and sustainer of all things!

Question: "What is the significance of how the four living creatures look and sound?"

---

[140] (1637--1711 AD)

23

SEVEN-SEALED SCROLL

5:1 "I saw, in the right hand of him who sat on the throne,
a **book written inside and outside**, sealed shut with **seven
seals**. ² I saw a **mighty angel** proclaiming with a loud voice,
"Who is worthy to open the book, and to break its seals?" ³
No one in heaven above, or on the earth, or under the earth,
was able to open the book or to look in it. ⁴ Then I **wept much**,
because no one was found worthy to open the book or to
look in it. ⁵ One of the elders said to me, "Don't weep. Behold,
the **Lion who is of the tribe of Judah**, the Root of David,
has overcome: he who opens the book and its seven seals."
(Rev. 5:1—5 emphases added).

5:1 | John of Patmos saw a similar vision to Ezekiel's. An
outstretched hand with a scroll, sometimes translated as "book"
written inside and out, unrolled before him. It was depressing
news containing "lamentations, mourning, and woe" (Ezek. 2:10).

5:1 | The seven-sealed document was not a modern **book**
with pages but a scroll in God's hand. In the Herculaneum ruins,
archaeologists unearthed a beautiful fresco from 79 AD depicting
a young man holding a papyrus scroll in his hands. The scroll form
is similar to the Dead Sea Scrolls from BC 300, which shepherds
discovered in desert caves in 1946 above its north shore. From
the ancient world to the second century AD, writing was on clay

tablets and then rolls rather than conventional books. Later, books on calfskin or other animal hide materials were called "vellum" or "parchment." Ten by eight-inch Papyri sheets were sewn together, rolled, and sealed with clay or wax. The leaves formed a long roll with two wooden rollers protruding at the top and bottom.

5:1 | Revelation's seven-sealed **scroll** contained the book's entire text. Scholars tell us that the writing would have been in narrow columns three inches wide, with margins of two and a half inches at the top and bottom and three-quarters of an inch between columns. This arrangement would be similar to many modern bibles with two columns of text and a space in between. A reader held it in the left hand, unrolled it with the right, and rotated the right hand roller to take up the slack.

5:1 | A Papyrus scroll's length varied according to its contents. John's second and third epistles, Jude and Philemon's, occupied one sheet, whereas the Romans' epistle required a twelve-feet roll. Mark's Gospel was nineteen feet, John's twenty-three feet, and Matthew's thirty feet. The combined Luke and Acts' roll was thirty-two feet. Revelation's roll required fifteen feet."

5:1 | Artisans made these **book** sheets from River Nile delta bulrushes. Each plant grew up to fifteen feet high, with six feet below the water, and its stem was sometimes as thick as a man's wrist. Egyptians used papyrus for writing, painting, rope, sandals, and even to make boats. Isaiah wrote that he "sends ambassadors by the sea, even in vessels of papyrus on the water" (Isa.18:2). Workers extracted the pith and cut it into thin strips with a sharp knife. They laid one layer of strips vertically and another horizontally moistened them with water and glue and pressed them together. They beat the papyrus with a mallet and then polished it with a pumice stone to produce a smooth sheet, not unlike brown paper.

5:1 | The word "papyrus" comes from the English word *paper*, but a Chinese court eunuch named Cai Lun[141] didn't invent paper until 105 AD. He got the idea after watching wasps build nests.

---

[141] (48--121 AD.)

The earliest surviving fragments of paper come from second-century China. Around 2000 BC, the Babylonians placed papyrus documents in baked clay envelopes, which survive today! In Egypt, locals sell beautifully colored papyrus **books**, bookmarks, and drawings of hieroglyphic writing and tomb paintings as souvenirs. On a trip to Egypt some years ago, my wife bought several lovely papyri drawings, which are displayed in our home today.

5:1 | Revelation's papyrus writing scroll had **writing inside and outside** to maximize the available space. Its grain ran horizontally on one side, known as the *recto,* and it was easier to write on that side along the line of the fibers. The vertical fibers' side was called the *verso,* but writers did not usually use the verso side. Papyrus was expensive and valuable, so if a person had a great deal to say, they wrote on both sides. The Revelation scroll described it as "a book written inside and outside, sealed shut with seven seals" (Rev. 5:1). British prisoners of war in Japan also wrote on the front and back of toilet paper sheets to save space.[142]

5:1 | The right hand of the one who sat on the throne held the Revelation **seven-seal**ed scroll. As the seals opened, events unfolded. God ordered the prophet, Daniel, to close and seal his book. "But you, Daniel, shut up the words and seal the book, even to the end time" (Dan. 12:4). On completion, scribes tied scrolls with threads and a "seal," called a *sphragida,* applied with wax or clay at the seven knots. Of the ten occurrences in the New Testament of this word meaning "seal," eight are in Revelation. Paul gives the seal a new meaning when he says, "he received the sign of circumcision, a seal of the righteousness of the faith" (Rom. 4:11).

5:1 | Each of the **seven seals** bears a witness' identity with a different impression in the wax. Revelation's documents had seven seals like many ordinary ones, such as wills, business agreements, or treaties. Important kings sometimes had seven ribbons and wax seals on their letters. I remember seeing King Henry the

---

[142] Some Victorians even wrote love letters in both diagonal directions as well as front and back!

Eighth's petition to the Pope for annulment of his marriage with many impressive wax seals of Lords and dignitaries attached with ribbons.

5:1 | Revelation's **seven-sealed** scroll contained secret information known only to God. The Lamb was the only one able to break the seals and view its contents. Under Roman law, documents could only be opened when witnesses or legal representatives were present. Revelation's scroll was God's will, his final settlement of universal affairs. The "seven seals" indicated its content's great secrecy, completeness, and importance. They were located throughout the scroll so that as they broke each one, another phase of God's plan unfolded. As they read more of the manuscript, it revealed other steps leading to the end of the age.

5:2 | A **mighty angel** asked, "who is worthy to open the scroll and break its seals?" Initially, there was despair when no one in creation could do it until Jesus came forward, for as "David's Root," he could fulfill the Old Testament's Messianic promise.

5:4 | The twenty-four elders cast their crowns before God's throne. They continuously worshiped at the seat of government and brought the people's prayers to God. One even encouraged John of Patmos when he was sad. John **wept much** because no one was found worthy to open the scroll or look into it. One of the elders told him not to cry, for the Lion of Judah's tribe had overcome and could open the seven seals.

5:5 | The **Lion, who is of the tribe of Judah,** is a title for Jesus.[143] Jacob blessed his sons and called "Judah a lion's cub" (Gen. 49:9). The Lion of the tribe of Judah" was a title transferred from King David to Jesus Christ. In Revelation, the conquering King Jesus, Judah's Lion, will lead the battle and defeat Satan with his ancestors' authority and power. He will then be the supreme victor!

Question: "Would you weep like John of Patmos because no one could open the seven-sealed scroll?"

---

[143] "The Lion of Judah's tribe" seemed to originate as an ancient title for the Messiah.

24

JESUS SLAIN LAMB

5:6 "I saw in the middle of the throne and of the four living creatures, and in the middle of the elders, a **Lamb** standing, as though it had been **slain,** having seven **horns** and seven **eyes,** which are the seven Spirits of God, sent out into all the earth. ⁷ Then he came, and he took it out of the right hand of him who sat on the throne. ⁸ Now when he had taken the book, the four living creatures and the twenty-four elders fell down before the Lamb, each one having a harp, and golden bowls full of incense, which are the prayers of the saints." (Rev. 5:6—8 emphases added).

5:6 | The **Lamb** of God is the fulfillment of all Israel's hopes and dreams. A temple worshipper presented "a lamb without blemish" for sacrifice, but the "Lamb of God" now becomes that offering and the culmination of centuries of Temple and Tabernacle gifts on earth. He turns tragedy into triumph, and shame becomes glory. According to H. B. Swete,[144] "we see Jesus Christ's majesty and meekness in the Lamb of God. In him are his deathly humiliation and risen glory."

5:6 | A **Lamb** appears with seven horns indicating his absolute power and seven eyes revealing his supreme knowledge. We find

---

[144] (1835-1917).

it difficult to visualize such a strange creature, but this describes Jesus. His appearance to receive God's scroll "as a Lamb" becomes a king's coronation, no less than a magnificent ceremony to crown a monarch in Westminster Abbey. The four living creatures encircle the throne, and the twenty-four elders surround Jesus as the focal point. The Lamb stands in the center of the heavenly pageant.

5:6 | "**Lamb** of God," one of the titles of Jesus, translates from the Latin *Agnus Dei*. When John the Baptist sees Jesus coming toward him, he says, "Behold, the Lamb of God, who takes away the sin of the world!" (John 1:29). This concept is central to our Christian beliefs, for he bears the crucifixion's wounds of weakness. Still, simultaneously God clothes him with might to defeat his enemies.

5:6 | The Greek word for "**Lamb**" in Revelation is significant. John of Patmos always uses the term *arnion* meaning "a young Lamb" or figuratively "a little lamb" or "a person with pure, innocent, virgin-like, gentle intentions." In all other Bible passages, the term used for "lamb" is *amnos*, meaning "a sacrificial lamb or a young sheep without blemish (especially a one-year-old lamb)." John the Baptist points to Jesus as the *amnos*, the Lamb of God. Peter described Christ as "a lamb without blemish or spot" (1 Pet. 1:19) using the same word, "amnos."

5:6 | An elder called John of Patmos to come and look at the "Lion," but John saw a Lamb when he turned around. The **Lamb** is the main title for Jesus and is used twenty-nine times in Revelation. Jesus utilized it elsewhere when he said, "Feed my lambs" (John 21:15). The prophet Jeremiah confessed, "I was like a gentle lamb that is led to the slaughter" (Jer. 11:19). In Revelation, by using *arnion* instead of *amnos*, John underlines that this concept is not a repeat of an Old Testament idea.

5:6 | John of Patmos sees the Lamb as if it had been **slain.** The wounds inflicted on the body of Jesus during his trial and crucifixion are still visible, asserting that Jesus is the final sacrifice for all sins. Although Christ is a sacrificial lamb, he is not weak. He died, but now he lives in God's strength and power. Even in heaven, Jesus is the one who loves us and gives himself for us. He erases all other wounds and blemishes on Christians in their new bodies, but not his. Jesus will retain the crucifixion marks on his hands, feet, head, and side for eternity. His wounds make us aware that the Lamb still remembers his crucifixion agony in heaven.

5:6 | The Lamb's seven **horns** and seven eyes indicate completeness. Seven horns show the Lamb's supreme power and seven eyes that he sees everything. None can withstand his all-conquering might or escape his all-seeing view. The horn takes on different meanings in different contexts. "Horns" stand for "sheer power" or "honor." In the Old Testament, Zedekiah made iron horns and said, "with these, you will push the Syrians until they are consumed" (1 Kgs. 22:11). Zedekiah's iron horns were a sign of God's unconquerable strength. "For you are the glory of their strength. In your favor, our horn will be exalted" (Ps. 89:17). The Lamb of God's seven horns also point to honor. "His horn will be exalted with honor" (Ps. 112:9). The "horn" also shows another quality, "dignity," for "he has lifted up the horn of his people, the praise of all his saints" (Ps. 148:14). It also points to "strength in praise." God increases the honor, dignity, and strength of those who trust him. The seven horns emphasize the Lamb's perfection, for his power is complete and irresistible.

5:6 | The Lamb's seven **eyes** represent the "seven spirits of God sent out into all the earth." Every place on earth is under his surveyance. The Lamb's seven eyes view everything as he stands in the center of God's throne encircled by the four living creatures and the elders.

Question: "Why does Jesus have the crucifixion wounds in heaven?"

25

NEW PRAISE SONG

5:9 "They sang a **new song**, saying, "You are worthy
to take the book and to open its seals: for you were
killed, and bought us for God with your blood out
of every tribe, language, people, and nation,
[10] and made us **kings and priests** to our God,
and we will **reign on the earth**." [11] "I saw, and I heard
something like a voice of many **angels** around the throne,
the **living creatures**, and the elders. The number of them
was **ten thousands of ten thousands, and thousands of
thousands**; [12] saying with a loud voice, **"Worthy is the
Lamb** who has been killed to receive the **power,** wealth,
wisdom, strength, honor, glory, and **blessing**!"
(Rev. 5:9—12 emphases added).

5:9 | One of Revelation's great surprises is that it is a book of
new things.

- "I will give him a white stone, and on the stone a new
  name written" (Rev. 2:17).
- "I will write on him the name of my God and the name of
  the city of my God, the New Jerusalem" (Rev. 3:12).
- "They sang a new song" (Rev. 5:9).
- "They sing a new song before the throne" (Rev. 14:3).

- "I saw a new heaven" (Rev. 21:1).
- "And a new earth" (Rev. 21:1).
- "I am making all things new" (Rev. 21:5).

5:9 | The Psalms frequently employ the phrase "a **new song**" as an outburst of praise for God's goodness and mercy. Here are some examples,

- "Sing to him a new song. Play skillfully with a shout of joy!" (Ps. 33:3).
- "Sing to Yahweh a new song, for he has done marvelous things!" (Ps. 98:1).
- "I will sing a new song to you, God. On the ten-stringed lyre" (Ps. 144:9).
- "Praise Yahweh! Sing to the Lord a new song" (Ps. 149:1).

5:9 | The nearest Old Testament parallel outside the Psalms to Revelation's **new song** is in Isaiah, where the people are encouraged to "sing to the Lord a new song, and his praise from the end of the earth" (Isa. 42:10). Why is Jesus worthy of this brand new Revelation song? John of Patmos explains, "You are worthy to take the book and open its seals. You were killed and bought us for God with your blood out of every tribe, language, people, and nation." This latest song is all about Jesus and his activities as our Savior! We will sing a fresh praise anthem to him.

5:9 | The four living creatures and the elders offer a **new song** to the slain Lamb and his shed blood. The sacrificial death of Jesus is not an accident of history, nor the tragic death of a good, heroic man in a righteous cause, but God's specific intention. The objective is to restore human beings' lost relationship with God. For that reason alone, Jesus Christ died on the cross. God wanted to make this praise an essential part of our earthly lives today and throughout heaven's eternity. What we glimpse in our Sunday worship, singing the Lamb's song, God wants to make a permanent feature in our lives. We are encouraged to

"Sing a new song unto the Lord,
Let your song be sung from age to age,
Sing a new song unto the Lord.
Singing, Alleluia." [145]

5:10 | Christians are made **kings and priests** to serve our God, for we have the privilege of being his royal servants. We have always been his created sons and daughters, but a new relationship has opened to us in that every Christian now has direct access to him. There is victory over sin and control over self in all circumstances, for he makes us "kings and priests to our God."

5:10 | In the ancient world, the Jewish High **Priest** alone had the privilege of approaching God on one specific day each year. When a Jewish male set foot in the Temple, he could enter through the Gentiles Court, into the Israelites' Court, but he could go no further into the Priests' Court nor to the Holy of Holies. But Jesus Christ, the great High Priest in the New Jerusalem, opens the way for all believers to enter God's presence. Every Christian becomes a priest with the same access to God as Jesus, the great High Priest!

5:10 | This Revelation passage tells us that the people of Jesus shall **reign on the earth.** Reigning is not a political triumph or material lordship but living a victorious life in all situations. Jesus said, "In the world, you have trouble, but cheer up! I have overcome the world" (John 16:33). He gives us victory over ourselves in all our circumstances.

5:11 | John of Patmos writes, "I saw, and I heard something like a voice of many **angels** around the throne." Angels are not human beings but spiritual entities serving and worshiping God as messengers and ministers. He made them before the creation. They have other roles, including protecting and guiding human beings. He expelled others, called fallen angels, like Satan from heaven. There is a clear hierarchy of angels in which archangels

---

[145] Written by Dan Schutte © as Track 1 on "Here I Am, Lord" (30th Anniversary Edition).

have greater authority over others. Gabriel seems to be God's primary messenger to human beings, whereas Michael is renowned as an outstanding military figure.

5:11 | I loved the movie "Michael,"[146] where John Travolta as Archangel Michael head-butted a bull in a field for fun! The comment was, "He's an **angel** and not a saint!" Angels walk amongst us today for our support and encouragement. "Don't forget to show hospitality to strangers, for in doing so, some have entertained angels without knowing it" (Hebr. 13:2). We never know who stands beside us in the coffee shop. It could be a heavenly messenger on an assignment on earth. Be kind to all you meet. I love the idea of passing it on and buying a coffee for someone in the line behind you without them knowing.

5:11 | John of Patmos writes, "I saw, and I heard something like a voice of many angels, the **living creatures**, and the elders around the throne." They sing a new heavenly song. It speaks of Jesus Christ's death and resurrection and his saving work on the cross for peoples from every tribe and nation. "We will reign" may be translated as "they do reign." It is as if the reign has begun already and is not just a future hope. At one time, the Jewish nation argued that God cared only for Jewish persons and wanted the destruction of others. The death of Jesus is for everyone, and in him, we meet a God who loves all the world. Therefore the church must tell everyone about it.

5:11 | In heaven, there were **ten thousands of ten thousands and thousands of thousands** of angels praising Jesus. A hundred million angels or "countless angelic beings" worship him. The number is just too enormous to comprehend. John of Patmos, no doubt, wanted to say they were like the stars in the sky or the grains of sand on the seashore but even that cannot describe it. In today's scientific language, thousands upon thousands would be 10 to the power of 8, or 100,000,000! Most would just say, "an

---

[146] 1996 Turner Pictures Worldwide Inc. 2009 Warner Brothers Entertainment Inc. Distributed by Warner Home Video 4000 Warner Blvd., Burbank, CA 91522. All rights reserved.

enormous number of angels!" They praise the Lamb of God, who is worthy to open the scroll.

5:12 | **"Worthy is the Lamb"** rings out loudly from the angels and all creation in heaven and earth. All heavenly creatures in the world, under the ground, and in the sea shout, "Worthy is the Lamb." The author of many devotional poems, Christina Rossetti,[147] wrote, "God revealed heaven to earth as the homeland of music." This Christ praise lifts our spirits too. We worship God and praise him for what he has done, what he is doing, and what he will do for all who trust him.

5:12 | Jesus, the Lamb, is now given praise and **power** worthy of his status. Paul writes, "To me, the very least of all saints, was this grace given, to preach to the Gentiles the unsearchable riches of Christ" (Eph. 3:8). The immense treasure of Jesus is "the power of God and the wisdom of God" (1 Cor. 1:24). He overcomes all his enemies and receives honor, praise, and power. The Father bestows on him grace and truth. Innumerable angels worship him, and all created beings with one great voice praise him.

5:12 | We will someday join these heavenly angels with our voices in Christ's **praise** from joyful and adoring hearts. God wants to make this a full-blown and permanent feature of our heavenly life!

Question: "What will a new praise song be like in heaven?"

---

[147] (1830--1894).

26

CREATURE PRAISE SONGS

5:13 "I heard **every created thing** which is **in heaven**, on the earth, **under the earth, on the sea,** and everything in them, saying, "To him who sits on the throne, and to the **Lamb** be the blessing, the honor, the glory, and the dominion, forever and ever! Amen!" ⁴ The four living creatures said, "Amen!" Then the **elders fell down** and worshiped" (Rev. 5:13—14 emphases added).

5:13 | **Every created thing** praises God, including the birds of the air singing out their morning chorus, the pasture's forest animals, the oceans' fish, and creatures, and every plant, insect, and flower.

5:13 | All the planets **in heaven** sound out their praise to God! Mercury whistles like a windswept desert. Venus clangs as a tolling bell. Mars whispers in its redness. Jupiter rings similar to a muffled xylophone. Saturn sounds the same as a plane taking off behind a curtain. Uranus whistles resembling a kettle in a storm. Neptune reminds us of deep breathing. Pluto comes over like railway wagons in the distance on a rusty track. The moon and stars' amazing songs also join in this grand celebration! The sun sings a song of praise to Almighty God in its fiery glory. An exciting documentary about the

Sun[148] explained that it gives off various notes combined into a chorus. Similarly, but with a different tune, planet earth also intones!

5:13 | The creature's praise songs extend to all **under the earth and on the sea.** Every creature everywhere and in all of nature joins together to glorify God. Whales click, and dolphins whistle in praise. Fish vocalizations may be pops, clicks, whistles, purrs, grunts, groans, growls, barks, hums, hoots, rattles, and even tinkles. Toadfish vocalizations in Honduras are like trumpet sounds. The midshipman fish snarls and snorts.

5:13 | The dead also worship the Lamb. All creation **under the earth** adds their praise to God. Hades' dead honoring God is something new, for it is a dark place and the dead souls' final destination. In the Old Testament, the dead are separated from God and live a shadowy existence. The Psalmist asks, "For, in death, there is no memory of you. In Sheol, who shall give you thanks?" (Ps 6:5). Do the dead under the earth have any God-consciousness? The Psalmist questions whether God shows his wonders to the dead. If so, do the departed spirits rise and praise you? Is your loving kindness declared in the grave? "Are your wonders made known in the dark? Or your righteousness in the land of forgetfulness?" (Ps. 88:12).

5:13 | All creation and every created thing worships and praises God and **the Lamb.** The elders fall down and worship. Songs to God and the Lamb meld together and reach throughout the universe's vastness and creation's entirety. "To him, who sits on the throne and to the Lamb be the blessing, the honor, the glory, and the dominion, forever and ever! Amen!" Jesus Christ is important, for he is seated with God. The phrase "every created thing" includes everything living, the elders, the myriads of angels, and heavenly beings. It takes in the rocks, mountains, seas, and smallest atoms in every tiny thing.

5:14 | The four living creatures worshiped the Lamb, and the **elders fell down.** Here is a Revelation vision that sweeps

---

[148] on Oasis TV

everything else away. Not even the land of the dead under the earth is beyond the risen Christ's reign. The heavenly creatures' songs are heard even from beyond the grave. Here is an all-inclusive response of "every creature in heaven and on earth" that is the whole of creation praising God.

Question: "Why are praise sounds of the planets so different from each other and so peculiar?"

27

FOUR APOCALYPSE
HORSEMEN

6:1 "I saw that the Lamb opened one of the seven **seals**, and I
heard one of the four living creatures saying, as with a voice of
thunder, "Come and see!" ² Then a **white horse** appeared, and
he who sat on it had a bow. A crown was given to him, and
he came out conquering, and to conquer. ³ When he opened
the second seal, I heard the second living creature saying,
"Come!" ⁴ Another came out: a **red horse**. To him who sat on it
was given power to **take peace from the earth**, and that they
should kill one another. There was given to him a great sword."
(Rev. 6:1—4 emphases added).

6:1 | The seven judgments began, and certain events in
human history started when each **seal** opened. The study of seals
is called *sigillography* from the Latin *sigillum* and the old French
scel. These impressions in wax were usually necessary for owners
to authenticate and validate documents. The unique stamp of
a person sending a letter was impressed with a *matrix* of cast
bronze called *latten*, silver, or occasionally gold. Whoever opened
them snapped each wax or clay seal, and the scroll revealed the
next part but not the whole text until the final seal.

6:2 | God's authority over human history unfolded, and scenes proclaiming his triumph interspersed these events. The riders were frequently called the "Four Horse" or the "Four **Horsemen** of the Apocalypse." In the Old Testament, we saw similar scenes. "In the first chariot were red horses; in the second chariot black horses; in the third chariot white horses; and in the fourth chariot dappled horses, all of them powerful" (Zech. 6:2—3).

6:2 | These four horsemen beginning with the **white horse,** brought violence upon the nations oppressing God's people. In Revelation, the four colors symbolized respectively "conquest, plague or disease," "war," "famine," and "death." As the seals opened, the "four horses" appeared. The "horses" represented God's vehicles of judgment, for he directed human history through them and used his enemies to accomplish his purposes.

6:4 | The scarlet, fiery or **red horse** caused people to fight and kill each other in wars and take peace from the earth. He carried a judgment sword and alluded to a conquering military empire like the Parthians on the Roman empire's eastern border, which God used to exercise punishment.[149]

6:4 | The "fiery scarlet horse" and its rider took **peace from the earth**. Warfare and mass slaughter were commonplace in John of Patmos' day, and on one occasion, a hundred thousand soldiers died in a single battle.[150] Queen Boudica,[151] the tribal queen of the British Iceni Tribe, led a British revolt which the Romans eventually crushed but only after one hundred and fifty thousand casualties! These were incredibly bloodthirsty times.

Question: "What do you think the white, red, black, and pale horses mean?

---

[149] Between BC 247 and 224 AD, the Parthians ruled large parts of Iran and Iraq. They were experts at riding horses in battle and humiliated the Romans with defeat at the Battle of Rhandeia in 62 AD.

[150] between BC 37 and 67.

[151] sometimes called "Boadicea, Boudicca, or simply as Budduc in Welsh,"

28

BLACK HORSE APOCALYPSE

6:5 "When he opened the third seal, I heard the third living creature saying, "Come and see!" And behold, a **black horse**, and he who sat on it had a **balance in his hand**. ⁶ I heard a voice in the middle of the four living creatures saying, "A **choenix of wheat** for a **denarius**, and three choenix of barley for a denarius! Don't damage the **oil and the wine!**" ⁷ When he opened the fourth seal, I heard the fourth living creature saying, "Come and see!" ⁸ And behold, a **pale horse**, and the name of he who sat on it was Death. Hades followed with him. Authority over one fourth of the earth, to kill with the sword, with famine, with death, and by the wild animals of the earth was given to him." (Rev. 6:5—8 emphases added).

6:5 | The rider of the **black horse** carried a pair of scales that symbolized severe famine. During shortages, they weighed bread when ordinary people could only afford a part of a loaf. Following a war in antiquity, famine inevitably resulted, creating devastation. Plagues and famines became a scourge in many parts of the ancient world and often resulted in the death of half or three-quarters of the population. Livy[152] described the first

---

[152] the Roman historian, (BC 59--17 AD) in "Founding of the City 4.12."

recorded plague in ancient Rome in BC 441, when the population fell by over ninety percent!

6:5 | In Europe and North Africa, the "**black** death"[153] occurred around c1350 AD after the Great Famine[154] and caused the demise of between seventy-five and two hundred million people. Compared to this, the Coronavirus has killed over six million people worldwide and infected over five hundred and forty-one million people.[155] The United States has seen over sixty-eight million cases and just over a million deaths. The term "black death" indicated the bubonic trademark gangrene finger and swellings of the lymph nodes due to infection. It brought a terrible toll on the population, and even today, black is still the standard mourning color because its horse and rider were death bringers.

6:5 | The black horse rider had a **balance in his hand** because to "eat bread by weight" indicated a significant bread shortage in society. The bread was made from flour or barley dough, salt, and water and was an essential staple. When the food supply in Jerusalem was about to be cut off in Ezekiel's time, "they will eat bread by weight, and with fearfulness. They will drink water by measure, and in dismay" (Ezek. 4:16).

6:5 | The main crops measured in the **balance** were probably bread, corn, and barley. A voice from the four living creatures dictated the prices for a day's wage in Greek *denarius* coinage. One denarius bought six pounds weight or a quart of barley. The famine shortages were God's punishment for disobedience. "When I break your staff of bread, ten women shall bake your bread in one oven, and they shall deliver your bread again by weight. You shall eat, and not be satisfied" (Lev. 26:26).

6: 6 | The four living creatures announced a reduced wheat flour measure for a day's labor. It was now not sufficient for an ordinary family. This statement came from the voice among the four living creatures, emphasizing the importance of necessities. It showed how vital the food price was to God and the people for

---

[153] From 1346 to 1353 AD.
[154] of 1315--1317 AD.
[155] from January 24, 2020, to June 21, 2022 (World Health Organization.)

a **choenix of wheat**[156] or two pints. One choenix of wheat flour or three of cheaper coarse barley flour cost one denarius in times of shortage. In his vision, John of Patmos realized that food was so expensive that a man needed a working wage to buy enough for himself. Nothing remained for his wife or children, a desperate situation for any family. Hardships caused widespread famines and subsequent riots, yet Revelation's four living creatures show concern for these practical situations.

6:6 | The people's desperation for **wheat** boiled over when an Alexandrian corn ship arrived from Puteoli, an important shipping center for goods from Egypt and other exotic places bound for Rome. The vessels delivered the merchandise to the Ostia port. Silt eventually closed off Ostia inland, but its merchant's streets and beautifully decorated mosaic tile floors remain today. The ship brought no food but only sand for the games, which was spread in the Colosseum to soak up any spilled blood!

6:6 | The Greek word for "a day's wages" is **denarius**, equivalent to twenty dollars today. It was a small silver coin first minted in BC 211 that Jesus mentioned to Peter as a tax payment. He told him to "go to the sea, cast a hook, and take up the first fish that comes up. When you have opened its mouth, you will find a stater coin. [157] Take that, and give it to them for me, and you." (Matt.17:27). The "stater" coin would pay the tax for two people ($40). The fish with the coin in its mouth may have been a tilapia or catfish called "St. Peter's Fish," which is still available on restaurant menus today! A four-drachma silver coin was worth four denarii or a Shekel of Tyre in Palestine, renowned in the ancient world for its standardized weight and silver quality.[158] A pay packet was essential for working people to buy bread

---

[156] a dry volume measure of a little more than a quart, or two pints.

[157] A stater is a silver coin equivalent to four Attic or two Alexandrian drachmas, or a Jewish shekel: just exactly enough to cover the half-shekel temple tax for two people. A shekel is about 10 grams or about 0.35 ounces, usually in the form of a silver coin.

[158] The Talmud explains that "Silver, whenever mentioned in the Pentateuch, is Tyrian silver" (Tosephta Kethuboth 13,20).

and pay their taxes! The availability of grain and the denarius' value determined a family's continued existence. The black horse apocalypse and scales were disaster omens for ordinary people.

6:6 | In Nero's time,[159] severe famines savaged the poor. Still, **oil and wine** remained relatively untouched, carefully rationed, protected from inflation, and readily available to the wealthy elite. Wheat was short but still obtainable but at prohibitive prices. Corn was a cereal crop rather than the North American maze. The olive tree and the grapevine were more deeply rooted than corn and could withstand a much harsher drought.

6:6 | When Jacob sent a plea to Egypt for **corn** in Joseph's time, Palestine still had an abundance of food delicacies. Jacob told his sons to place some of these products in their bags. He said, "Carry a present for the man, a little balm, a little honey, spices and myrrh, nuts, and almonds" (Gen. 43:11).

6:6 | In 92 AD, Emperor Domitian issued a **wine** proclamation, banning new vineyard planting in Roman Italy,[160] but his mandate caused great hardship for the poor. Domitian was Emperor for fifteen years, one of the longest reigns. He was a cruel, paranoid tyrant who ordered uprooting half of the vineyards in the Roman provinces to control taxation and force farmers to grow more cereals. The wine edict occurred at the same time as John of Patmos was writing Revelation. Domitian's law, however, had the opposite effect as it caused a provincial rebellion in Asia, where grapes were one of their principal revenue sources. Because of this hostile reaction, Domitian rescinded this law and ordered the prosecution of anyone who stopped cultivating their vineyards! Interference in the Emperor's wine supply was forbidden, further protecting the wine and oil prices and indirectly inflating the bread price.

6:8 | The fourth seal's opening revealed the **pale horse**, the last of the "four apocalypse horsemen." It represented the coming of death and famine, leaving people white with fear. *"Pale"* was

---

[159] (37—68 AD).

[160] The Roman Emperor Augustus created this area officially with the Latin name "Italia," uniting the Italian Peninsula under the same name and government..

a person's face color when they were terrified or about to die. It described the dead's ashen appearance and came to symbolize death itself. The rider of the *"pale horse"* was the only horseman named "Death" and "Hades," which was the equivalent of the Hebrew "Sheol" and the "place of departed souls" or "hell." The pale horse and its rider caused a terrible famine upon the earth, but Jesus assures us that he is still in control as he holds the keys of Hades and Death's domain.

Question: "What does this passage teach us about the necessity for a minimum or living wage?"

29

WHITE ROBED MARTYRS

6:9 "When he opened the fifth seal, I saw underneath the altar the souls of **those who had been killed** for the Word of God, and for the testimony of the Lamb which they had. [10] They cried with a loud voice, saying, "**How long, Master**, the holy and true, until you judge and avenge our blood on those who dwell on the earth?" [11] A long white robe was given to each of them. They were told that they should rest **yet for a while**, until their **fellow servants and their brothers**, who would also be killed even as they were, should complete their course. [12] I saw when he opened the sixth seal, and there was a **great earthquake**. The sun became black as sackcloth made of hair, and the whole **moon became as blood**. [13] The stars of the sky fell to the earth, like a fig tree dropping its unripe figs when it is shaken by a great wind. [14] The sky was removed like a scroll when it is rolled up. Every mountain and island was moved out of its place. [15] The kings of the earth, the princes, the commanding officers, the rich, the strong, and every enslaved person and free person, hid themselves in the caves and in the rocks of the mountains. [16] They told the mountains and the rocks, "Fall on us, and hide us from the **face of him who sits on the throne**, and from the wrath of the Lamb, [17] for the great day of his wrath has come; and **who is able to stand**?" (Rev. 6:9—17 emphases added).

6:9 | The Old Testament describes various features of the altar sacrifices. Here, instead of animals' blood flowing under the altar, John of Patmos sees the souls of the martyrs **who had been killed.**

6:10 | They cry out, **"how long, Master?"** God works according to his timetable, promising a final redress. While we may wish for justice immediately, we must be patient like the martyrs. For the kingdom of God's sake, no suffering is needless. He calls upon Christians to stand firm for their beliefs in the face of earthquakes, warfare, famine, persecution, and even death. He rewards those who endure to the end.

6:11 | Martyrs must wait **for a while.** God is holding back until a certain number of disciples have been killed. These are their fellow servants, brothers, and sisters who would die like them. This incident reminds us of Jesus waiting for several days after Lazarus' death before coming to raise him. When he heard that Lazarus was sick, he stayed two more days. Then he said to his disciples, "Let's go into Judea again" (John 11:7). Jesus explained that sickness and death are not final but for God's glory. He promised that those who suffer and die for their faith will not be forgotten but cleared of blame and honored. Jewish belief held that the coming Messiah[161] would not arrive until a certain number of souls had been born.

6:11 | The Greek phrase for **their brothers** in this passage is *adelphoi* and refers to siblings, brothers, and sisters. *Martyrs*[162] are each given a pure white robe, and God tells them to wait until more believers give their lives for their faith.

6:12 | Revelation's **great earthquake** was significant not as a natural disaster but as God's intended punishment. We read later, "For the great day of his wrath has come, and who can stand?" People are so afraid they cry out for protection from God and the Lamb. The list includes many occupations in society, including kings, princes, commanding officers, the rich, strong, and every

---

[161] "anointed one" or "Christ"
[162] from the Greek meaning "witnesses."

enslaved and free person. This list indicated the breadth of those experiencing the great earthquake's widespread terror.

6:12 | When the **moon became like blood**, a great earthquake caused people to retreat to caves from fear. It was so frightening and enormous that people hid themselves in the crags of the mountains. We can compare this terrible earthquake to the Great Chilean earthquake of 1960,[163] when the death toll was seven thousand, and an eighty-feet high tsunami tidal wave caused over six billion dollars in damage. By comparison, the San Francisco earthquake and fire in California in 1906 caused three thousand deaths and the destruction of eighty percent of the city. My wife and I had a short holiday in one of the few buildings that survived the San Francisco blaze called the Palace Hotel. The orange juice each morning was "to kill for!" The magnificent glass-enclosed dining room took one's breath away!

6:16 | At the sight of the **face of him who sits on the throne**, all human beings are terrified. They call for the mountains to fall on them to hide them from God's face! Hosea prophesied a similar disaster for Samaria's occupants when their king died. The "high places" would be destroyed, and thorns and thistles would grow on their altars. They will beg the mountains, "Cover us!" and the hills, "Fall on us!" (Hosea 10:8).[164]

6:17 | These verses remind us that Jesus may not promise an easy ride in life, but all will be well in the end. He asks the question, **who is able to stand?** Annie Johnson Flint[165] expressed it so clearly in her poem.

"God has not promised skies always blue,
Flower-strewn pathways all our lives through;
God has not promised sun without rain,

---

[163] Also called the Valdivia earthquake The Chilean Quake recorded 9.4 to 9.6 on the magnitude scale. It lasted just ten minutes but sent out an eighty-foot-high tsunami tidal wave, which affected Southern Chile, Japan, Hawaii, the Philippines, Australia, and New Zealand.

[164] The "high places of wickedness" uses the Hebrew word *aven*, referring to Beth Aven, a derogatory name for Bethel.

[165] (1866-1932) from Vineland, New Jersey,

Joy without sorrow, peace without pain."

"But God has promised strength for the day,
Rest for the labor, light for the way,
Grace for the trials, help from above,
Unfailing sympathy, undying love."

Question: "In times of need, do you ask for God's strength, rest, light, grace, help, sympathy, or love."

30

THE SEAL MARK

7:1 "After this, I saw four angels standing at the four corners of the earth, holding the four winds of the earth, so that no wind would blow on the earth, or on the sea, or on any tree. ² I saw another angel ascend from the sunrise, having the **seal** of the living God. He cried with a loud voice to the four angels to whom it was given to harm the earth and the sea, ³ saying, "Don't harm the earth, the sea, or the trees, until we have sealed the bondservants of our God on their foreheads!" ⁴ I heard the number of those who were sealed, one hundred forty-four thousand, sealed out of every **tribe of the children of Israel**:
⁵ of the tribe of **Judah** twelve thousand were sealed,
of the tribe of Reuben twelve thousand,
of the tribe of Gad twelve thousand,
⁶ of the tribe of Asher twelve thousand,
of the tribe of Naphtali twelve thousand,
of the tribe of Manasseh twelve thousand,
⁷ of the tribe of Simeon twelve thousand,
of the tribe of Levi twelve thousand,
of the tribe of Issachar twelve thousand,
⁸ of the tribe of Zebulun twelve thousand,
of the tribe of Joseph twelve thousand, and
of the tribe of Benjamin twelve thousand were sealed."
(Rev. 7:1—8 emphases added).

7:2 | The total number of those **sealed** from every tribe of the children of Israel was one hundred and forty-four thousand. Seals appeared on wills, title deeds, and, in this case, people. A seal mark typically identified and protected a document's contents, and a broken one indicated an information leak. Some commentators suggested that "a seal on God's servants' foreheads" could be invisible, but that is doubtful because a person often reveals their identity to others. Prostitutes in Rome wore a nameplate on their foreheads.

7:2 | Owners in the Roman empire stamped ceramic amphora for wine or oil with a **seal**. Archeologists have identified over two hundred unique inscriptions.[166] The stamp contained production, content, ownership, and other information. A signet ring's wax impression also indicated confidential contents. Daniel was told to "shut up the words and seal the book, even to the end time" (Dan. 12:4). In some senses, the small red square seal mark on Japanese and Chinese pottery is another parallel to the owner's seal. The Oriental seal on plates and pots tells who made them, also when and where.

7:2 | As circumcision is the Jewish person's **seal** mark, and baptism is the Christian's seal mark, the Revelation seal mark signifies and protects all God's faithful followers. Our physical bodies may be beaten, maimed, or even destroyed, but nothing can remove our souls' seal. God protects us because we are supremely valuable to him.

7:2 | A parallel to the Revelation seal mark is the beast's **seal** mark. It forced everybody, whether important or not, rich or poor, enslaved or free, "to be given a mark on their right hands or their foreheads" (Rev. 13:16). God's and the beast's marks place people in two very distinct camps, those subject to love in Jesus Christ's service and those owned by Satan. God will safely bring all his sealed followers to himself, and no one will be overlooked or left behind. I am reminded of the scenes in Kabul airport in

---

[166] *Amphora* comes from a Greek compound word, *amphi* for "on both sides" and *pherein*, meaning "to carry." Therefore, an amphora is a ceramic container with double-sided handles used to carry a liquid.

Afghanistan, with crowds holding up their passports and papers urging the soldiers to let them onto a plane. Some would have the necessary documents to go, and others would not. Similarly, those with the correct seal will join Christ in glory, and others will not.

7:4 | This record of the **tribes of the children of Israel** does not correspond with any of the eighteen Old Testament lists. Twelve thousand were sealed per tribe, totaling one hundred and forty-four thousand. Each of Israel's twelve tribes had its tribal seal, the best known being Judah's tribe with its Lion motif.[167] Israel's twelve tribes were descendants of the Patriarch Jacob, his two wives, Leah and Rachel, and his two concubines, Zilpah and Bilhah.

7:5 | **Judah** from the tribe of David is listed first.[168] The Levites were God's priests in the Temple with no tribal allotment, but they received a reward for their faithfulness by being included as a tribe. The list omits Dan's tribe, no doubt, because of his unfaithfulness. He would "be a serpent on the trail, an adder in the path that bites the horse's heels so that his rider falls backward" (Gen. 49:17). They may also have omitted Dan, whose most famous leader was Sampson because the tribe adopted pagan practices. This new Israel embraces the faithful from every nation, race, people, and tongue - an army of true believers and those Israeli tribes dedicated to God's service.

Question: "What would the seal mark be like on Christians?"

---

[167] Leah had six sons, Reuben, Simon, Levi, Judah, Issachar, and Zebulun. The other women had two sons each. Rachel bore Joseph and Benjamin, Zilpah bore Gad and Asher, and Bilhah bore Dan and Naphtali.

[168] *Judah* sounds like and may originate from the Hebrew word for *praise* (Genesis 29:35).

31

GREAT THRONE MULTITUDE

7:9 "After these things I looked, and behold, a **great multitude**, which no man could count, out of every nation and of all tribes, peoples, and languages, standing before the throne and before the Lamb, dressed in white robes, with **palm branches** in their hands. [10] They cried with a loud voice, saying, "Salvation be to our God, who sits on the throne, and to the Lamb!" [11] All the angels were standing around the throne, the elders, and the four living creatures; and they fell on their faces before his throne, and worshiped God, [12] saying, "Amen! Blessing, glory, wisdom, thanksgiving, honor, power, and might, be to our God forever and ever! Amen." [13] One of the elders answered, saying to me, "These who are arrayed in the **white robes**, who are they, and where did they come from?" [14] I told him, "My Lord, you know" He said to me, "These are those who came out of the **great suffering.** They washed their robes, and made them white in the Lamb's blood." (Rev. 7:9—14 emphases added).

7:9 | Who are the people in this **great multitude**? John of Patmos sees those of every nation and all "tribes, people, and languages." They are dressed in white robes with palm branches in their hands in the Lamb's honor. The elders, all the angels, and the four living creatures sing God's praises. This vast heavenly gathering includes the faithful of every generation. They praise God that salvation comes only from the "Lamb," the Lord Jesus Christ. A great multitude that no one could count encircled the one hundred and forty-four thousand, including all faithful followers, Jewish persons, and Gentiles, holding palm branches in their hands."

7:9 | John of Patmos would undoubtedly have remembered another similar occasion he witnessed during the earthly life of Jesus. The crowds took up **palm branches** by the roadside on the hill going into the Golden Gate on the eastern side of Jerusalem. They shouted in praise to welcome him, the prince, as heaven's multitudes do now. The palm branches remind me of an Easter parade in my home church in Birkenhead, where the Sunday School boys carried banners, and the girls held flowers as we processed around the town. We stopped at specific places to sing hymns and hear an Easter reading or a word of testimony. I remember carrying a red shield on a broomstick, saying, "God is love!"

7:9 | The Temple Mount's Golden Gate is the oldest gate on the northeastern side of Jerusalem. Jesus passed through an earlier gate that we know little about except that there is a possibility that it was called the Shushan Gate. Tradition attributes its construction to King Solomon. An arch, possibly of a former gate, lies directly beneath the blocked-up entranceway. Emperor Justinian[169] built the present gate in c520 AD on top of the ruins of the earlier gate in the wall. He was a prolific builder of churches, dams, bridges, and fortifications. According to Jewish tradition, the eastern gate was where the "Shekinah" or "Divine Presence" entered the Temple courts. It was also where the crowds greeted the Messiah with **palm branches**.

7:9 | The Golden Gate's two doors from the Temple Mount were named "Mercy" and "Repentance." Many Jewish people prayed for mercy at the gate as they were not allowed into the city through the Western Wall during the Crusader period. The

---

[169] also called Justinian the Great, (483--565 AD).

Ottoman Turks transformed the walled-up Golden Gate into a watchtower to prevent the Messiah from entering and being greeted with **palm branches.** Its vaulted hall is divided by four columns into two aisles on the ground floor, leading to the Mercy and Repentance doors and an upper floor room with a domed ceiling. Muslims built a cemetery outside the Golden Gate because they believed it was a holy place that no pious Jewish person would cross, especially the messiah.

7:9 | Closed by the Muslims in 810 AD, the Crusaders reopened the **Golden Gate** in 1102 AD, but Saladin walled it up again after regaining Jerusalem in 1187 AD. Ottoman Sultan Suleiman[170] rebuilt the gate but walled it up in 1541 AD, which has stayed that way to the present. Suleiman's empire was large, and he ruled at least twenty-five million people.

7:9 | Ezekiel described the **Golden Gate,** the sanctuary's outer gate that looks toward the east. The Lord said, "no man shall enter in by it; for Yahweh, the God of Israel has entered in by it" (Ezek. 44:2). Ezekiel continues, "As for the prince, he shall sit in it to eat bread before Yahweh." (Ezek. 44:3). "The Prince" may refer to Jesus, to Israel who wrestled with God or one of Israel's kings like King David

7:9 | Interestingly, the "Golden Gate,"[171] where the people waved **palm branches,** may be the same as the "Beautiful Gate," where Peter healed a lame beggar. Both gates led into the Temple courts on the east side of Jerusalem. We read that a man lame from birth was carried and laid daily at the temple door called "Beautiful" to beg from those entering the temple. Seeing Peter and John about to go into the Temple, he asked for a gift. "Peter, fastening his eyes on him and, with John, said, 'Look at us.' He listened to them, expecting to receive something from them. But Peter said, 'I have no silver or gold, but what I have, I give you. In

---

[170] Suleiman the Magnificent (1494-1566 AD) broke with tradition and married a converted Orthodox Christian woman from his harem. Her name was "Roxelana," which translates as "Russian" or "Ruthenian." She reputedly had beautiful red hair.

[171] possibly named for the golden sandstone masonry in the sunshine.

Jesus Christ of Nazareth's name, get up and walk!'" (Acts 3:4—6). The Golden Gate became a beautiful healing place, for the man stood up, leaped, and danced with joy!

7:13 | An elder in Revelation asked John of Patmos, "who are these arrayed in white robes, and where did they come from?" John explained that they wear **white robes** washed in the Lamb's blood. How can this be? Usually, blood is a challenging stain to remove from a shirt or dress, but Christ's blood is the world's most effective detergent! It removes even sin's blemish from the saint's robes. White symbolizes sinless perfection and holiness, which only the Lamb of God's death can give a person. The gowns represent human souls, which bear dark sin stains, but the blood of Jesus bleaches clothes to a glowing, dazzling white like fresh snow in the sunshine! The elder explains that those in white robes came out of the great suffering.

Question: "What would it be like to worship with a hundred million other Christians?

32

TEMPLE COURT THRONE

7:15 "Therefore they are before the **throne of God,** they serve him day and night in his temple. He who **sits on the throne** will **spread his tabernacle over them**. ¹⁶ They will never be **hungry or thirsty** any more. The sun won't beat on them, nor any heat; ¹⁷ for the Lamb who is in the middle of the throne **shepherds** them and leads them to springs of life-giving waters. And God will wipe away every tear from their eyes." (Rev. 7:15—17 emphases added).

7:15 | Those from every race, tribe, and tongue with pure hearts enter God's presence and serve him day and night before his throne. Here is an astonishing revolution. In Jerusalem's earthly temple, no non-Jew could go beyond the Gentiles' Court on the threat of death. But here, every Christian stands before and near God, no matter who they may be.

7:15 | Most devout Jewish people could never hope to do this. They could cross the Temple courts but not go into the Holy of Holies, which was reserved for the High Priest to enter alone once a year. In the heavenly temple, the way to **the throne** of God is now open to all faithful believers. Heaven has an open temple court with no barriers, and distinctions of race and status no longer exist for loyal followers. The pure in heart can enter Almighty God's presence.

7:15 | I recall attending Westminster Abbey in London for the Church Army centenary celebration in 1982. Afterward, I stood about six feet from the Queen in the Rose Garden reception. I took her photograph, though I learned later that I shouldn't have. I didn't realize how special that moment was, being so close to a reigning monarch, one of the most influential and wealthiest women on earth, with extraordinary power at her fingertips. But here is a more unusual situation in heaven where Christians stand together before him who **sits on the throne**! One day, Her Majesty, a well-saved Christian, and I will stand together before God!

7:15 | The Hebrew verb translating "filled" in "Yahweh's glory filled the Temple" in Exodus 40:35 is in the present continuous tense, reflecting an "ongoing, dynamic situation." To say that God sits on **the throne** says that his glory is there forever. Many Jewish people came to think of him as remote from the world. They did not even consider it right to speak of him in human terms, so they called him *Shechinah* or "glory" instead, but he and his people are to come together.

7:15 | There is more to the words **"spread his tabernacle over them"** than meets the eye. The Greek for "spread" is *skenoun*, from *skene*, meaning a "tent" or a "shelter." Over the throne, the Lord spreads his glory tent like a canopy shading his saints from hunger, thirst, and scorching heat. God's blessed ones then live and serve in his presence and glory. Those who faithfully work on earth for the Lord Jesus also enjoy his Shekinah glory dwelling on them and their ministry. Surprisingly, "dwelt" or "lived" describes how "the Word became flesh and lived among us" (John 1:14). John of Patmos says that God became like a human being and lived next door to us. Many Jewish people connected *skene*, meaning "tent," with another Hebrew word, *Shechinah*,[172] meaning "dwelling" or "glory."

7:15 | God will **spread his tabernacle over them**. When the Lord gave the Ten Commandments, we read that "Yahweh's glory

---

[172] This word is sometimes written as *shekinah*, indicating the actual visible presence of God's glory.

settled on Mount Sinai"[173] and "The appearance of Yahweh's glory was like a devouring fire" (Ex. 24:16—17). His tabernacle glory sheltered the people and went before them on their march like a fire at night and a cloud in the day. Jacob said the Lord "is in this place, and I didn't know it" (Gen. 28:16).

7:15 | In their wisdom, reverence, and fear of speaking **God's** holy name, the Rabbis changed the word "Lord" or "Yeh" "to "Lord Shekinah." Jewish scholars then altered the verse, "My eyes have seen the King, the LORD of hosts!"[174] to read, "My eyes have seen the Lord's Shekinah glory of the king of the world" (Isa. 6:5). Rabbis were not setting out to change the scriptures but, out of reverence, to avoid saying God's holy name, whether "the LORD," "Yahweh," or "the King Almighty."

7:15 | When God **spreads his tabernacle** over them, hunger, thirst, and scorching heat will not even be a memory. He who loves them "will guide them by springs of water" (Isa. 49:10). They will be forever under the Lamb of God's protection, and he will wipe away every tear from their eyes.

7:16 | Never again would the Lord's people be **hungry or thirsty any more,** for God's presence and fullness dwells in the temple. Even Moses could not enter the Old Testament's Tent of Meeting because the glory of the Lord "filled the tabernacle" (Ex. 40:34). The priests could not enter either. In the sight of all, the cloud hovered over it by day and a column of fire by night. The people would set out whenever it lifted, but they would not move if it did not rise.

7:16 | **Hunger and thirst** were common in the time of Jesus, for there was often famine or drought. At times, the wells ran dry, and the unrelenting heat scorched them. Isaiah promised they would neither hunger nor thirst nor have the sun beat down on them. "For he who has mercy on them will lead them. He will guide them by springs of water" (Isa. 49:10). No one will suffer

---

[173] *Mount Sinai* means Moses' mountain and is also known as Mount Horeb *or* Jebel Musa in the Egyptian Sinai Peninsula. It is a 7,497 feet peak surrounded by higher mountains.
[174] King James Version

these everyday stresses in heaven, for there will be shade, peace, and plentiful crystal clear water from the River of Life.

7:17 | The Lamb now **shepherds** God's people, a curious transformation. From a helpless animal like a lamb to a strong leader like a shepherd is quite a step! But here, the shepherd, Jesus, leads the chosen people to living water. When you are suffering physically or emotionally, take comfort that God will give you his "living water" and refreshment for body and soul. The Lord "will wipe away tears from off all faces" (Isa. 25:8). As in the wilderness, where the tabernacle marked God's presence, he now spreads a tent out over his chosen ones. Instead of standing outside, the faithful people can come into the Holy of Holies. No harm can come to those under Almighty God's shade.

Question: "How did God spread his tent over Christians during Covid-19?"

33

HEAVEN'S GLOWING COAL

8:1 "When he opened the seventh seal, there was **silence in heaven** for about half an hour. [2] I saw the seven angels who stand before God, and seven trumpets were given to them. [3] Another angel came and stood over the **altar**, having a golden censer. Much **incense** was given to him, that he should add it to the **prayers of all the saints** on the golden altar which was before the throne. [4] The smoke of the incense, with the prayers of the saints, went up before God out of the angel's hand." (Rev. 8:1—4 emphases added).

8:1 | There is an intensely dramatic **silence in heaven** for about half an hour before the woes. After the previous trumpets, singing, and earthquakes, this stillness must have been shattering for John of Patmos. I recall college life in Blackheath, London. The principal insisted that all the students and staff meet weekly in the main hall without a plan. One week there had been some arguments among students, and no one talked. A stunning quietness descended, and nobody spoke for an hour! It was an intensely dramatic stillness.

8:3 | Another angel stands at the Temple incense **altar**. The word "altar" frequently appears in Revelation and is usually "a place of slaughter or sacrifice," but this golden altar only burns incense. It cannot be the burnt-offering altar, for there can be no animal sacrifices in heaven. When the Lamb opened the fifth seal, "I saw underneath the altar the souls of those who had been killed for the Word of God, and for the testimony of the Lamb" (Rev. 6:9). The incense altar[175] stood before the Holy Place, which could have been a floor model with fragrances burned on the top like those used in Ancient Rome. They were common in Roman times at the entrance to affluent homes. On a trip to Port Sunlight near Liverpool, I was impressed to discover a collection of such stone Roman incense altars at the "Lady Leverhulme Art Gallery," many of which had Latin inscriptions.

8:3 | The **incense** altar instructions were to "take a censer full of coals of fire from off the altar before Yahweh, and two handfuls of sweet incense beaten small, and bring it within the veil" (Lev. 16:12). Moses also told Aaron to take his censer, add fire from the altar, lay incense[176] on it, and "carry it quickly to the congregation and make atonement for them" (Num.16:46).

8:3 | Burning **incense** is typically associated with rising prayers, but it is separate from intercession, and one does not represent the other. The Bible speaks of the fragrant incense and the saints' invocations rising together. The Psalmist writes, "Let my prayer be set before you like incense; the lifting up of my hands like the evening sacrifice" (Ps. 141:2).

8:4 | The angel pours out the **saints' prayers**, and they rise to God with incense. Heaven holds a breathtaking stillness, even more memorable than the thunder and the lightning. This silence may be a breathing space or a preparation moment before another shattering revelation. There is also something much more beautiful in it. The saints' prayers in heaven are about to ascend to God, and everything halts so that God may hear them. R. H. Charles suggested, "The saints' needs are more important to God than all heaven's psalmody." The music and thunder of heaven are stilled so that God's ear may catch the humblest people's

---

[175] The incense altar was made of gold, eighteen inches square and three feet tall, and had a horn at each corner. A small railing kept the burning coals from rolling off.

[176] "Incense" comes from the Latin *incendere*, meaning "to burn."

whispered intercessions. A touching moment! The people's offerings, the invocations of all the saints, rise to God wrapped in an envelope of aromatic fragrance. People may have no other gift to offer, but they can submit their prayers to God, who is always waiting to receive them.

Question: "Do you feel you can whisper a prayer at any moment, and God will hear you?"

34

THE CENSER ANGEL

8:5 "The **angel** took the censer, and he filled it with the fire of the **altar**, then threw it on the earth. **Thunders, sounds, lightnings, and an earthquake** followed. [6] The **seven angels** who had the **seven trumpets** prepared themselves to sound. [7] The **first sounded**, and there followed **hail and fire, mixed with blood**, and they were **thrown to the earth.** One third of the earth was burned up, and one third of the trees were burned up, and all green grass was burned up. [8] The second **angel** sounded, and something like a great burning mountain was thrown into the sea. One third of the sea became blood, [9] and one third of the living creatures which were in the sea died. One third of the ships were destroyed." (Rev. 8:5—9 emphases added).

8:5 | Since the beginning of time, **angels** have acted as messengers, ministers, and guardians to Almighty God. He commanded this attendant to take the censer, fill it with altar coals and incense and then dash it to the ground. Then came thunder, rumblings, flashes of lightning, and an earthquake. God tells a linen-clothed angel to fill "both your hands with coals of fire from between the cherubim, and scatter them over the city" (Ezek. 10:2). In Revelation, a linen-clothed individual may be the same censor angel, as they seem to live forever. Jesus confirms that angels do not die, speaking about those resurrected from the dead, "For they can't die anymore, for they are like the angels" (Luke 20:36).

8:5 | The incense **altar** did not receive any sacrifice, and they took no coals from it, for it existed solely to fulfill the commandment for a permanent fire[177] burning in the Temple. There was no commandment regarding the type of wood used on the incense altar except that the Rabbis forbade olive and grapevine woods, as these did not burn well and were conserved because of their commercial value.

8:5 | Hurling fire on the earth brings peals of **thunders, sounds, lightnings, and an earthquake.** These are the curtain-raisers to more terrors as the coals represent new woes. H. B. Swete writes, "The saints' prayers return to the earth in wrath." They cry out for vengeance upon those who have tortured and killed them.

8:6 | The **seven angels** are known as "the presence angels" and are considered archangels. According to Enoch, the traditional names of the seven senior angels[178] are "Uriel, Raphael, Raguel, Michael, Saraqael, Gabriel, and Remiel." Some of these names vary according to their source. Some scholars link the seven archangels to the seven days of the week or the seven classical planets visible to the naked eye. Apart from these names, we know little about them except for Gabriel and Michael. Mary and Zechariah met with Gabriel, who said, "I am Gabriel, who stands in the presence of God. I was sent to speak to you and to bring you this good news" (Luke 1:19). Michael led a battle in heaven, for "there was war in the sky. Michael and his angels made war on the dragon" (Rev. 12:7).

8:6 | In Old and New Testament visions, angel **trumpet** blasts are signs of God's intervention in history. The trumpet blare is like a smoke alarm that awakens us from sleep or warns us of danger.

---

[177] The Persians called this "permanent fire" the *orismada* or "continual holy fire." They would carry it solemnly before the king in public ceremonies.
[178] Archangels are sometimes called "Princes."

In Russia's invasion of Ukraine, sirens warned householders of impending air raids, and people scurried for shelter.

8:6 | Similarly, God's **trumpet** will sound when Christ returns and comes down from heaven. Paul confirms, "the Lord himself will descend from heaven with a shout, with the voice of the archangel and with God's trumpet" (1 Thess. 4:16). Matthew writes, "he will send out his angels with a great sound of a trumpet, and they will gather together his chosen ones from the four winds, from one end of the sky to the other" (Matt. 24:31). When Moses gave God's Law, "there were thunders and lightnings, and a thick cloud on the mountain, and the sound of an exceedingly loud trumpet; and all the people who were in the camp trembled" (Ex. 19:16).

8:6 | What kind of trumpets did they use? The Greek words for "trumpet" are *salpingosor* or *salpinx* and mean "a straight, narrow bronze (or silver) tube with a mouthpiece and a bell." The **seven trumpets** may have been similar to Moses' trumpets of hammered silver. The Lord said, "Make two trumpets of silver. You shall make them of beaten work. You shall use them for the calling of the congregation, and for the journeying of the camps" (Num. 10:2).

8:6 | Archeologists discovered one such beautiful silver and gold engraved **trumpet** and its wooden mute in the Tomb of Tutankhamun.[179] Ancient trumpets did not resemble modern instruments, but the player still produced the horn's sound by blowing air through partly closed lips. Trumpeters also sounded the traditional Hebrew sacred ram's horns called *shofars* on Rosh Hashanah, "a day of shouting and blasting." It is also the beginning of the civil new year and the traditional anniversary of the creation of Adam and Eve. Trumpets have become a permanent part of the "Day of the Lord" apparatus. One day a great trumpet will summon exiles from every land.

8.6 | I was introduced to **trumpets** as a boy when I went to a brass band practice in Liverpool with my brother-in-law

---

[179] (1326–1336 BC).

George Williams, who played the trombone. As they warmed up, George let me have a go – though all I could produce was a puffing sound! He showed me how he pursed his lips to make his trombone sing! I fondly remember going with him and my sister Joan to the Royal Albert Hall in London, England, for a brass band competition with some of the best bands from all across Britain. It seemed too good to be true until I discovered that all the bands played the same piece of music in the first part! Even I could tell the absolute best from the average players after that!

8:6 | Seven **trumpets** sounded the alarm on the Day of the Lord in the Old Testament visions. "Blow the trumpet in Zion, and sound an alarm in my holy mountain." (Joel 2:1). Paul wrote about the last trumpet, "we will all be changed, in a moment, in the twinkling of an eye, at the last trumpet. For the trumpet will sound and the dead will be raised incorruptible, and we will be changed" (1 Cor. 15:51—52). Each of the seven blasts cues apocalyptic events, and an attack happens in a different part of the world. Destruction is not total, for this is only a prelude to the end. Devastation falls on the earth, the sea, the freshwater rivers and springs, and the heavens. Every part of the created universe feels this destruction.

8:7 | Aside from being an alarm, the **trumpet sound** indicates military strength or a battle summons. It is an instrument to signal directions, to advance or retreat. It may also be a trumpet fanfare to announce an eminent person's arrival. An angel trumpet blast is a fitting symbol for the Lord's entry. It can also be God's way of summoning us to stand up for truth as the King of Kings' soldiers. It marks his active involvement in punishing the world's evil. He hurls nature's elemental forces in judgment on the planet.

8:7 | The first angel pours out **hail and fire mixed with blood** on the world. John of Patmos sees his visions in the light of his life experiences. He may have recalled blood rain from what he had seen in Palestine. Similar well-documented occurrences of red-colored hail have occurred in Spain, Italy, and Morocco. In 2014, a mild red blood-like rain descended like a thick smog engulfing parts of England, notably Liverpool. Many people suffered from breathing difficulties as a result. There is also a record of red rain in Italy in 1901 when "fine red sand blew from the Sahara Desert caught up into the upper air, then when the rain came, the red particles descended with the rain and looked just like blood." High air currents can carry red sand from the Sahara across Europe, the Atlantic Ocean, Canada, and even the United States.

8:7 | We have no immediate explanation for the supernatural origin of **hail and fire**. Only once before, during Egypt's ten plagues, do we encounter a calamity in the seventh plague caused by frozen hail and fire mixed with blood. It was the worst storm in Egypt since it had become a nation. The hail struck everything in the fields, both people and animals. "Only in the land of Goshen, where the children of Israel lived, there was no hail" (Ex. 9.26).

8:8 | **Angels** in the heavenly court enjoy the unique honor of being close to God himself. To be a servant was a special privilege. In an Asian court, the king gave the right to enter or remain only to the most favored courtiers. It meant exclusive rewards and immediate readiness for the king to dispatch them on errands or service elsewhere. We, too, should aspire to be "presence angels" on earth, ready to go without hesitation at our Lord's command!

Question: "Are you a presence angel willing to go wherever the Lord sends you?

35

GREAT STAR BLAZING

8:10 "The third angel sounded, and a **great star** fell from the sky, burning like a torch, and it fell on one third of the rivers, and on the springs of the waters. [11] The name of the star is called "**Wormwood.**" One third of the waters became wormwood. Many people died from the waters, because they were made bitter. [12] The fourth angel sounded, and one third of the sun was struck, and one third of the moon, and one third of the stars; so that one third of them would be **darkened**, and the day wouldn't shine for one third of it, and the night in the same way. [13] I saw, and I heard an eagle, flying in mid heaven, saying with a loud voice, "Woe! Woe! Woe for those who dwell on the earth, because of the other voices of the trumpets of the three angels, who are yet to sound!" (Rev. 8:10—13 emphases added).

8:10 | A **great star** blazing like a torch descends from heaven. This colossal rock, named *Wormwood*, meaning "bitterness," wipes out a third of the rivers and water springs that become bitter. People died because of the poisoned waters' toxicity. Many years ago, a similar giant asteroid broke up as it entered the earth's atmosphere and landed in the Gulf of Mexico. The Chicxulub crater marks the impact site of this asteroid[180] that struck planet Earth. The impact of this great star may have caused worldwide planet disruption and mass extinction of seventy-five percent of plant and animal species. Its crater is ninety-three miles in diameter and twelve miles deep.

8:10 | The single largest meteorite or **great star** to be recovered was the nine-foot by nine-foot by three-foot "Hobo Meteor."[181] Asteroids, like this, fly around the sun as moons that have not cleared their orbit. Currently, the four largest asteroids we know about are named "Ceres," which is a five-hundred and seventy-seven-miles diameter dwarf planet, "Vesta" at three hundred and twenty-six miles across, "Pallas," and "Hygies." One of these could feasibly strike the earth with devastating effects in the future.

8:10 | Interestingly, a **great star**, a giant rock fifty meters in diameter, fell from space and struck the earth in Palestine some three thousand six hundred years ago. Archeologists believe it burst in the air, melting stones and mud bricks. It hit a town of eight to ten thousand people whose bones were shattered into tiny pieces and scattered over a wide area. The estimated force of the explosion was a one-megaton yield event. In this Revelation picture, John of Patmos has a terrifying vision of God using nature's elemental forces to warn us of our final destruction. The Wormwood star crosses the sky, blazing like a torch at the third angel's trumpet call.

8:11 | **Wormwood** is also the name of a plant in the Artemisia group. It occurs seven times in the Hebrew Bible and means a "curse" or a "bitter substance." These herbs are mildly poisonous and not usually fatal, but Jewish people hate their bitterness. However, certain plant parts produce valuable oils and medicines that help with digestive problems, gall bladder disease, and intestinal spasms.

8:11 | **Wormwood** turns the waters bitter, and many die. God

---

[180] 6.2 miles in diameter. It is suggested that this occurred 66 million years ago.
[181] *Hobo* comes from the South African *Khoekhoegowab* word meaning "gift."

threatens to give his people bitter food and "gall"[182] or "bitter" waters to drink because of their sins. It represents God's judgment on the people for their detestable images and idols of wood, stone, silver, and gold. Deuteronomy warns us to make sure there is no root among us that produces such bitter poison.

8:11 | The name **Wormwood** may also refer to a celestial event, an "enormous rock flying through space," a "meteor," or a "shooting star." These produce streaks of light as they burn up in the earth's atmosphere. Meteor colors give us a clue as to their geological makeup. They vary from red (nitrogen/oxygen,) white (iron,) purple (calcium,) yellow (sodium,) and green (magnesium.) Scientists and astronomers track asteroids and meteors continuously and believe that four billion of these fall on the earth daily. Thankfully, most are minuscule!

8:12 | At the fourth angel trumpet blast, God strikes a third of the sun, moon, stars, and a third of them are **darkened**. There is also a daytime darkening. A recent TV documentary from a deep South African mine described how visitors turned off their helmet lights and one person commented, "the utter darkness was shattering! You could barely see the floor in front of your feet with one light." The Lord told Moses to stretch his hand toward the sky to spread darkness over Egypt that they could feel. Darkness covered all of Egypt for three days, "They didn't see one another, and nobody rose from his place for three days; but all the children of Israel had light in their dwellings" (Ex. 10:23).

Question: "How would a great star event affect you and your family?"

---

[182] Gall is "greenish bile duct fluid, from the gall bladder, and liver."

36

ABYSS LOCUST DEMONS

9:1 "The fifth angel sounded, and I saw a **star from the sky** which had fallen to the earth. The key to the pit of the abyss was given to him. ²He opened the pit of the **abyss**, and smoke went up out of the pit, like the smoke from a burning furnace. The sun and the air were darkened because of the smoke from the pit. ³Then out of the smoke came **locusts** on the earth, and power was given to them, as the scorpions of the earth have power. ⁴They were told that they should not hurt the grass of the earth, neither any green thing, neither any tree, but only those people who don't have God's seal on their foreheads. ⁵They were given power, not to kill them, but to torment them for five months. Their torment was like the torment of a scorpion when it strikes a person. ⁶In those days people will seek death, and will in no way find it. They will desire to die, and death will flee from them." (Rev. 9:1—6 emphases added).

9:1 | An angel, described as a **star from the sky,** falls from heaven with the abyss key to open the underworld. Here, "hell" is called the *abyss* in Greek, meaning "bottomless." When Jesus spoke to the demon-possessed man named Legion, he used the same word. "Jesus asked him, 'What is your name?' He said, 'Legion,' for many demons had entered into him. They begged him that he would not command them to go into the abyss" (Luke 8:30). The fifth angel receives the key to access the abyss' shaft under God's control and authority.

9:2 | The **abyss** represented the locust demons' abode. The Hebrews pictured a three-level cosmos. The "heavens" *shamayim* were above, the "earth" *eres* were in the middle, and the "underworld" *Sheol* was below. The "heavens" contained the "upper seas" or "waters above the firmament" and the "chambers in heaven." Underneath were the "sun, moon, and stars." Then there were the mountains, the earth, and *Sheol* below, resting on the "pillars of the earth." After the fourth century AD, a Greek scientific cosmology of a round world and multiple concentric heavens replaced the Hebrew cosmos. The underworld's locust demons were below the surface, and the dead without Christ lived in the Abyss in hell with the beast. It was Satan's prison during the millennium or "one thousand years" with a vast underground fire-filled cavern, and its only link to the earth was a locked shaft. God controlled these places and evil powers, but here they were released to wreak havoc on the planet.

9:3 | When they were released, a plague of scorpion-stinging **locusts** tortured those without God's seal on their foreheads. In the Old Testament, locusts figured prominently in Egypt's eighth and ninth plagues before the Exodus and were symbols of destruction because they devoured crops and food. Here the stings of the Revelation scorpion torture people who do not believe in God. Scorpion stings are significant in Israel for the excruciating pain they inflict. The one limitation placed on locusts in Revelation is that they can only torment people for five months, but they are still under God's power.

Question: "What do the Abyss locust demons do?"

37

DESTROYER LOCUST DEMONS

9:7 "The shapes of the **locusts** were like horses prepared
for war. On their heads were something like golden
crowns, and their faces were like people's faces. [8] They
had hair like women's hair, and their teeth were like those
of lions. [9] They had breastplates, like breastplates of iron.
The **sound** of their wings was like the sound of chariots,
or of many horses rushing to war. [10] They have tails like
those of **scorpions**, and stings. In their tails they have
power to harm men for **five months**. [11] They have over
them as king the angel of the abyss. His name in Hebrew
is "**Abaddon**," but in Greek, he has the name "Apollyon."
(Rev. 9:7—11 emphases added).

9:7 | Revelation describes the destroyer **locust** demons in vivid
detail. Their golden crowns indicate their power to succeed like
kings, and their faces may refer to their human-like intelligence.
Locusts move like an army. They advance in a regular column
that climbs hills, enters houses, and leaves scorched earth behind
them. People have dug trenches, lit fires, and even fired cannons to
stop them without success. There is no more destructive visitation
than a destroyer locusts' plague.

9:7 | The Old Testament mentions several **locust** types. "The
swarming locust has eaten, the great locust, the grasshopper, and

the caterpillar, my great army" (Joel 2:25). The precise meaning of some Hebrew words for different locusts are uncertain, but translators try to differentiate between them. The King James Version calls the locusts in this same Joel passage the "cankerworm," the "caterpillar," and the "palmerworm" (Joel 2:25).

9:7 | Many **locust** characteristics account for their name. The "shearer" describes how they cut down all living vegetation in their path. *Arbel*, or "the swarmer," tells of its immense numbers. Another called *hasil* means the "finisher," which pictures the utter devastation left behind after they have invaded. Some locusts are named *solam*, the "swallower," or the "annihilator." *Hargol*, meaning the "galloper, "describes the scorpion locust's rapid progress across the land. *Tzelatzel*, the "creeker," explains the particular sound this variety makes. Another locust type is called *gazam* or the "gnawing locust."[183] In Revelation, demonic locusts, whose king is Satan, do not attack vegetation but advance against those people without God's forehead seal.

9:9 | Scorpion locusts **sound** like the thundering of a troop of horses and chariots rushing into battle. In nature, some hiss, but most crackle like crickets by rubbing body parts against one another.[184] Witnesses describe millions of them eating like "a prairie fire crackling." They remind one of "waters dashing in a mill-wheel" or a "great waterfall." Marching scorpion locusts seem like "heavy rain falling on a distant forest." When the swarm leaves an area, the land looks scorched, like after a wildfire. No green plant, grass blade, or other vegetation remains, and they even strip the bark of trees. A swarm causes darkness like a solar eclipse. Swarms breed in desert places and then invade cultivated lands for food. They are usually about two inches long, with a four to five inches wingspan, and belong to the cricket and grasshopper family. Locust swarms can be a hundred feet deep and four miles long. One such plague caused a famine in Algiers in 1866, resulting in 200,000 deaths.

---

[183] Strong's Concordance
[184] known as "stridulation."

9:10 | Scorpions' attacks last **for five months**, the total life span of a *"locust."* Five months represents the birth, larval stage, maturity, and death of a generation launched simultaneously. The destroyer locust demons resemble undersized lobsters with large claws to clutch prey. Unlike the lobster, its long tail curves over its back and head. A curved rear claw and a "telson stinger" inject poison to paralyze its captive.

9:10 | Deathstalker scorpion stings are still one of Palestine's greatest scourges. This **scorpion** may be six inches long, and its claw strikes and secretes poison into its victim. They live in cracks in walls and under stones. Before pitching their tent, Near Eastern campers lift and examine rocks to see if a "deathstalker scorpion" or the "Palestine yellow scorpion" hides underneath. A scorpion's sting is worse than a hornet's bite but is not necessarily fatal. It can sometimes kill a human being, but only two of fifteen hundred worldwide scorpion species have venom that can cause a person's death. The pain caused by it is so bad that victims are in terrible agony. Some "long for death, but it doesn't come" (Job 3:21). Cornelius Gallus[185] said that the scorpion sting was "worse than any wound. One would wish to die and yet cannot do so."

9:11 | John of Patmos sees the terrible devastation caused by the destroyer locust demons. They are different and far more destructive than any earthly insect he may have seen before. The leader of the locusts is called **Abaddon** in Hebrew or *Apollyon* in Greek, meaning "destruction." Both names describe "the destroyer, the destruction place or destruction," and refer to "Hell," as Satan's abode.

9:11 | John of Patmos' wordplay on the leader's name as "Abaddon," or in Greek as "**Apollyon**," indicates that both Greek and Roman worshippers of Apollo serve the destroyer locust demon. Emperor Domitian thought of himself as Apollo's reincarnation and an enlightened leader destined to guide the Roman empire into a brilliant new era. The play on the words *Apollyon* and *Abaddon* may be John of Patmos' way of referring

---

[185] The Roman orator (BC 70--26).

in a subtle way to the terrible evil of the worst Roman Emperor, who was, however, more than a little mad.

Question: "Who was the worst Roman emperor in your mind, Nero, Domitian, Elagabalus, Caligula, Commodus, or Caligula?"[186]

---

[186] https://www.thoughtco.com/worst-roman-emperors

38

TWO HUNDRED
MILLION TROOPS

9:12 "The first woe is past. Behold, there are still two woes coming after this. [13] The sixth angel sounded. I heard a voice from the horns of the golden altar which is before God, [14] saying to the sixth angel who had the trumpet, "Free the four angels who are bound at the great river Euphrates!" [15] The **four angels** were freed who had been prepared for that hour and day and month and year, so that they might kill one third of mankind. [16] The number of the armies of the horsemen was **two hundred million**. I heard the number of them. [17] Thus I saw the horses in the vision, and those who sat on them, having breastplates of fiery red, hyacinth blue, and sulfur yellow; and the horses' heads resembled lions' heads. Out of their mouths proceed **fire, smoke, and sulfur**. [18] By these three plagues were one third of mankind killed: by the fire, the smoke, and the sulfur, which proceeded out of their mouths. [19] For the power of the horses is in their mouths and in their tails. For their tails are like serpents, and have heads, and with them they harm. [20] The rest of mankind, who were not killed with these plagues, **didn't repent** of the works of their hands, that they wouldn't worship demons, and the idols of gold, and of silver, and of brass, and of stone, and of wood; which can't see, hear, or walk. [21] They didn't repent of their murders, their sorceries, their sexual immorality, or their thefts." (Rev. 9:12—21 emphases added).

9:15 | The judgment is still not complete, as **four angels** appear who are "exceedingly destructive." However, they do not have the power themselves to inflict their evil work on earth. God holds them back until a specific date and time, doing what he allows them to do. Here, he destroys one-third of all humanity. In earlier chapters, one-fourth of the population died. More than half the world's people have perished during this great judgment. If God had not set limits, even more would have expired.

9:16 | The number of horsemen in the Lord's army is **two hundred million**. In Greek, this number is " ten thousand of ten thousand" or "two myriads of myriads." Two hundred million is an exceedingly large army and would be a frightening military opponent. In John of Patmos' day, millions of troops were almost inconceivable. King Xerxes 1,[187] who ruled over one hundred and twenty-seven provinces stretching from India to Egypt, is reported to have assembled two and a half million men to invade Greece.

9:16 | Compare **two hundred million** heavenly troops with one hundred and fifty-six thousand American, British, Canadian, and others who landed at Normandy during the Second World War. The thirty-four-nation coalition that liberated Kuwait deployed roughly one million troops. Recently, Russia massed one hundred eighty thousand soldiers in their Ukraine invasion. An army of two hundred million soldiers would cover an area one mile wide and eighty-five miles deep. However, large nations like China or India could theoretically gather this many soldiers today.

9:17 | John of Patmos sees the horsemen in his vision "having breastplates of fiery red, hyacinth blue, and sulfur yellow; and the horses' heads resemble lions' heads. Out of their mouths proceed

---

[187] King Xerxes, "Xerxes the Great," also called "Ahasuerus," or "Artaxerxes," appears in the Book of Esther (BC 519--465).

fire, smoke, and sulfur." This vast army, led by the four demons, is dispatched to destroy one-third of humanity with **fire, smoke, and sulfur** from the horses' mouths.

9:17 | These natural elements of **fire, smoke, and sulfur** were also responsible for destroying the ancient city of Gomorrah. The archaeological researcher Ron Wyatt documented the five cities destroyed by fire and brimstone in the days of Abraham and Lot. Layers of sterile white ash cover the entire area, and numerous golf ball-sized sulfur pellets are on the ground. Wyatt tested these and found they were ninety-eight percent pure sulfur with a trace of magnesium. Naturally occurring sulfur usually is forty to forty-five percent pure. These brimstone balls would have burned at a high temperature! A thin crust of rock-like slag encased some of them. Once broken open, they gave off an intensely pungent sulfur smell which ignited violently with a flame. Interestingly, modern tourists can still see the remains of Gomorrah's window and door openings on the cliff face not far from the Masada fortress.

9:20 | The earth's inhabitants were so hard-hearted that despite the fire, smoke, and sulfur, they **didn't repent**. Like Exodus' Egyptian pharaoh, the remaining people on earth "did not repent of the work of their hands." People don't usually fall into immorality suddenly, but they slide into it a little at a time until they hardly realize what has happened. Today's temptation becomes tomorrow's sin, then a habit, and in the end, death and separation from God for eternity.

Question: "Can you imagine a huge hostile army gathered at your borders as the Ukrainians did. How would you feel?"

39

CLOUD ROBED ANGEL

10:1 "I saw a mighty angel coming down out of the sky, **clothed with a cloud. A rainbow** was on his head. His face was **like the sun**, and his feet like pillars of fire. [2] He had in his hand a little open book. He set his right foot on the sea, and his left on the land. [3] He cried with a loud voice, as a lion roars. When he cried, the seven thunders uttered their voices. [4] When the seven thunders sounded, I was about to write; but I heard a voice from the sky saying, "**Seal up** the things which the seven thunders said, and don't write them." [5] The angel whom I saw standing on the sea and on the land lifted up his **right hand to the sky,** [6] and swore by him who lives forever and ever, who created heaven and the things that are in it, the earth and the things that are in it, and the sea and the things that are in it, that there will **no longer be delay**, [7] but in the days of the voice of the seventh angel, when he is about to sound, then the **mystery of God** is finished, as he declared to his servants, the prophets." (Rev. 10:1—7 emphases added).

10:1 | This section is an interlude between the sixth and seventh trumpet blasts[188] when terrible things happen. The description of the angel, **clothed with a cloud** and a rainbow

---

[188] The sixth trumpet sounds in Rev. 9:13, and the seventh occurs in Rev. 11:15.

above his head, indicates that he comes straight from Almighty God and the risen Christ's presence. The Psalmist writes that the Lord "makes the clouds his chariot." (Ps. 104:3).

10:1 | The angel **clothed with a cloud** comes from heaven, with a rainbow over his head. His shout is like a lion's roar, and the seven thunders sound. Some think this "mighty angel" is none other than the glorified Christ himself, or an Archangel like Gabriel, coming from God's presence. He has his right foot on the sea, and his left on the land and holds a little open scroll.[189] He gives John of Patmos a partial revelation, and the seven thunders crash when he speaks. "The God of glory thunders, even Yahweh on many waters" (Ps. 29:3).

10:1 | The angel's face was radiant **like the sun,** similar to Jesus at the Transfiguration, and a light shone from his skin and robes. He comes from God's glorious throne, reflecting his divine brilliance as "the appearance of the likeness of Yahweh's glory" (Ezek. 1:28).

10:4 | A voice from heaven then commands John to **seal up** what he had seen and heard. A great chasm exists between the present and the future, and God prevents him from recording these details. Many people want to know what will happen in the future leading to a misplaced and dangerous fascination with fortune-telling, horoscopes, Ouija boards, and tarot cards. Far from being harmless, these are Satan's temptations to lead people away from God and eventually destroy them. Some people think they would feel better about their present circumstances if they could see what would happen to them. They want to know whether they are destined to inherit a fortune, marry a beautiful wife, or have a handsome husband. They imagine a crack in heaven and the all-knowing God somehow leaking out information. I am glad I do not know what is coming tomorrow. I don't believe I would be any happier if I did!

10:5 | The angel raises his **right hand** and affirms all creation's final judgment. John seems to be on earth, for he sees this mighty angel coming down from heaven wrapped in a cloud.

---

[189] The word *scroll* comes from the old French *escroe,* meaning "a deed, or a bond."

10:6 | The mighty angel now announces that there will be **no longer a delay**[190] and swears it with an oath. The Antichrist, a figure of concentrated evil, is about to burst upon the scene in all his destructive terror.

10:7 | When the seventh angel sounds his trumpet, the **mystery of God** will be accomplished. He will reveal what tomorrow holds, how the future will unfold, and human history's purpose. Much in life is difficult to understand, but as John of Patmos sees it, there will be a reckoning at the end. God's angel army, led by the archangel Michael, will battle with the Antichrist and his forces and defeat them. When he settles it, he will answer all questions, right every wrong, and solve great mysteries. Beyond all these strange word pictures, history moves towards his inevitable triumph. Wise people understand that events will only be understood when God reveals them.

10:7 | The words of Jesus clearly describe the **mystery of God** and how he has fixed an impassable gulf between the beggar Lazarus and the rich man Dives. "Those who want to pass from here to you are not able, and that no one may cross over from there to us" (Luke 16:26).

10:7 | The Lord's plan is predetermined and will eventually reveal the **mystery of God**. Paul writes that we are "chosen" and "assigned an inheritance in him, having been foreordained according to the purpose of him who does all things after the counsel of his will" (Eph. 1:11). Like firstborn children, we will receive our inheritance. God has told us all we need to know. We must not overly speculate about the last days but live for him today to be ready for the end. At that time, all prophecies will finish, and the end of the age will come.

Question: "Would you like to know your future on earth? What if it is not what you would like?"

---

[190] which may also mean, "time shall be no more." That is to say, "time as we know it is at an end, and eternity begins."

40

SWEET LITTLE SCROLL

10:8 "The voice which I heard from heaven, again speaking with me, said, "Go, take the book which is open in the hand of the angel who stands on the sea and on the land." ⁹ I went to the angel, telling him to give me the **little book**. He said to me, "**Take it, and eat it. It will make your stomach bitter, but in your mouth it will be as sweet as honey**." ¹⁰ I took the little book out of the angel's hand, and ate it. It was as sweet as honey in my mouth. When I had eaten it, my stomach was made bitter. ¹¹ They told me, "You must prophesy again over many peoples, nations, languages, and kings." (Rev. 10:8—11 emphases added).

10:9 | The Greek word for a **little book** or "little scroll" is *Biblaridion,* from which *Biblia,* meaning "the books" or "Bible," also comes. "Little book" is an unusual phrase only occurring once before, where a mighty angel "had in his hand a little open book" (Rev. 10:2). John of Patmos then went to the angel and asked him for it.

10:9 | This **little book** or scroll reminds me of my visit to the Dead Sea Scrolls exhibit in "The Shrine of the Book"[191] in western Jerusalem. The texts were on parchment, papyrus, and copper.

---

[191] at the Israel Museum in Jerusalem

One scroll, the twenty-four feet long "Isaiah," was stretched out in a circular viewing case for all to see. After displaying a scroll for three to six months, it was removed and placed temporarily in a special storeroom, where it "rested" from exposure to light and people's corrosive breaths! The fragility and sheer quantity of scrolls make it impossible to display them continuously. The Isaiah scroll dates from the second century BC and its close similarity to the modern text prove Isaiah's authenticity and historicity beyond doubt. Shepherds found the Dead Sea Scrolls in the "Qumran Caves."[192] They were written as early as the 3rd century BC and contained forty percent of the Old Testament Books, which were surprisingly almost identical to those we read today.

10:9 | The heavenly voice told John of Patmos to take a little scroll, which would typically have been a roll of papyrus, parchment, or animal hide. The voice then said, **take and eat it**! The prophet Ezekiel speaks of a similar scroll God told him to eat. "Son of man, eat what you find. Eat this scroll, and go, speak to the house of Israel" (Ezek. 3:1). John of Patmos describes the same experience as Ezekiel when he eats the little scroll. Each special scroll contained unfolding judgments, initially as comforting prophecies as sweet as honey in his mouth but then with disturbing consequences which tasted sour to his stomach. Believers find God's word sweet because it brings encouragement. However, it also leaves a bad taste because of the coming judgments it contains. If we knew the future today, it might seem initially sweet, but it would hold bitterness for us.

10:9 | To John of Patmos, the scroll was sweet and sour. Heaven's voice told him twice to **take and eat it**. Even when he asked the angel to give it to him, the angel said he had to take it for himself. The inference is that God never forces his wishes on anyone, but people must take the scroll of life for themselves. God's messengers must digest the Lord's word with negative and positive consequences into their very beings. Such is a messenger's duty!

---

[192] in the Judaean Desert on the West Bank.

10:9 | Behind the words, **sweet as honey,** lies an unusual Jewish educational custom. A Jewish boy learning his alphabet's characters wrote his letters in a mixture of flour and honey on a slate. He needed to know what they were and how they sounded. The teacher then pointed to a letter and asked, "What is this, and how does it sound?" If a boy answered correctly, he was permitted to lick the letter's honey off the slate as a reward! When the prophet and the psalmist spoke about God's words and judgments being sweeter than a scroll, they may have thought about this quaint and unusual Jewish custom. Wouldn't you want to "lick the slate too?"

10:9 | The scroll was as **sweet as honey** from the angel's hand. There are at least twenty-six references to "honey" in the Bible. The Lord's commands are "sweeter also than honey, and the extract of the honeycomb" (Ps. 19:10) and "How sweet are your promises to my taste, more than honey to my mouth!" (Ps. 119:103). The book of Proverbs adds, "Pleasant words are a honeycomb, sweet to the soul, and health to the bones" (Prov. 16:24). King David's friend, Jonathan, loved honey, for "he put out the end of the rod that was in his hand and dipped it in the honeycomb, and put his hand to his mouth; and his eyes brightened" (1 Sam. 14:27). Bright eyes are good!

10:9 | Interestingly, President Biden used a related and unusual word in one of his speeches. When addressing the police who had served in the capital during the attack on the Congress building, he said, "This must seem bittersweet." He meant that though the officers received a gold medal for protecting the officials, they had to live with the memory of being attacked. **Honey** is precious for the Christian because it is a great privilege to be a messenger. The message itself may be painful also. For John of Patmos, it was a joy to be privy to heaven's secrets, but at the same time, it was challenging to proclaim a time of terror, even if it had a triumphant conclusion.

Question: "Would you like to lick the honey from a school boy's slate? What would that mean for you?"

41

TWO WITNESSES PROPHESY

11:1 "A reed like a rod was given to me. Someone said, "Rise, and measure God's **temple**, and the altar, and those who worship in it. [2] Leave out the court which is outside of the temple, and don't measure it, for it has been given to the nations. They will tread the holy city under foot for forty-two months. [3] I will give power to my **two witnesses**, and they will prophesy one thousand two hundred sixty days, **clothed in sackcloth**." [4] These are the **two olive trees** and the two lamp stands, standing before the Lord of the earth. [5] If anyone desires to harm them, fire proceeds out of their mouth and devours their enemies. If anyone desires to harm them, he must be killed in this way. [6] These have the power to **shut up the sky**, that it may not rain during the days of their prophecy. They have power over the waters, to turn them into blood, and to strike the earth with every plague, as often as they desire."
(Rev. 11:1—6 emphases added).

11:1 | In his vision, John of Patmos is encouraged to participate in measuring the temple. He computes the building and altar sizes but is told not to measure the outer gentiles' court. The Greek word for **temple** comes from the Latin *templum* and an earlier root *tem*, meaning "to cut." "Temple" indicates a "space cleared" or "cut down" for an altar. As it developed, a temple became a "building for a god's worship" or a "consecrated section of land."

11:3 | The **two witnesses** prophesied, for they experienced death and resurrection. They remind us of Moses and Elijah, two of God's mighty men representing the Law and the Prophets. Moses called plagues upon Egypt, and Elijah defeated Baal's[193] prophets with fire. They both appeared at the Transfiguration with Jesus.

11:3 | The two witnesses were **clothed in sackcloth,**[194] sometimes called "haircloth," made of black goat's hair as a self-imposed means of mortifying the flesh. In Christianity, wearing a sackcloth hair shirt in the Middle Ages acted as a deliberate personal punishment of one's body. Penitents wore it on Ash Wednesday, Good Friday, and during the Lenten season. People put it on under their clothes as a sign of repentance.

11:3 | The Archbishop of Canterbury, Thomas a Becket,[195] was murdered in his Cathedral by four of King Henry the Second's[196] knights. When the servants of Thomas removed his ornate outer clothing to prepare his body for burial, they were astonished to find underneath a vermin-infested **sackcloth** hair shirt! There is also an unusual story of Aramean soldiers wearing haircloth seeking mercy from Israel's king. "So they put sackcloth on their bodies and ropes on their heads and came to the king of Israel" (1 Kgs. 20:32).

11:4 | The **two olive trees** and the two lamp stands symbolize the Old Testament's two great heroes, Moses and Elijah. The angel awakened John of Patmos and asked him what he saw. He answered that he could see two lamp stands and two olive trees.

---

[193] *"Baal"* was a pagan god associated with the "storm and fertility deity Hadad."
[194] Sackcloth could be an empty sack with holes for the head and arms or a loincloth made from goat's hair, flax, or hemp, a coarse, rough woven material, often symbolizing mourning.
[195] (1119--1170 AD).
[196] (1133--1189 AD).

11:6 | God gave Moses and Elijah miraculous powers. Elijah **shut up the sky,** so it did not rain, and Moses turned water into blood. These are two characteristics of the olive trees, and the lamp stands in Revelation.

Question: "Why were the two witnesses there?"

42

LIFE AFTER DEATH

11:7 "When they have **finished their testimony**, the beast that comes up out of the abyss will make war with them, and overcome them, and kill them. [8] Their dead bodies will be in the street of the great city, which spiritually is called **Sodom and Egypt**, where also **their Lord was crucified.** [9] From among the peoples, tribes, languages, and nations, people will look at their dead bodies for three and a half days, and **will not allow their dead bodies to be laid in a tomb**. [10] Those who dwell on the earth rejoice over them, and they will be glad. They will give gifts to one another, because these two prophets tormented those who dwell on the earth. [11] After the **three and a half** days, the breath of life from God entered into them, and they stood on their feet. **Great fear fell on those who saw them.** [12] I heard a loud voice from heaven saying to them, "Come up here!" They went up into heaven in the cloud, and their enemies saw them."
(Rev.11:7—12 emphases added).

11:7 | The two witnesses had **finished their testimony**. The beast from the abyss attacked, overpowered, and killed them. Their bodies lay in the Jerusalem public square for three and a half days. Even worse, the people's hatred for them was such that they regarded their deaths as a reason for celebrating and exchanging gifts. Though they had died, God's life-breath[197] entered them, and they arose. John of Patmos added that terror struck those who saw it when the two witnesses recovered. The horrific pictures from Bucha in Ukraine show ordinary people's dead bodies strewn about a street where they had been killed with no one to bury them. Friends and family have a deep-rooted need for closure and to bury their loved ones, no matter the circumstances.

11:8 | These events happened in Jerusalem, called by the derogatory names **Sodom and Egypt**. Isaiah also cynically addressed "Jerusalem" and "Jerusalem's people" as "you rulers of Sodom" and "you people of Gomorrah" (Isa. 1:9—10). Sodom and Gomorrah were two of the five Canaanite cities mentioned in Genesis in the Hebrew Bible, New Testament, and the Quran and located near the Dead Sea in southern Israel. This fertile plain appeared like the "Garden of Eden" or the "Garden of the Lord." When Lot arrived, he "saw all the plain of the Jordan, that it was well-watered everywhere" (Gen. 13:10).

11:8 | In the Genesis account, fire and brimstone consumed **Sodom**, Gomorra, and three other plain cities. Neighboring Zoar was the only city spared. Lot's wife disobeyed the angels, looked back as she left the town, and turned into a pillar of salt. So Jerusalem was allegorized as Sodom and Egypt on which the Lord sent plagues, which became bywords for destruction, shame, and punishment.

11:8 | Jerusalem, where **their Lord was crucified,** welcomed the two witnesses' death. Its people hated the two witnesses so much that they left their bodies unburied in the street. Our Lord died that we might live! When they have laid their eggs, some octopuses stop eating to dedicate themselves to caring for their young. They blow oxygenated water over them to prevent microbes from attacking the eggs. Eventually, the female dies caring for their offspring. The male also expires after fertilizing

---

[197] God's "life breath" may mean the "life spirit" or the Holy Spirit here. The word for "breath" may equally be "wind or spirit" and is the same word used in the creation account of the Spirit moving over the waters.

the eggs. The sacrificial act of both parents reminds us of the death of Jesus on the cross.

11:9 | When the heathen attacked and killed God's people, the greatest tragedy was that they would **not allow their dead bodies to be laid in a tomb.** The Psalmist foresaw this distress. "God, the nations have come into your inheritance. They have defiled your holy temple. They have laid Jerusalem in heaps. They have shed their blood like water around Jerusalem. There was no one to bury them" (Ps. 79:1,3). The greatest threat to a disobedient prophet was to refuse their funeral. "Your body will not come to the tomb of your fathers" (1 Kgs. 13:22).

11.9 | The two witnesses lie dead on the streets, and the people refuse them interment. Then suddenly, after **three and a half days,** God raises them to life. Breath returns to their bodies, and they stand up, much to the crowd's astonishment and terror. God summons them into heaven, possibly like Elijah's heavenly departure in a whirlwind as the people watch.

11.11 | The two witnesses' resurrection makes you wonder about rising again. Death is stone cold and final, but rising from the dead is amazing. Their organs and brains stopped when the witnesses died, and their heart's pumping slowed to zero. When the two witnesses revived, **great fear fell on those who saw them.** Every committed Christian will experience this transformative resurrection one day and enjoy heavenly life with God!

11:11 | The Roman General Titus ordered Jerusalem's destruction in 70 AD, slaughtered a million Jewish people, and plundered the Temple treasures. John of Patmos wanted the Christian victims of this carnage and their families to know their sacrifice was not in vain. He desired them to understand the reality of **life after death.**

11:11 | I had a personal experience of seeing resurrection firsthand in my church one Sunday. In the middle of a service, an elderly gentleman passed out in a pew without a heartbeat or breathing. A nurse tended to him as best she could, and a group of us prayed over him and laid hands upon his head. Suddenly, to our great relief, he revived!. **Great fear** fell on those who saw it! Strangely, the same thing happened the following week. It was scary to see him return to life after his breathing and heart had stopped a second time. Sometime later, it happened again, but no one was there to pray for him, and he died. Life after death is astonishing and wonderful, but the dying experience is frightening even for Christians.

Question: "What is the significance of three and a half days here? Are you prepared for life after death?"

43

JERUSALEM CITY EARTHQUAKE

11:13 "In that day there was a **great earthquake**, and a **tenth of the city** fell. **Seven thousand people** were killed in the earthquake, and the rest were terrified, and gave glory to the God of heaven. [14] The second woe is past. Behold, the third woe comes quickly. [15] The seventh angel sounded, and great voices in heaven followed, saying, "The kingdom of the world has become the **Kingdom of our Lord, and of his Christ**. He will reign forever and ever!" (Rev. 11:13—15 emphases added).

11:13 | **Great earthquakes** are not unusual in Israel. Palestine lies on the Syrian African rift, which experiences large ones every fifty to a hundred years.[198] In 1927, a major eruption occurred at the northern end of the Dead Sea. It was a "six-point two magnitude tremor that killed five hundred people and injured seven hundred." A previous earthquake in 749 AD had its epicenter in Galilee and destroyed the city of Tiberias. There were many deaths and injuries, including several thousand in Jerusalem.

11:13 | Many scholars believe that Sodom and Gomorrah's

---

[198] It is part of the Great Rift Valley from Mozambique in the south to Syria in the north.

destruction with its sulfur, brimstone, and salt in Lot's time resulted from a significant **earthquake** further south on the same fault. These three materials come to the surface during an eruption. Even though the rest of the Judean Desert is composed of desert limestone, Mount Sodom is made up of salt, as are two interesting geological features called "Lot's wife." These are salt pillars that visitors can view today near the Dead Sea. Lot's wife's name may have been "Ado" or "Edith," according to some Jewish traditions. The historian Josephus claimed to have seen it, as did Clement of Rome and Irenaeus.

11:13 | Another Jewish legend says that because Lot's wife sinned with **salt,** God punished her with salt. The night the two angels visited Lot, he requested that his wife prepare a feast for them. Not having any salt, she asked her neighbors, which alerted them to the presence of their guests, resulting in the mob action that endangered Lot's family. Jesus mentions her, "Remember Lot's Wife," in Luke 17:32 in the context of warning his disciples not to waver in the future when the Son of Man returns.

11:13 | In the event of another earthquake, Archeologists believe Jerusalem's old city and the Temple Mount would be the worst affected because their foundations are on layered debris rather than solid rock, and a **tenth of the city** could collapse. Jerusalem is a tell built on layers of garbage from previous centuries like other towns and cities in the area. In the Revelation vision, survivors are terrified, yet God spares those who give glory to him.

11:13 | The Jewish News Syndicate[199] reviewed the possible impact of an earthquake in Israel. "In 2016, the Knesset[200] estimated that a seven-point five magnitude earthquake would kill **seven thousand people,** injure another eight thousand six hundred, leave four hundred thousand homeless, and cause approximately fifty-six billion dollars in damages." This forecast of a significant tremor concurs with the Revelation eleven vision, "In that day

---

[199] on May 16th, 2019.
[200] Foreign Affairs and Defense Committees Home Front Readiness Subcommittee chaired by Colonel Itzik Bar.

there was a great earthquake, and a tenth of the city fell. Seven thousand people were killed in the earthquake, and the rest were terrified and gave glory to the God of heaven." This biblical passage matches the Jewish Knesset report and gives us an idea of what will likely happen.

11:15 | The seventh angel announces that the **Kingdom of our Lord and of his Christ** has arrived, and he has installed his sovereign on Zion, his sacred mountain. The Psalmist echoes this truth, "Yet I have set my King on my holy hill of Zion" (Ps. 2:6). The Messianic reign has begun. William Barclay writes, "This is a picture of the coming of the full glory of God, a terrifying threat to his enemies but an uplifting promise to his covenant people."

Question: "How does God use earthquakes for his glory for Christians and non-Christians?"

44

THRONE ROOM ELDERS

11:16 "The **twenty-four elders,** who sit on their thrones before God's throne, fell on their faces and worshiped God, [17] saying: "We give you thanks, Lord God, the Almighty, the one who is and who was; because you have taken your great power and reigned. [18] The nations were angry, and your wrath came, as did the time for the **dead to be judged,** and to **give your bondservants the prophets, their reward,** as well as to the saints, and those who fear your name, to the small and the great, and to destroy those who destroy the earth." [19] **God's temple** that is in heaven was opened, and the **ark of the Lord's covenant** was seen in his temple. Lightnings, sounds, thunders, an earthquake, and great hail followed." (Rev. 11:16—19 emphases added).

11:16 | The twenty-four elders erupt in thanksgiving and praise because of God's great victory. He will assume his supreme authority in the thousand-year reign of peace and prosperity.[201] Hostile powers will attack at the millennium's end, but their final defeat will come and begin his absolute rule.

11:18 | It is time to reward God's heavenly servants and

---

[201] The word "millennium" comes from the Latin *Mille* for "thousand" and *Annus* for a "year."

for the **dead to be judged**. There is no turning back for future rulings as they are no longer partial but complete, and he is in control.

11:18 | Humans want immediate justice and rewards but do not want to wait until later. It doesn't seem fair when evil people prosper, and the good suffer but God's way is different. We are told not to judge because true justice belongs to him. It is time to **give your bondservants, the prophets, their reward** with the saints. He does not shower his covenant blessings on people in this life according to what they wish or deserve, but a time for recompense is coming. Obedience often brings benefits in the Old Testament, but faithfulness and immediate appreciation are not always linked. If they were, virtuous people would always be rich, and suffering would always signify sin. While it is true that God promises to reward our earthly deeds, the greatest prize is the gift of God's eternal life in Jesus Christ.

11:19 | **God's temple** in heaven opens, and we see the Ark of the Covenant. We enter the Holy of Holies, which only a very few High Priests have ever seen, and only once a year on the Day of Atonement. Even then, bells were attached to his robe so that people could still hear him moving about, and a rope was tied around his waist so that if he should collapse, the other priests could haul him out without defiling themselves. Even today, a devout Jewish person will not set foot on the Temple Mount or Al-Aqsa Compound in the event that they should inadvertently step upon what would have been the "Holy of Holies"[202] in the old Jerusalem temple.

11:19 | The Dome of the Al Aqsa Mosque was completed in 692 AD, making it one of the oldest Islamic structures in the world. It is built on the southern side of the Mount, facing Mecca. It currently sits in the middle, occupying or close to the area where **God's Temple** previously stood before its destruction by the Romans in 70 AD. Visitors access it through eleven gates, ten reserved for Muslims and one for non-Muslims, with guards

---

[202] The Holy of Holies was a 20 feet cube space and the center of the Temple worship.

on each. Muslims revere it as the destination of Muhammad's journey to Jerusalem and ascension to heaven. Orthodox Jewish tradition maintains that they will build the third and final Temple there when the Messiah comes. Jewish people turn towards the Temple Mount when they pray. Western Christian churches often align east to west with the sanctuary at the eastern end facing Jerusalem.

11:19 | In the fictional adventure movie "Raiders of the Lost Ark," archeologists discover the **ark of the Lord's covenant** in Egypt. It is also known as the "Ark of the Testimony" and contains the stone tablets inscribed with the Ten Commandments brought down from God by Moses on Mount Sinai, Aaron's rod that budded, and a pot of manna.[203] The ark of the Lord's covenant reminds us of his agreement with his people.

11:19 | What is the **ark of the Lord's covenant**? The craftsman Bezalel, in Exodus, made it of acacia wood, overlaying it inside and out with pure gold, and formed a molding around the top. He cast four gold rings and fastened them to the feet, with two rings on either side. He then inserted carrying poles of acacia wood and sculpted the cover of pure gold with two cherubim, one at each end. "The cherubim spread out their wings above, covering the mercy seat with their wings, with their faces toward one another" (Ex. 37:9). The Ark of the Covenant was constructed to God's pattern one year after the Israelite's exodus from Egypt.

11:19 | Interestingly, Moses appears to have made an earlier **ark of the Lord's Covenant** out of acacia wood. He chiseled out two stone tablets like the first ones and went up the mountain with them. The Lord wrote the Ten Commandments on these tablets and gave them back to him, and he descended from the mountain. He wrote, "I put the tablets in the ark which I had made" (Deut. 10:5). We do not know whether this is the same ark of the covenant we read about later. God gave ten commandments to Israel, but the new covenant is for those from every nation who

---

[203] (Heb. 9:4).

love and believe in the Messiah. Whatever the terrors to come, he will not break his promises. His coming is a threat to his enemies and an encouragement to his covenant people.

Question: "Did you see the movie "The Raiders of the Lost Ark?" What did you think would happen when the Nazi officer opened the Ark's top?

45

HEAVENLY BIRTH OF JESUS

12:1 "A great sign was seen in heaven: **a woman clothed with the sun**, the moon under her feet, and a crown of twelve stars on her head. ²She was **with child**. She cried out in pain, laboring to give birth. ³**Another sign** was seen in heaven. Behold, a **great red dragon**, having seven heads and ten horns, and on his heads seven crowns. ⁴His tail drew one third of the stars of the sky, and threw them to the earth. The dragon stood before the woman who was about to give birth, so that when she gave birth he might devour her child. ⁵She gave birth to a son, a male child, who is to rule all the nations with a rod of iron. Her **child was caught up to God,** and to his throne." (Rev. 12:1—5 emphases added).

12:1 | The birth of a child is a special moment for any mother, father, or family. Here, the writer describes the immense, eternal significance of the birth of Jesus for his family in heaven. The sun, moon, and stars, representing God's faithful people, clothe and encircle the **woman** in this passage and await the Messiah's birth. "A crown of twelve stars" over her head indicates the twelve tribes of Israel or the twelve apostles. God set apart the Jewish people for himself, and that nation gave birth to the Messiah, born in Bethlehem in Judea.

12:1 | **A woman clothed with the sun** was a virgin girl called

Mary,[204] from the ancient Hebrew name "Miriam," derived from Moses' sister's title with a root meaning "beloved," "bitter," or "rebellious," a reference to her life as an enslaved person in Egypt. Mary's Aramaic name was probably "Maryam," meaning "beloved" or "rebellious," and envisions a "strong, independent person." "Marian" is of French origin and is a blend of the Latin for "Mary, star of the sea" and the Hebrew for "Ann," meaning "grace."

12:1 | Three Gospels[205] affirm that Mary was a virgin when she conceived Jesus by the Holy Spirit. John's Gospel refers to the mother of Jesus in seven places but never by name. She was there at the cross with John of Patmos, "Therefore when Jesus saw his mother, and the disciple whom he loved standing there, he said to his mother, "Woman, behold, your son!" (John 19:25-26). At this moment, Jesus instructed John of Patmos to care for Mary and take her in as if she was his mother.

12:2 One of my earliest memories as a four-year-old **child** was the birth of my brother Alan at home in my parent's bedroom in their large double bed. So many people were milling around with my elder sisters, our doctor, nurses, and close neighbors. I recall peeping into the bedroom and then quickly being sent away! But it was an extraordinary moment that I remember. My brother, who was born almost as handsome as I am, has been a close friend and Christian brother for many years, for which I am very grateful.

12:2 | We can compare this birth episode in heaven with what we know of the historical delivery of Jesus by a young Jewish woman. On hearing the news of the **child**, a jealous and cruel King Herod immediately attempted to destroy the baby Jesus as he perceived him as a threat to his throne. Satan, portrayed in Revelation as an "enormous red dragon," wanted to kill him.

12:3 | A silver star in a cave grotto marks the birthplace of

---

[204] Mary comes from the Greek. Maryam as she is known in Islam, or Marian from the Aramaic language.
[205] Matthew 1:16,18, 21 and 23. Mark 6:3 and Luke 1:26—27.

Jesus in the Church of the Nativity in Bethlehem.[206] The heavenly pageant is **another sign** depicting Christ's birth in King David's birthplace. Today's basilica over the cave where Jesus was born is the oldest complete church in the Christian world. The emperor Justinian built it in the 6th century to replace the original one constructed by Constantine the Great and dedicated in 339 AD.

12:3 | Today, Bethlehem is a Palestinian town in the West Bank. When I visited it many years ago, large banners of Yasser Arafat,[207] the Palestinian leader, lined the main street leading to the Church of the Nativity. He was awarded the Nobel Peace Prize for efforts to create peace and was a Palestinian political leader as chairman of the Palestine Liberation Organization. He acknowledged Israel's right to exist and sought a two-state solution to the Israeli–Palestinian conflict. In 1990, he married Suha Tawil, a Palestinian Christian, when he was sixty-one years old, and Suha was twenty-seven. She said she regretted the marriage and would not repeat it if given a choice. Arafat remains a controversial figure today. Many Palestinians view him as a martyr, but many other Israelis regard him as a terrorist.

12:3 | The birth of Jesus in Bethlehem is **another sign** that corresponds to a strange myth of a monster that pursues a pregnant goddess, and her baby is saved only by miraculous intervention. She bore a son who then killed the beast. However, the earthly birth of Jesus is no myth but a historical occurrence with a cosmic significance.

12:3 | Revelation describes Satan as the **great red dragon**[208] with seven heads, ten horns, and seven crowns, representing his power and the kingdoms over which he rules. The birth of the male child occurs, but he is protected. The abyss dragon gives the first beast "out of the sea" authority and power, and the second beast, the "false prophet," comes "from the earth." The stars that plunge to earth with the seven-headed dragon represent the

---

[206] *Bethlehem* means the "house of bread" in Hebrew and the "house of meat" in Arabic.
[207] (1929—2004),
[208] The word "dragon," in Greek, *therion*, refers to two beasts in Revelation.

wicked angels or demons expelled with Satan, and the "dragon" symbolizes all evil earthly forces.

12:5 | The woman's **child was caught up to God** and his throne, referring to Christ's ascension. She found spiritual rest from the dragon in the desert, the traditional refuge place for the afflicted. Because God aided her escape, we know he offers security to all other true believers. He keeps all his people safe and secure.

Question: "Can you compare the earthly and heavenly births of Jesus?"

46

MICHAEL'S ANGELS FIGHT

12:6 "The **woman fled** into the wilderness, where she has a place prepared by God, that there they may nourish her **one thousand two hundred sixty days**. ⁷ There was war in the sky. Michael and his angels made war on the dragon. The dragon and his angels made war. ⁸ They didn't prevail. No place was found for them any more in heaven. ⁹ The great dragon was thrown down, the old serpent, he who is called the devil and **Satan**, the deceiver of the whole world. He was thrown down to the earth, and his angels were thrown down with him. ¹⁰ I heard a loud voice in heaven, saying, "Now the salvation, the power, and the Kingdom of our God, and the authority of his Christ has come; for the accuser of our brothers has been thrown down, who accuses them before our God day and night. ¹¹ They overcame him because of the Lamb's blood, and because of the word of their testimony. They didn't love their life, even to death. ¹² Therefore rejoice, heavens, and you who dwell in them. Woe to the earth and to the sea, because the devil has gone down to you, having great wrath, knowing that he has but a short time."
(Rev. 12:6—12 emphases added).

12:6 | John of Patmos described two similar pictures from the Old Testament, how the **woman fled** and the dragon's attack.

Running is reminiscent of the prophet Elijah's flight to the "Brook Cherith"[209] from persecution to escape King Ahab. When Jezebel threatened him: "he arose, ran for his life, and came to Beersheba" (1 Kgs. 19:3). John of Patmos would also have recalled how Mary and Joseph fled with baby Jesus to Egypt from another monster, King Herod. I was reminded of a scene in the 1971 movie "Kidnapped" when the actor Michael Caine, as a Scottish highlander, was fleeing from persecution from the British. He tells his colleague, "When I say run, hide! Our lives will be like the hunted deer." I'm sure this is how the pregnant woman felt as she fled from the dragon.

12:6 | Two other incidents were no doubt in John's mind when thinking about how the **woman fled**. Antiochus Epiphanies,[210] the invading Greek king, desecrated the Jerusalem Temple in 167 BC by offering the sacrifice of a pig. Many sought safety then and retreated to hide in the desert. H. B. Swete commented, "The church fled into the wilderness, and it is lonely. For early Christians, life was lonely and isolated in a pagan world." Sometimes, we are bound to experience loneliness, but divine companionship comes even in human abandonment. Times of persecution brought terrible bloodshed and revolution. Jesus told his followers that when they saw the abomination of desolation standing where it ought not, "let those who are in Judea flee to the mountains" (Mark 13:14).

12:6 | We read that the woman fled into the desert for **one thousand two hundred sixty days** or "three and a half years." These numbers represent an incomplete time at the end of which something more substantial will happen. According to Eusebius,[211] this reference is to the church's flight from Jerusalem to Pella on the other side of the Jordan before Jerusalem's obliteration. A prophet or an angel of God warned Christians to leave before this disaster.

---

[209] sometimes called *Kerith* or "Brook Chorath."
[210] (BC c215-164), He was called "the Mad."
[211] the Greek historian and commentator in "Ecclesiastical History 3.5" (263-339 AD).

12:9 | The Lamb throws **Satan**[212] down, who is enraged and goes off to hurt other family members. His critical blow came when our Lord Jesus Christ was victorious on the cross. He steps up his persecution because he knows his time is limited. He continues to accuse Christ's disciples today, even though God's special providence protects them. We live in the last days, even though we don't know the actual time, the day, or the hour of the end. Satan's defeat results in the heavens rejoicing because of Christ's victory and the earth mourning because the accuser is now wreaking havoc there.

Question: "Would you flee under the same circumstances? Consider the millions of refugees who escaped from Ukraine."

---

[212] *Satan* is a Hebrew term meaning "adversary" or "accuser" and is the equivalent of the Greek word *diablos* meaning "accuser, slanderer, or opponent."

47

WOMAN GIVES BIRTH

12:13 "When the dragon saw that he was thrown down to the earth, he **persecuted** the woman who gave birth to the male child. ¹⁴ **Two wings of the great eagle** were given to the woman, that she might fly into the wilderness to her place, so that she might be nourished for a time, and times, and half a time, from the face of the serpent. ¹⁵ The **serpent spewed water** out of his mouth after the woman like a river, that he might cause her to be carried away by the stream. ¹⁶ The earth helped the woman, and the earth opened its mouth and swallowed up the river which the dragon spewed out of his mouth. ¹⁷ The dragon grew angry with the woman, and went away to make war with the rest of her offspring, who keep God's commandments and **hold Jesus' testimony**."
(Rev.12:13—17 emphases added).

12:13 | There is no worse feeling than being **persecuted** and chased, especially for a woman about to give birth. One's life seems to hang on the ability to outrun and outfox a predator. The heart pounds, and the mind races through possible escape routes. The woman fears for her life and her newborn child as she gives birth.

12:13 | The chase and **persecution** begin in heaven as the Lamb overcomes Satan and dispatches him to the earth. Many believe that Satan has access to God until this time, as in Job, where he argues the case against God's righteous servant. Now his entrance is barred. He can no longer accuse people before God, so he turns his wicked ways elsewhere. When the dragon crashes to the ground, "he pursued the woman." The serpent spewed water like a river on the seashore to drown her and sweep her away, but the earth opened up, and she soared away on a great eagle's wings. In fleeing from Egypt during the Exodus, the Lod told Moses, "You have seen what I did to the Egyptians, and how I bore you on eagles' wings and brought you to myself" (Ex. 19:4).

12:14 | **Eagle wings** symbolize God's supporting, rescuing, and bearing arms. "As an eagle that stirs up her nest, that flutters over her young, he spread abroad his wings, he took them, he bore them on his feathers" (Deut. 32:11). There are several different eagles native to Palestine. John of Patmos may have been familiar with the "White-tailed," the "Greater Spotted," the "Bonellis," or even the osprey. When its chicks are ready to fly after twelve weeks in the nest, the American or Bald Eagle encourages them to flap their wings and practice jumping on the breeze. When they have the confidence, they launch themselves solo into the air. Many succeed in their inaugural flight, but sadly some do not, as the first venture comes with a forty percent mortality rate! God assures us that we can be one hundred percent confident in the Almighty's eagle wings to rescue and support us despite persecution.

12:14 | American **eagles** came north to nest beside my riverside home during winter. They were superb at flying and fishing and seemed to be able to swoop in and snatch a fish without a problem. On one occasion, three or four boats were on the river with anglers patiently waiting for a bite. Suddenly, an American eagle swept in and picked out a three-foot-long trophy fish. As the anglers looked on with their mouths open, it sat calmly feeding on the ice. Three or four crows waited at a safe distance for any leftovers!

12:14 | A **great eagle** rescued the woman and her newborn baby. She soared from her pursuer to the desert or wilderness, a traditional place of refuge. The woman's pursuit parallels the Egyptians' chase of Israel by Pharoah into the Exodus wilderness.

12:14 | The **two wings of the great eagle** echo God's assurance in Sinai that he would bring his people out of Egypt, "I bore you on eagles' wings and brought you to myself" (Ex. 19:4).

12:14 | Hippolytus of Rome[213] saw in the **two wings of a great eagle** "the two holy arms of Christ outstretched upon the Cross." The words of Jesus to Paul on the Damascus road were, "Saul, Saul, why do you persecute me?" (Acts 9:4). The church also received the same persecution as Paul, but the abuse against the church was the persecution of Jesus himself. To harm the church was to harm Jesus Christ.

12:15 | When the **serpent spewed water** like a river, the earth swallowed it, and the woman survived. In Asia Minor, rivers routinely appear, disappear, and travel underground in the sand to come up later. This phenomenon may have been in John of Patmos' mind. In the Old Testament, an overwhelming flood illustrated hardship and persecution. The Psalmist wrote that "all your waves and billows have swept over me" (Ps. 42:7). David prayed, "If it had not been Yahweh who was on our side, let Israel now say. Then the waters would have overwhelmed us, the stream would have gone over our soul" (Ps. 124:1,4). Isaiah added reassuringly, "When you pass through the waters, I will be with you, and through the rivers, they will not overflow you" (Isa. 43:2).

12:15 | Because Israelis feared **water** and drowning, they employed Phoenician sailors to carry goods backward and forward by boat to and from Israel. During Solomon's reign, merchants exported all kinds of goods across the Mediterranean Sea. Non-Jewish sailors crewed the ship Jonah boarded for Nineveh, for many Israelis firmly believed that demons killed anyone who fell overboard. As a result, Jewish people did not like to sail out of sight of land but stayed inshore.

12:17 | Nature itself is on the side of those who **hold the**

---

[213] The third-century theologian, (170-235 AD).

testimony of Jesus. James Froude[214] wrote, "In the world, there is a moral order, and in the long run, it is well with the good, and ill with the wicked." This story of the dragon at war with the woman's family points to the coming persecution of Christians, but all will turn out well in the end. As John of Patmos sees it, Satan's last terrible convulsion will involve the whole church family in the agony of Christian persecution.

Question: "Why did the devil battle with the woman about to give birth?"

---

[214] (1818-1894)

48

ROMAN EMPIRE BEAST

13:1 "Then I **stood on the sand of the sea**. I saw a **beast** coming up out of the sea, having ten horns and seven heads. On his horns were ten crowns, and on his heads, blasphemous names. [2] The beast which I saw was like a leopard, and his feet were like those of a bear, and his mouth like the mouth of a lion. The dragon gave him his power, his throne, and great authority. [3] One of his heads looked like it had been wounded fatally. His fatal wound was healed, and the whole earth marveled at the beast. [4] They worshiped the dragon, because he gave his authority to the beast, and they **worshiped the beast**, saying, "Who is like the beast? Who is able to make war with him?" [5] A mouth speaking great things and blasphemy was given to him. Authority to make war for forty-two months was given to him. [6] He opened his mouth for blasphemy against God, to blaspheme his name, and his dwelling, those who dwell in heaven. [7] It was given to him to make war with the saints, and to overcome them. **Authority** over every tribe, people, language, and nation was given to him."
(Rev. 13:1—7 emphases added).

13:1 | Here, we see John of Patmos standing **on the sand of the sea**, staring out and seeing a beast emerging from the water. It represented the Roman Emperors who controlled vast

Mediterranean resources, governed seventy million people and instituted Caesar worship to keep firm control over the population. However, Caesar worship was a blasphemy against God. The Romans incurred extreme Jewish anger by erecting images of their deities in the Temple's Holy of Holies. However, the Jewish nation would suffer extermination rather than submit to such heresy, for Caesar worship was an insult to God.

13:2 | John of Patmos thought that the Roman empire, as the **beast,** had insulted God and the Jerusalem Temple. Some Emperors were embarrassed by Caesar worship, but not Caligula.[215] He was a noble and moderate ruler for the first six months of his reign but became an insane tyrant. He insisted all his subjects worship him, including Jewish people and Christians. Every empire dweller was required to burn incense yearly to his image.

13:4 | Jewish persons were ordinarily exempt from Caesar worship. The Romans were well aware of Jewish and Christians' monotheistic beliefs and their unwavering allegiance to one God. Across the empire, they did not require Jewish persons to do military service because of their strict adherence to food laws and Sabbath observance. However, certain emperors' decided to introduce it to gain control over the people and consolidate their power.

13:4 | Caligula insisted on mandatory worship yearly even though Christians were considered a Jewish sect. Every January, the army swore the annual Sacramentum oath to the emperor in all military units and consecrated a new altar to Jupiter Optimus Maximus, described as "the best and greatest god." John of Patmos wrote that the Romans also **worshipped the beast.** This incident may have been in his mind when he spoke of the torments launched against God's dwelling place. The Praetorian Guard, senators, and courtiers assassinated him[216] while forming an army to enforce his demands.

---

[215] Caligula had epilepsy and was, unfortunately, more than a little mad. As a child, he was nicknamed "the little soldier's boot" by his father's militia when he accompanied their Northern European campaigns. (12-41 AD).
[216] in 41 AD.

13:7 | The beast was given **authority** and allowed to make war on the earth. The beast's mouth showed that Satan, a higher power, controlled it when it cursed God and slandered his name.

Question: "Would you, under pressure, worship another God or accept persecution instead?"

49

LAMB'S BOOK OF LIFE

13:8 "All who dwell on the earth will worship him, everyone whose name has not been written **from the foundation of the world** in the **book of life of the Lamb** who has been killed. ⁹If anyone has an ear, let him hear. ¹⁰**If anyone is to go into captivity, he will go into captivity. If anyone is to be killed with the sword, he must be killed.** Here is the **endurance and the faith** of the saints." (Rev. 13:8—10 emphases added).

13:8 | All who dwell on the earth will worship Christ the Lamb who was slain **from the foundation of the world.** Jewish mythology believed that the Archangel Michael originated as the mediator between Israel and God before the world's creation. Moses also existed before the beginning of time, and there would be nothing unusual in Jewish thought in saying that Jesus was also present before the Creation.

13:8 | The **book of life** is mentioned at least seven times in Revelation[217] and six times in the rest of the Bible. Translators note that "the book of life of the Lamb" may mean "the book of life belonging to the Lamb," emphasizing who owns it.

13:8 | Those whose names are written in the **book of life**

---

[217] The Book of Life is mentioned in Revelation 3:5, 13:8, 17:8, 20:12, 20:15, 21:27, 22:19.

"will marvel when they see that the beast was, and is not, and shall be present" (Rev. 17:8). Here, the beast's name mimics the "I am name" for the Lord God, the Almighty, "who was and who is and who is to come" (Rev. 4:8). Christians can be encouraged that all eternity belongs to God. Nothing in life or death, nothing the Devil nor any secular society can ever do can pluck them from his hand nor remove them from the Lamb's book of life. The names of those not written in "the book of life" are given to the beast.

13:8 | Keeping a **book of life** is similar to an ancient ruler's practice of maintaining citizens' registers for their realms. When a man died or lost his citizen's rights, the ruler removed his name from his ledger. "The Lamb's life book" registers only those belonging to God through Jesus Christ.

13:10 | Several manuscripts translate **if anyone is to be killed** as "if anyone kills," adding a cause and effect to this verse. If something is sure to happen, God has already decided and will not prevent or change it. Predestination acknowledges that God wills all events into being, but this belief is often set opposite to free will, where people are free to do as they wish. However, these two sides often conflict with God's omniscience or all-knowing nature. His predetermination indicates that If anyone is meant to die, they will die. Jeremiah wrote, "Such as are for death, to death; such as are for the sword, to the sword; such as are for the famine, to the famine; and such as are for captivity, to captivity" (Jer. 15:2).

13:10 | The controversy between predestination and free will has engaged the church periodically over the centuries. If anyone is to be killed with the sword, **with the sword, he must be killed.** Many devout men and women died for their cause on both sides of this debate. In sixteenth-century Reformation times, John Calvin[218] led the "predestination argument." In 1529 AD, he had an enlightening experience. He wrote, "God by a sudden conversion subdued and brought my mind to a teachable frame, which was more hardened in such matters than might

---

[218] (1509-1564), the French theologian and reformer. Quotation from J. Calvin, preface to *Commentary on the Book of Psalms*, trans. James Anderson, vol. 1 (Grand Rapids: Eerdmans, 1948).

have been expected from one at my early period of life. Having thus received some taste and knowledge of true godliness, I was immediately inflamed with so intense a desire to make progress therein that although I did not altogether leave off other studies, yet I pursued them with less ardor."[219] Calvin had experienced an enlightenment.

13:10 | To give the opposite side of the argument to **"with the sword, he must be killed,"** Jacobus Arminius, a Dutch Theologian, presented the "free will view." It asked, "Is all we do God's predestined will, or do we make our own choices?" The question arises, "can we genuinely choose between one belief and another?" A friend and theologian Theodore Beza[220] wrote of Arminius, "God has given him an intellect well-suited both to the apprehension and to the discrimination of things." These two arguments are only partially valid, for as Christians may accept free will and choice, they can also believe in God's predetermined will. Christians are not one or the other but both Calvinist and Arminian simultaneously. This position is OK, even if challenging for a tiny mind like mine to comprehend!

13:10 | The inevitability of the unforgiving phrase, **with the sword he must be killed,** is illustrated by the example of a person holding a balloon on a string. It displays the balance between predestination and free will. God holds the line and leads the balloon along while we move freely inside it. We have some choices, but he determines where we will go. The balloon's direction and speed are decided entirely by the one pulling the string. You and I have numerous limited life choices, yet he directs the overall trend.

13:10 | We must submit to God's will with **endurance and faith**. There is an unavoidable certainty in death, for even the time of our demise cannot change without "God's say so." We have to be patient and faithful. Perseverance, however, is not passive but a powerful reaction. We are not fatalists, for he fills us with the hope that he will overrule on our behalf whatever happens.

---

[219] *Brandt, Kaspar (1854). The Life of James Arminius. London: Ward and Co.* pp. 40–41. (1560-1609).
[220] (1519-1605).French reformer and scholar, Geneva.

13:10 | This calls for patient **endurance and faith**. I recall one Saturday evening when Captain Ken Weaver and I were giving out tracts and preaching in Piccadilly Circus in London's West End. As we stood opposite the Eros statue, a crowd of raucous football fans passed by, and one suddenly stepped out and punched our elderly friend in the face, and he went down. Slowly, he got back on his feet and, not complaining, continued as if nothing had happened. He turned the other cheek.

13:10 | His reaction of **endurance and faith** was particularly appropriate for the Statue of Eros, the Greek God of love, was standing on the island directly in front of us. Sir Alfred Gilbert[221]designed the aluminum statue 'The God of Selfless Love' to commemorate Anthony Ashley Cooper.[222] He was known for his courageous efforts to reform child labor practices, improve the care of the mentally challenged, stop using young boys as chimney sweeps, and end the opium trade. He died in 1885, and though he had been offered a state funeral and burial in the prestigious Westminster Abbey before his death, he declined, expressing his wish to be buried on his family estate in Dorset. His was a selfless love.

13:10 | Patient **endurance and faith** are encouraged in God's people and reflected in this beautiful song by Andrae Crouch[223]

> "I've had many tears and sorrow,
> I've had questions for tomorrow,
> There were times I didn't know right from wrong,
> But in every situation,
> God gave me blessed consolation.
> That my trials only come to make me strong."

Question: "During tears and sorrow, have you found that you've learned to trust in God through it all?"

---

[221] (1854-1934)

[222] 7th Earl of Shaftesbury (1801-1885)

[223] (1942-2015).

50

SECOND EARTH BEAST

13:11 "I saw **another beast** coming up out of the earth. He had two horns like a lamb, and he spoke like a dragon. [12] He exercises all the authority of the first beast in his presence. He makes the earth and those who dwell in it to worship the first beast, whose **fatal wound** was healed. [13] He **performs great signs**, even making fire come down out of the sky to the earth in the sight of people. [14] He deceives my own people who dwell on the earth because of the signs he was granted to do in front of **the beast**, saying to those who dwell on the earth that they should **make an image** to the beast who had the sword wound and lived. [15] It was given to him to give breath to it, to the image of the beast, that the image of the beast should both speak, and cause as many as wouldn't worship the image of the beast to be killed. [16] He causes all, the small and the great, the rich and the poor, and the free and the slave, to be given **marks on their right hands, or on their foreheads;** [17] and that no one would be able **to buy or to sell**, unless he has that mark, which is the name of the beast or the number of his name. [18] Here is wisdom. He who has understanding, let him calculate the number of the beast, for it is the **number of a man.** His number is **six hundred sixty-six."** (Rev.13:11—18 emphases added).

13:11 | Revelation's unholy trinity comprises the dragon, **another beast**, and the sea beast. These three are opposed to the Holy Trinity of Father, Son, and Holy Spirit, but their power is limited to a short time, and God still maintains control over them. The term "Trinity" is derived from the Latin *Trinitas*, meaning "three," and defines God as three persons together in one in which though they are distinct; they are still of one substance. Jesus instructed his disciples at the close of his earthly ministry to use the trinitarian formula and commanded them to "make disciples of all nations, baptizing them in the name of the Father, and of the Son, and the Holy Spirit" (Matt. 28:19).

13:11 | "The second earth **beast's** power" points to the organization enforcing Caesar worship in a general sense. The beast speaks and performs great signs and wonders, such as bringing down fire from heaven. It has "two horns like a lamb," a grim parody of the Lamb of God "having seven horns and seven eyes" (Rev. 5:6). It also speaks "like a dragon." "Dragons" or "serpents." appear in different cultures, some four-legged and others serpentine, that is, without legs like snakes. The year two thousand and twenty-two commemorates the Chinese "Year of the Dragon."

13:12 | John of Patmos saw believers exercise patient endurance and faithfulness during the great persecutions under this unholy trinity. Tough times are spiritual growth opportunities. The Devil here compels the earth's inhabitants to worship the beast. The second beast has a **fatal wound**, which some early Christians believed indicated a revived Nero. He had ruthlessly and relentlessly persecuted them during his reign and was responsible for thousands of innocent deaths. The significance of the beast's deadly injury may be that Nero committed suicide[224] from a self-inflicted knife wound in his throat!

13:13 | In ancient religions, priests knew how to **perform signs**, illusions, tricks, wonders, and even create a speaking image by throwing their voices. WickiHow tells us, "throwing your

---

[224] on the 9th of June, 68 AD.

voice is known as the 'distant effect' and makes your voice sound as if it comes from far away." Pharaoh employed such magicians to conjure similar deceptions and trickery in Moses' time.

13:14 | The Romans erected **an image** to test citizens' loyalty and punish Christians and others who refused to participate. The imperial priesthood could easily appeal to the people. "Look what Rome has done for you." "Look at the peace and prosperity you enjoy. Have you ever known a greater benefactor than the emperor? Surely you can offer him this small worship act in simple gratitude?"

13:16 | Those People who worshiped the beast received a mark on their right hand o**r forehead.** The King James Version translates "on their right hands" or "on their foreheads" as "in their right hands" or "in their foreheads," so the "mark" could mean a computer chip under the skin. Scientists can insert an integrated circuit in an animal as a locator or even in a person's frontal brain to control mood changes. A small wafer of semiconductor material embedded in the hand can be swiped like a credit card to pay a bill!

13:16 | Leviticus prohibits marking or "tattooing." [225] "You shall not make any cuttings in your flesh for the dead, nor tattoo any **marks** on you for I am the Lord" (Lev. 19:28). The King James Version translates "print" instead of "tattoo" in this verse. "Tattoo" appeared as the mid-seventeenth century *tap-too* from the Dutch command *taptoe,* meaning literally "to shut the taps of the cask!" A drum performance at a military display such as the Royal Edinburgh Military Tattoo also uses this same word.

13:16 | Joseph Banks[226] described "tattowing" in the South Sea Islands. In his journal, he wrote, "I shall now mention the way they **mark** themselves indelibly; each of them by their humor or disposition." Aspiring warriors and their wives between twelve and fourteen years of age expressed their individuality with

---

[225] "Tattoo" comes from two 18th-century terms, *tattow* and the Polynesian *tatau* Tattooing was known as "painting, scarring, or staining."

[226] Captain Cook's naturalist on board HMS Endeavour. (1743-1820).

individual markings. It was an ancient rite of passage and custom in the South Sea Islands and is still so today.

13:16 | To produce a tattoo, a bone or metal point inscribes a **mark**, symbol, or ornamental pattern with ink into a person's skin, creating a permanent scar. Archaeologists discovered them on a two thousand five-hundred-year-old Scythian chieftain's mummified arms in Siberia. Tattoos may have special meanings. Today, one modern and popular design with great significance is the semicolon, inked on the wrist of a young person. The punctuation mark isn't just trendy; its display indicates solidarity against suicide, depression, and other mental health issues. However, a tiny semi-colon tattoo can cost two hundred dollars in New York City today!

13:16 | The Romans practiced human branding widely. It was performed either with the person's consent, as a punishment, or as an enslavement **mark**. Sometimes, soldiers stamped themselves with their general's name if they were especially devoted to him. This practice corresponds with the present-day custom of displaying the name of a husband, girlfriend, wife, mother, or even a regimental emblem upon one's person. It has become a significant art form, with enthusiasts embellishing large parts of their bodies with multicolored scenes and images!

13:16 | Sometimes, enslaved persons were branded by their owners like livestock animals are today. Owners often **marked** runaways with "FGV" for *fugitivus,* meaning "they are fugitives." Usually, owners only did this if they might attempt to flee or were guilty of a serious misdemeanor. The British Army placed the capital letter "D" on deserters. Concentration camps like Auschwitz burned an identifying forearm number on the prisoners who would be allowed to live.

13:16 | A **mark** was called a *stigma,* which meant "a mark made by a pointed instrument denoting disgrace." This word from the late 16th century denotes "a mark made by pricking or branding." It links to the account of Cain murdering Abel when the Lord declared that "whoever slays Cain, vengeance will be taken on him sevenfold." A warning follows, "Yahweh appointed a sign for Cain so that anyone finding him would not strike him" (Gen. 4:15). Cain was cursed and marked for life with a "sign."

13:16 | The word "beast **mark**" is *charagma*, meaning a "stamp or an imprinted mark," and appears seven times in Revelation and once in Acts. In the Roman empire, jars of oil or wine were impressed by a potter before firing. One such pot read "ATTICVS. FEC" with "KANABIS.BON." This translates as "Atticus made this at the canaba at Bonna," meaning Bonn in Germany.[227]

13:16 | The beast tattoo **mark** on the right hand or the forehead is a grim parody of a sacred Jewish custom. The phylactery, or *tefillin*, is a little leather prayer box containing Hebrew texts from the Law on a leather strap worn during weekday morning prayers. Devout Jewish persons follow the commandment to "bind them for a sign on your hand, and they shall be for frontlets between your eyes. You shall write them on the doorposts of your house and on your gates" (Deut. 6:8-9). Jewish believers also nail a small leather box on the doorpost as a reminder of the Law. "You shall tell your son in that day, saying, 'It is because of that which Yahweh did for me when I came out of Egypt'" (Ex. 13:8). These tiny portions mark the owner's relationship with their God.

13:16 | The "**mark** on his forehead" appears nine times in the New Testament. Other parts of Revelation contain it, particularly when a third angel shouted, "If anyone worships the beast and his image, and receives a mark on his forehead, or his hand, he also will drink of the wine of the wrath of God" (Rev. 14:9).

13:16 | Connecting ownership and a **mark** also occurs in our money. "Jesus said to the Pharisees and Herodians, 'Why do you test me? Bring me a denarius that I may see it.' They brought it. He said to them, 'Whose is this image and inscription?' They said to him, 'Caesar's.' Jesus answered them, 'Render to Caesar the things that are Caesar's, and to God the things that are God's'" (Mark.12:15—17). Roman coinage bore the emperor's outline as a stamped head and inscription. Today, presidents' heads appear on American coins and banknotes, and British and Canadian

---

[227] from c1250 AD.

currencies similarly carry the British sovereign's profile. As Jesus said, all money belongs to the person marked on it.

13:17 | The second beast is given power so those who do not offer worship can be killed, imprisoned, and unable **to buy or sell** goods. If Christians refused to burn incense to Caesar's image, they were liable to death, punishment, or denied the ability to do business. They could not engage in any transaction and become destitute. They may be forced to choose between material success and loyalty to Jesus Christ. The world knows how to pressure those who will not accept its standards. Each inhabitant worshipped the beast in the town square and received a certificate to buy or sell. The beast number six hundred sixty-six may refer to this worship declaration, which Christians could not obtain without denying their faith. It was necessary to do business.

13:18 | John of Patmos used the number **six hundred sixty-six** to identify a person without the Roman authorities realizing it. Each alphabet letter in Hebrew, Greek, and Latin has a numerical value.[228]

13:18 | In the nineteenth century, James Austin Bastow[229] identified the number **six hundred sixty-six** as having a symbolic correlation to Emperor Nero. The Greek name "Nero Emperor" was transliterated into Hebrew letters, reading "N-R-O-N Q-S-R," which has a numeric value of "50+200+6+50+100+60+200," adding up to "six hundred sixty-six!" This number pointed to Revelation's beast as a hidden reference to Nero Caesar. The beast marks or tattoos his adherents with the number "six hundred sixty-six."

13:18 | John of Patmos challenges his readers to understand this number's meaning. He says, "Here is wisdom. Let him that has understanding count the number of the beast." He then gives his readers a clue, "it is the number of a man." The number **six hundred sixty-six** may suggest other candidates such as communism, Napoleon, the European Union, Adolph Hitler, or in today's context, President Putin of Russia!

---

[228] Assigning a numerical value to a word or phrase is technically known as *gematria* from the Greek word meaning "geometry."

[229] (1810-1894), a Primitive Methodist Minister in Lancashire England.

13:18 | Other sources give **Six hundred sixty-six** as the sum of all the numbers on a roulette wheel from zero to thirty-six. It is also the original name of the Macintosh SevenDust computer virus discovered in 1998. If the number seven is the Bible's perfect number, and three sevens represent complete perfection, then three sixes fall short of this standard and indicate absolute imperfection or evil in a person or thing. Chinese culture, however, considers "six hundred sixty-six" very lucky because it means "everything goes smoothly!"

13:18 | Interestingly, in Christian numerology, the number "eight hundred eighty-eight" has been found to represent "Jesus" or, more specifically, "Christ the Redeemer." Some believe it has good connotations meaning success and financial achievement. It is also the **number of a man.**

13:18 | The Septuagint is the oldest version of the Hebrew Bible from about BC 250. The Hebrew names Yehoshua, Yahoshua, and Yeshua were all translated from Hebrew into Greek as *Iesous*. This word becomes "JESUS" in Greek and has six letters. The value of the letters adds up to "10+8+200+70+400+200=888." The name of Jesus as "eight hundred eighty-eight" is always superior to **six hundred sixty-six.** "Although some Bible numbers hold great significance, they are not to be treated as having magical powers in Judaism or Christianity. That is not God's intent in providing us with these numerical patterns."[230]

Question: "What do the numbers 666, 777, and 888 mean to you?"

[230] Bibles for Israel and the Messianic Bible Project are ministries of The Messianic Jewish Bible Society, a Non-profit 501c-3 Charity. © copyright Bibles For Israel 2022

51

FATHER'S NAME WRITTEN

14:1 "I saw, and behold, the **Lamb** standing on Mount Zion, and with him a number, **one hundred forty-four thousand**, having his **name**, and the name of his Father, **written on their foreheads**. ²I heard a sound from heaven, like the sound of many waters, and like the sound of a great thunder. The sound which I heard was like that of harpists playing on their harps. ³They sing a new song before the throne, and before the four living creatures and the elders. No one could learn the song except the one hundred forty-four thousand, those who had been redeemed out of the earth. ⁴These are those who were not defiled with women, for they are virgins. These are those who follow the Lamb wherever he goes. These were redeemed by Jesus from among men, the first fruits to God and to the Lamb. ⁵In their mouth was found no lie, for they are blameless." (Rev. 14:1—5 emphases added).

14:1 | The vision of John of Patmos opens with Jesus as a **lamb**. There are twenty-nine references to a lamb in Revelation where he delivers victory like a slain but standing Lamb. He is worthy of taking God's scroll and opening the seals. Augustine,[231] in 375 AD, wrote,

---

[231] (354-430 AD).

"Why a passionate Lamb?
Because he underwent death without being guilty
of any iniquity.
Why a lion in his passion?
Because in being slain, he slew death.
Why a resurrected Lamb?
Because of his everlasting innocence.
Why a resurrected lion?
Because of his everlasting might."

14:1 | John of Patmos sees the Lamb before him and **one hundred forty-four thousand** chosen ones with his name and his father's name on their foreheads. This number constitutes the believers who have endured persecution and will receive eternal life's blessings. Twelve by twelve by one thousand represents all humanity being three, God's number, multiplied by four, humanity's number. These are the Lamb's followers on Mount Zion, where they gather for the messianic reign. Their signs show they belong to him and are unblemished, like Temple sacrificial lambs. They are "spiritually pure," resistant to evil, and sing the redeemed ones' song. Surrounding them are a countless host of faithful believers from all ages and places. They are loyal followers of Jesus from Old Testament times up to today, with his name on their foreheads.

14:1 | A **name** could refer to a god's ownership of a devotee. Plutarch[232] said, "Most Athenians were branded on the forehead with a horse's mark when sold." After the Athenians' defeat under Nicias, the Sicilians took many captives and branded a galloping horse, Sicily's emblem, on their foreheads.

14:1 | Ptolemy[233] did a similar injustice to Jewish people and ordered the demotion of all Jews to enslaved people. They killed any who spoke out, and the rest were branded not with a **name** but with an ivy leaf mark, the emblem of Bacchus, Ptolemy's god."

14:1 | The Syrians offered sanctuary for those fleeing a death

---

[232] (45-127 AD) (Nicias 29).
[233] Ptolemy the Fourth of Egypt (BC 244-204)

threat at Heracles' temple.[234] "if any man's servant takes refuge and is branded with sacred marks, delivering himself to the deity, they may not touch him." They tattooed enslaved people in the sanctuary with their deity's **name** on the wrist or the neck.

14:1 | The Lamb's **name** could stand for dependence. William Robertson Smith [235] told how powerful Arab chieftains controlled clients by branding them with the same symbol as his camels to show their subservience.

14:1 | A fourth-century papyrus letter from a son serving in the Roman army to his father, Apollo, recently appeared. He sent his greetings and asked, "I have told you before of my grief at your absence from among us and my dreadful fear that something might happen to you and that we may not find your body. I often wished to tell you that, regarding the insecurity, I wanted to stamp **a mark** upon you." The son wished to label his father's body to identify and recover it in a worst-case scenario after a battle. Likewise, the Lamb's company is known and marked with the Lamb's and the Father's names on their foreheads. They are recoverable in life and death.

Question: "How do you picture the Lamb and the gathering on Mount Zion?"

---

[234] Herodotus 2.113:2 mentions the asylum place.
[235] (1846-1894) Reader of Arabic in Christ's College, Cambridge.

52

ANGEL'S MIDAIR FLIGHT

14:6 "I saw an **angel flying in mid heaven**, having an eternal **Good News** to proclaim to those who dwell on the earth, and to **every nation, tribe, language, and people.** [7] He said with a loud voice, "**Fear the Lord, and give him glory**; for the **hour of his judgment** has come. Worship him who made the heaven, the earth, the sea, and the springs of waters!" [8] Another, a second angel, followed, saying, "**Babylon the great has fallen**, which has made all the nations to drink of the **wine of the wrath of her sexual immorality.**" [9] Another angel, a third, followed them, saying with a great voice, "If anyone worships the beast and his image, and receives a mark on his forehead, or on his hand, [10] he also will drink of the wine of the wrath of God, which is prepared unmixed in the cup of his anger. He will be tormented with fire and sulfur in the presence of the holy angels, and in the presence of the Lamb. [11] The smoke of their torment goes up forever and ever. They have no rest day and night, those who worship the beast and his image, and whoever receives the mark of his name." (Rev. 14:6-11emphases added).

14:6 | The **angel flying in mid-heaven** is necessary, so everyone will hear the Good News everywhere. The phrase "Good News" comes from the Anglo-Saxon term "god-spell," meaning "good story" or "gospel." It is a rendering of the Latin *evangelium* and the Greek *euangelion*, meaning "good news" or "good telling." John of Patmos asserts that God created everything, controlled them, and called upon them to "Fear the Lord and give him glory." The good news is valid forever, for even in a world crashing to its doom, its truth still stands. The angel flying in mid-heaven is followed immediately by a destructive one, revealing a double-edged aspect of this gospel. It is welcomed by those who receive it, but it is a terrible judgment on those who reject it.

14:6 | Jesus instructed his disciples to preach the gospel to **every nation, tribe, language, and people** as a prelude to the end. He told them, "This Good News of the Kingdom will be preached in the world for a testimony to all the nations, and then the end will come" (Matt. 24:14).

14:7 | The first angel loudly proclaimed that Christians were to **fear the Lord and give him glory** because the hour of his judgment had come. Significantly, this is the fiercest of all of Revelation's dooms. As John of Patmos saw it, the church was battling for its existence. Individual Christians were preparing for suffering, trial, imprisonment, and even death, for the church would die if they yielded. Christians must protect the faith and be ready to commend it to others. All give him glory, for the Lord "has a day of vengeance, a year of recompense for the cause of Zion" (Isa. 34:8). The angel's words, "Worship him who made the heaven, the earth, the sea, and the springs of water!" are a summons from the creator.

14:8 | Another reason to give God glory is to see the **hour of his judgment**. When Chrysostom[236] encouraged Olympias in Constantinople to be steadfast in martyrdom, he told her that she would see her persecutors' eternal torture like Lazarus saw Dives tormented in flames. The heathen looked down from crowded arenas on them being killed, savaged by wild animals, and tortured. They knew that someday heaven's divine justice would rectify earth's brutality, and the persecutors would become

---

[236] (349-407 AD).

the persecuted! We have no right to speak about forgiveness and mercy until we have gone through the same suffering as martyred Christians.

14:8 | Babylon, the great,[237] was notorious in the ancient world for corruption and excessive luxury, but it has fallen. Its armies swept through Israel multiple times, stealing crops, subduing people, and forcibly resettling and enslaving them. The second angel proclaims, "Fallen, fallen is Babylon; and all the engraved images of her gods are broken to the ground" (Isa. 21:9). Babylon's fall was a cloaked way of pointing to the Roman empire's demise.

14:8 | Babylon the Great was the incarnation of power and sin in ancient days, but it was reborn in Rome's immorality and corruption. Its fall to the Persian king Cyrus was one of the most unexpected events in ancient history. The prophets declared, "Babylon has suddenly fallen and been destroyed! Wail for her!" (Jer. 51:8). The "wrath of her fornication" is an oblique reference to immorality in Rome.

14:8 | Babylon was a corrupting influence that lured the nations with the **wine of the wrath of her sexual immorality.** Ancient Rome was like a glittering prostitute seducing the world and filling a man full of wine to persuade him to sin. Behind this image remains the eternal truth that governments or people who encourage others to do evil will not escape God's avenging wrath.

Question: "What did the angel flying in mid-heaven announce?"

---

[237] Founded in Mesopotamia in BC 2300 and finally abandoned in c1000 AD.

53

PATIENT ENDURANCE

14:12 "Here is the perseverance of the saints, those who keep the commandments of God, and the faith of Jesus." [13] I heard a voice from heaven saying, "Write, '**Blessed are the dead** who die in the Lord from now on.'" "Yes," says the Spirit, "that they may **rest from their labors**; for their **works follow with them**." [14] I looked, and saw a white cloud, and on the cloud one sitting like a **son of man**, having on his head a golden crown, and in his hand a sharp sickle." (Rev. 14:12—14 emphases added).

14:13 | "Blessed are the dead," says the voice from heaven. An old maxim[238] advises, "You can't take it with you when you die." An "Inverted Jenny," a valuable and rare American stamp produced in 1918, illustrates this truth. Philatelists know it as the "Upside Down Jenny" or "Jenny Invert." It shows a Curtiss JN-4 airplane in its frame printed upside down by mistake. One such postage stamp went missing when its owner died. The family searched everywhere for the treasured object but to no avail. Finally, someone thought to look in their dead loved one's waistcoat pocket in his casket and found it! They thwarted his plan to take his prized possession with him when he died!

---

[238] from a 1936 comedic play in three acts by George S. Kaufman and Moss Hart

How valuable are "Inverted Jennies?" A block of four was sold at auction in New York for nearly three million dollars! How precious are you to God? You are of much more significance. You are of infinite worth.

14:13 | The phrase that they may **rest from their labors** refers to those who die or "fall asleep in the Lord" and occurs in several New Testament passages. The writer to the Hebrews advises, "Let's fear, therefore, lest perhaps anyone of you should seem to have come short of a promise of entering into his rest" (Heb. 4:1). Later, he says, "For he who has entered into his rest has himself also rested from his works, as God did from his" (Heb. 4:10). Jesus agreed, "Come to me, all you who labor and are heavily burdened, and I will give you rest" (Matt. 11:28). Many things and people may seek to separate Christians from him. However, those at their lives end who are still loyal are supremely happy. The promise to those dying in him is the end of their labors, for a well-deserved breather is sweet after the most strenuous toil. They will receive their due reward.

14:13 | When we leave this world, we only take our human values, personality, and relationship. We came into it with nothing and will leave the same way. John of Patmos writes that only their **works will follow them**. While it is true that we can't take money, fame, or belongings with us from this life, God's people can produce eternal fruit. Those who follow Jesus and point others to him will survive death. Here, deeds follow faith, and works bear fruit to instill character. According to Jewish thought, "people's actions follow them like witnesses into God's court." The seeds of faith you sow in this life will bear fruit in the next.

14:13 | The idea that **works will follow them** sounds like Revelation preaches a "salvation by works doctrine." What does John of Patmos mean by "works"? He speaks of the Ephesians' actions, labor, and patience and emphasizes "your works, and your toil and perseverance" (Rev. 2:2) and the resultant increases in a giver's Christian character.

14:13 | John of Patmos describes the Thyatira Christians' actions, "I know your works, love, faith, service, patient endurance, and that your last **works** are more than the first" (Rev. 2:19). Patient endurance is a particular virtue. We have a window sill outside our living room on the second floor, and one day discovered a pair of mourning doves making a nest there. Watching them and seeing the mother bird sitting on the eggs all night, sometimes for fourteen hours, was fascinating. The male bird took the day shift and patiently tolerated the elements from early morning to before sunset. The eggs hatched in precisely fourteen days, and the hatchlings or "squabs," which my wife named "Little Maddie" and "Little Ronnie," after much feeding and devoted care, flew from the nest exactly fourteen days later. The Creator God's magnificent timing and provision for these little "birds of the air" overawed us. Both adult birds were devoted parents and models of patient endurance!

14:13 | John of Patmos suggests that all you can take with you when you leave this earth is yourself and **your works**. If you come to the end of this life still one with Christ, you will carry over into the next world a character tried and tested like gold, bearing something of Jesus' reflection. Those who accept him because of our witness will join us in heaven.

14:14 | Revelation pictures Christ as the **son of man**. This theme reminds us of Daniel, who wrote, "I saw in the night visions, and behold, there came with the clouds of the sky one like a son of man, and he came even to the ancient of days, and they brought him near before him" (Dan. 7:13). The "Ancient of Days" is an Old Testament description of Almighty God. The phrase "son of man" is *bar enash* in Aramaic, meaning, in simple terms, "a human being." Jesus calls himself the son of man because he wants to be known and treated like an ordinary guy!

Question: "What can we learn from the perseverance of the saints?"

54

EARTH HARVEST SICKLE

14:15 "Another angel came out of the temple, crying with a loud voice to him who sat on the cloud, "Send your **sickle**, and reap; for the hour to reap has come; for the harvest of the earth is ripe!" [16] He who sat on the cloud thrust his sickle on the earth, and the earth was reaped. [17] Another angel came out of the temple which is in heaven. He also had a sharp sickle. [18] Another angel came out from the altar, he who has power over fire, and he called with a great voice to him who had the sharp sickle, saying, "Send your sharp sickle, and gather the clusters of the vine of the earth, for the earth's grapes are fully ripe!" [19] The **angel thrust his sickle** into the earth, and gathered the vintage of the earth, and threw it into the great **wine press of the wrath of God.** [20] The wine press was trodden outside of the city, and blood came out of the wine press, even to the bridles of the horses, as far as **one thousand six hundred stadia.**"
(Rev. 14:15—20 emphases added).

14:15 | This Revelation passage depicts earth's judgment with a harvest **sickle**, a serrated or toothed metal or stone instrument for cutting grass, hay, grapes, or grain. Interestingly, a serrated edge is not a modern adaption but dates from 3,000 BC in Iraq. When the prophet Joel wished to say the punishment was near, he called out, "Put in the sickle; for the harvest is ripe. Come, tread, for the winepress is full, the vats overflow, for their wickedness is great" (Joel 3:13). In John of Patmos' vision, an angel calls for the sickle to be swung to harvest the judged. This blood tide from the winepress is as deep as a horse's bridle and flows for one hundred and eighty-four miles.[239]

14:19 | The words "the great **wine press of the wrath of God**" are reputed to have inspired Rev James Freeman Clarke to ask the abolitionist Julia Ward Howe to write the famous "Battle Hymn of the Republic," the popular American patriotic song. In a Washington Hotel, she later recorded,

"I went to bed that night as usual and slept, according to my wont, quite soundly. I awoke in the gray of the morning twilight, and as I lay waiting for the dawn, the long lines of the desired poem began to twine themselves in my mind. Having thought out all the stanzas, I said to myself, 'I must get up and write these verses down, lest I fall asleep again and forget them.' So, with a sudden effort, I sprang out of bed and found in the dimness an old stump of a pencil that I remembered to have used the day before. I scrawled the verses almost without looking at the paper."[240] Her first published version began

> "Mine eyes have seen the glory of the coming of the Lord;
> He is trampling out the vintage where the grapes of wrath are stored;
> He hath loosed the fateful lightning of His terrible swift sword;
> His truth is marching on.
> Glory, Glory, Hallelujah!
> His truth is marching on."

Her original attempt included the following verse,

---

[239] Equals one thousand six hundred stadia in the text.
[240] Howe, Julia Ward. *Reminiscences: 1819–1899*. Houghton, Mifflin: New York, 1899. p. 275.

"He is coming like the glory of the morning on the
wave,
He is Wisdom to the mighty, He is Succour to the
brave,
So the world shall be His footstool, and the soul of
Time His slave,
Our God is marching on."

14:19 | Harvesting of grapes occurred every year in villages,
and the people trod the **wine press**. A typical one was built from
brick or as a trough hollowed out in the rock. Workers crushed
the grapes with their feet in the upper bath, and the juice flowed
down a connecting channel into a lower basin.

14:19 | God's judgments are like the trampling of grapes from
the harvest in a **wine press.** Lamentations says, "The Lord has
trodden the virgin daughter of Judah as in a winepress" (Lam.
1:15). Isaiah adds the Lord's words, "I have trodden the winepress
alone. Yes, I trod them in my anger. Their lifeblood is sprinkled
on my garments, and I have stained all my clothing" (Isa. 63:3).

14:19 | Many Jewish people believed they would set up the
judgment **wine press** outside Jerusalem's walls in the end times.
Gentiles would be brought there and tried in Jehoshaphat's Valley
between the city and the Mount of Olives. *Jehoshaphat* means "the
Lord judges." Joel writes, "I will gather all nations, and bring them
down into the valley of Jehoshaphat, and I will execute judgment
on them there for my people, and for my heritage, Israel" (Joel 3:2).

14:20 | The tide of equity flows like a blood tsunami from the
winepress for **one hundred and eighty-four miles,** the length
of Palestine from north to south! It rose "as high as the horses'
bridles" to five or six feet above the ground. The harvest angel
reaps this massive blood punishment on the earth.

Question: "What was the purpose of this earth harvest judgment?"

55

SEVEN LAST PLAGUES

15:1 "I saw another great and marvelous sign in the sky: seven angels having the **seven last plagues**, for in them God's wrath is finished. ²I saw something like a **sea of glass mixed with fire**, and those **who overcame the beast**, his image, and the number of his name, standing on the sea of glass, having **harps** of God. ³They **sang the song of Moses, the servant of God**, and the **song of the Lamb**, saying, "**Great and marvelous are your works, Lord God, the Almighty!** **Righteous and true** are your ways, you **King of the nations.**
⁴Who wouldn't fear you, Lord, and glorify
your name? For you only are **holy.**
For all the nations will come and worship before you.
For your righteous acts have been revealed."
(Rev. 15:1—4 emphases added).

15:1 | John of Patmos heard a loud voice from the temple telling the angels to pour out the **seven last plagues.** These afflictions cause terrible sores on those with the beast's mark. The second one turns the sea into blood, and all life in the waters dies. The third causes rivers and springs to be blood-filled. The fourth makes the sun so hot as to scorch people, and they curse him. The fifth brings complete darkness, but people refuse to repent. The sixth affects the Euphrates River, which dries up. As a result, armies can travel to Armageddon's great battle eighteen miles southeast of modern Haifa. The assembled troops advance towards Jerusalem for a final battle against Jesus Christ, and the seventh angel ushers in thunder, lightning flashes, and a mighty earthquake.

15:1 | John of Patmos arranges the last plagues in two sets of **seven,** typical of how other apocalyptic writers organized groups of ten, seven, or three. Two groups of seven would symbolize perfection. Before John of Patmos describes the seven angels with the last afflictions, he paints a picture of those martyred for Christ.

15:2 | The martyrs stand beside a **sea of glass mixed with fire**. In antiquity, artisans made glass into jewelry, beads, windowpanes, and tableware, but it was rare and precious. It appears here intermingled with fire, symbolic of judgment.

15:2 | Heaven's martyrs, having **overcome the beast** emerge victorious from their contest with evil forces and the antichrist. They often died the most savage deaths, yet they are triumphant here. It is the very fact that they died that makes them victors.

15:2 | God gives the heavenly martyrs **harps** to sing Moses' servant song and the Lamb's refrain. Moses' sister Miriam sang the Lord's praise and danced after triumphantly crossing the Red Sea. H. B. Swete commented, "The saints have now come safely through the martyrdom sea and have arrived at heaven's shore."

15:3 | The martyrs **sang the song of Moses** and danced with joy. The early church records described martyrdom as a victory day and a time for celebration when faithful Christians processed to a martyr's tomb, sang and worshiped God. The prison diary of a young woman in Carthage[241] recounted others being martyred, "The victory day dawned, and they walked from prison to the amphitheater as if they were walking to heaven, happy and serene in countenance."

15:3 | At each Sabbath evening synagogue service, Jewish worshippers sing **the song of Moses.** They recite the *Shema,*

---

[241] "The Martyrdom of Perpetua," in c202 AD.

Israel's equivalent to the Lord's Prayer. "The delivered sang a new song to your name by the sea-shore, all praised together and owned you king, and said that the Lord shall reign, world without end. Blessed be the Lord who saves Israel." Moses' praise commemorates the extraordinary deliverance of the people of Israel. In the same way, the martyrs come through the persecution seas to sing a new melody to the Lord in heaven's promised land.

15:3 | Jesus confirms this joy in **the song of the Lamb** when he says, "Whoever will lose his life for my sake will find it." (Matt. 16:25). The real victory is not to prudently preserve one's life but to face the worst that evil can do and, if need be, to be faithful in death. Miguel de Unamuno y Jugo[242] once said, "May God deny you peace and give you glory."

15:3 | The victorious martyrs sing, **great and marvelous are your works, Lord God, the Almighty**. They sang Moses' and Miriam's songs of deliverance after the Red Sea's crossing. It begins with "*Ya* is my strength and song. He has become my salvation. This is my God, and I will praise him; my father's God, and I will exalt him" (Ex. 15:2). *Ya* is another name for "Lord." The phrase, "the Lord is my strength, and my song," may also mean "the Lord is my strength and defense." Our song encourages, supports, and defends us as our resolve strengthens in praise!

15:3 | Heaven is where people focus on the Lamb of God and the Heavenly Father. The martyrs sing, "**Great and marvelous are your works, Lord God, the Almighty!**" R. H. Charles believed, "In the perfect vision of God, one wholly forgets self." When we become absorbed in God's wonder, we no longer consider our trivial needs. H. B. Swete agreed, "In God's presence, the martyrs forget themselves. New wonders surrounding them absorb their thoughts. Their sufferings form a tiny, infinitesimal part in the mighty scheme of things. They begin to see the great world drama and hear the expression of praise to God with which they greet their first unclouded vision of the true king and his works."

15:3 | For the martyrs, righteousness, truth, and holiness join

---

[242] A famous Spanish poet, philosopher, and mystic (1864-1936).

together like links in a chain. **Righteous and true are your ways, for you only are holy.** The king regards truth as imperative. His perfect justice matches his supreme righteousness and purity. He is scrupulously fair in his judgment because his holy standards are clear. But we will find no true justice without holiness and transparency!

15:3 | The **King of the nations** and the "Lord God, the Almighty" emphasize the geographical control of Jesus and his eternal power. Jeremiah asks, "Who shouldn't fear you, King of the nations?" (Jer. 10:7). The Psalmist adds, "All nations you have made will come and worship before you, Lord" (Ps. 86:9) for he "has openly shown his righteousness in the sight of the nations" (Ps. 98:2). Heaven's victorious ones sing their martyr's song to the Lord and praise the Sovereign of all.

15:3 | Interestingly, the **song of Moses** is composed of oblique references to Old Testament passages. There may be four hundred and forty verses in Revelation, but Steve Moyise points out, "it contains more Old Testament allusions than any New Testament book, but it does not record a single quotation."

15:3 | The martyrs do not dwell on their achievements or experiences but instead make a lyrical outburst of praise for God's greatness. They sing, "**Great and marvelous are your works**, Lord God, the Almighty! Righteous and true are your ways, you King of the nations. Who wouldn't fear you, Lord, and glorify your name? For you only are holy. For all nations will come and worship before you. For your righteous acts have been revealed." We, too, join in that heavenly chorus of praise!

Question: "Jesus is called the king of the nations. What does that mean today?"

56

SEVEN AVENGING ANGELS

15:5 "After this I looked, and I saw in heaven the temple—that is, the **tabernacle of the covenant law**—and it was opened. [6] Out of the temple came the **seven angels** with the seven plagues. They were dressed in **clean, shining linen** and wore **golden sashes** around their chests. [7] Then one of the **four living creatures** gave to the seven angels seven golden bowls filled with the wrath of God, who lives for ever and ever. [8] And the temple was filled with smoke from the glory of God and from his power, and no one could enter the temple until the seven plagues of the seven angels were completed." (Rev. 15:5—8 emphases added).

15:5 | The "**tabernacle of the covenant law**" is also called the "tent of witness" or "tent of the testimony." The word "tabernacle" means a "residence," as it was "the portable earthly dwelling place of the divine" during the wilderness wanderings. John of Patmos viewed the new temple not in terms of the Jerusalem temple before its fall in 70 AD but the ancient wilderness tabernacle. "On the day the tabernacle was raised up, the cloud covered the tabernacle, even the Tent of the Testimony. At evening it was over the tabernacle, as it were the appearance of fire, until morning. So it was continually. The cloud covered it, and the appearance of fire by night" (Num. 9:15-16).

15:6 | **Seven angels** came from this heavenly tabernacle wearing white linen robes, described as "clean shining linen," with golden sashes around their chests, similar to the son of man's attire. They wore these robes as ambassadors of the Lord God Almighty.

15:6 | **Linen** was a greatly valued textile made from flax plant fibers, and its manufacture was very labor-intensive, but its cloth was cool in hot weather. "Linen" gives us the word "line" from the use of a flax thread to determine a straight line or "plumb line." "A plumb bob, plumb bob level, or plummet" is derived from the Latin *plumbum* (lead) and is a metal weight, usually with a pointed tip, suspended from a string and used as a vertical reference line."[243] Today, electronic devices have mainly replaced the plumb line, the level, and other measuring devices in construction.

15:6 | The **clean shining linen** of the angels' holy garments symbolizes purity and innocence, like a bride's white dress. The fine linen and the gold-embroidered sash around the chest resemble the High Priest's robes. He was the Jewish faith's chief religious official from the Exile in Babylon in BC 411 to the Temple's destruction in 70 AD. Archaeologists have discovered ancient linen cloth in good condition with the Dead Sea Scrolls near the Red Sea.

15:6 | The angel's robes were also royal regalia. The clean, shining linen and **golden sashes** around their chests came with the radiance of the King of Kings upon them. An angel or archangel appeared in Christ's empty tomb. When the disciples arrived, "they saw a young man sitting on the right side, dressed in a white robe, and they were amazed" (Mark 16:5). Heavenly angels traveled from God's presence to fulfill his decrees upon the earth, and they glowed, having been in God's vicinity.

15:7 | One of the **four living creatures** handed the angels the seven golden bowls filled with God's wrath. "The first creature was like a lion, and the second creature like a calf, and the third creature had a face like a man, and the fourth was like a flying

---

[243] Wikipedia

eagle" (Rev. 4:7). They were the ultimate throne room bodyguards with eyes everywhere! The bowls of wrath brought natural disasters to the world, signaling that all nature was handing itself over to God to serve his purposes.

Question: "What is the significance of the angel's clean, shining linen robes and golden sash?"

57

SEVEN WRATH BOWLS

16:1 "I heard a loud voice out of the temple, saying to the seven angels, "Go and pour out the **seven bowls of the wrath of God on the earth!**" [2] **The first** went, and poured out his bowl into the earth, and it became a harmful and evil sore on the people who had the mark of the beast, and who worshiped his image. [3] The **second angel** poured out his bowl into the sea, and it became blood as of a dead man. Every living thing in the sea died. [4] The third poured out his bowl into the rivers and springs of water, and they became **blood.** [5] I heard the angel of the waters saying, "You are righteous, who are and who were, O Holy One, because you have judged these things. [6] For they poured out the blood of saints and prophets, and you have given them blood to drink. They deserve this." [7] I heard the altar saying, "Yes, Lord God, the Almighty, true and righteous are your judgments." (Rev. 16:1—7 emphases added).

16.1 | The seven angels were instructed to pour the **seven bowls** of God's wrath upon the earth. God had confronted Pharaoh in Egypt with similar bowls and painful plague sores. "Yahweh said to Moses and to Aaron, 'Take handfuls of ashes of the furnace and let Moses sprinkle it toward the sky in the sight of Pharaoh. It shall become small dust over all the land of Egypt and shall be boils and blisters breaking out on man and animal throughout the land of Egypt." (Ex. 9:8—9).

16.1 | The **seven bowls** of God's wrath in Egypt were,

- Loathsome sores on the people.
- The sea turned to blood.
- The rivers became blood.
- The sun burned the planet.
- Thick darkness descended.
- The Euphrates River dried up.
- A global earthquake occurred.

16:1 | The terrors from the **seven bowls** resulted in everyone breaking out in ulcerous sores. William Barclay commented that in this final series of terrors, John gathered the horrors from the stories of God's avenging wrath and hurled them on the unbelieving world in one last terrible, disastrous deluge.

16.2 | **The first** angel poured out his bowl on the land producing harmful, evil sores on those with the beast's mark. Every living thing in the waters died.

16.3 | The **second angel** poured his bowl into the sea, which became like blood. Earlier, a great burning mountain was hurled into the sea with a similar effect. "One-third of the sea became blood." (Rev. 8:8).

16.4 | **Blood** terrors and destruction upon the earth were justifiable punishments by God. Hail, darkness, blood in the waters, ulcerous sores, and the coming of the hordes are all experiences Christians in those days could have known. There is a difference between terrors after trumpets and those after bowls. Punishment for God's enemies in the former is limited, but destruction in the latter is complete.

Question: "What punishments do we find in this passage? How do they compare with the Egyptian ones?"

58

FOURTH ANGEL CURSE

16:8 "The fourth (angel) poured out his bowl on the sun, and it was given to him to scorch men with **fire.** ⁹ People were scorched with great heat, and people blasphemed the name of God who has the power over these plagues. They didn't repent and give him glory. ¹⁰ The fifth poured out his bowl on the throne of the beast, and his kingdom was **darkened.** They gnawed their tongues because of the pain, ¹¹ and they **blasphemed the God of heaven** because of their pains and their sores. They **still didn't repent** of their works." (Rev. 16:8—11 emphases added).

16.8 | **Fire** is often connected with judgment in the scriptures. The fourth terror is that the sun scorched people with fire. Individuals receive God's punishment, curse him, and refuse to repent. Christians should not be surprised at an unbeliever's hostility and hardness of heart. While attending the Bible Training Institute in Glasgow, I was involved in open-air street meetings. One Saturday, we were preaching in Barlinnie to crowds at the marketplace. Afterward, I talked with a young man and referred to the Psalms saying, "The fool has said in his heart, 'There is no God.' They are corrupt. They have done abominable deeds. There is no one who does good." (Ps. 14:1) Though I had meant it in a general sense, he took it as a personal insult and angrily raised his clenched fist and shouted. He showed the unbeliever's hostility. However, he kept coming back, and we got to know him after a while. He was living rough in a condemned building with his girlfriend, who turned out to be very pregnant. He was proud of his Mercedes outside, even though it had no wheels! One afternoon they came over for tea to our tenement home in Anderson, and my wife put out a plate of biscuits and other goodies. John's girlfriend grabbed the cookies and stuffed a plateful in her mouth. We figured she was eating for two!

16.8 | The fifth terror, thick **darkness,** is reminiscent of Egypt's blackness. The Lord God said to Moses, "Stretch out your hand toward the sky that there may be darkness over the land of Egypt, even darkness which may be felt." (Ex. 10:21). There was thick blackness for three days, and the Egyptians couldn't see one another, but all the people of Israel had light where they lived.

16.10 | John affirms, "the light shines in the **darkness,** and the darkness hasn't overcome it" (John 1:5). The word "overcome" can also be translated as "comprehended" or "mentally grasping or gripping an enemy to defeat him." The darkness attempted to grab hold of the light to subdue it, but the fifth angel's action "plunged its kingdom into darkness."

16.10 | **Darkness** is the "absence of light." Scientists tell us that the darkest blackness reflects ninety-eight percent of sunlight. A one hundred percent black surface would theoretically not be visible. A "black hole" is one heavenly body of extremely intense gravity from which nothing, not even light, can escape. The velocity required for matter to escape from the gravitational field of a black hole exceeds the speed of light so that not even rays of light can escape into space hence the blackness of the hole![244] This "blackness" is so intense that people feel it. In the countryside in Ontario, where my wife and I lived for many years, there were no visible city lights on some nights, and it was pitch black! One could almost feel the darkness! Light, however, enthrones God,

[244] Information from Britannica, The Editors of Encyclopedia. "black hole". *Encyclopedia Britannica*, 12 May. 2022, https://www.britannica.com/science/black-hole. Accessed 19 May 2022.

and there can be no darkness around him. The Psalmist writes, "For with you is the spring of life. In your light we will see light" (Ps. 36:9). We are also reminded about the very nature of God, "In him, there is no darkness at all" (1 John 1:5).

16.11 | The people on whom these terrors fell **blasphemed the God of heaven** because they were impervious to his goodness. An unrepentance refrain runs through this section. We are bound to ask ourselves if we are any different today. We may not doubt God's existence, for we know of his love for us and concern for the created world. We may know of his laws and goodness, but we still experience his kindness and sternness toward those who fall.

16.11 | Repeatedly, we exhibit selfish and sinful ways like those who **still didn't repent**. Marcus Eremita[245] wrote of Mark the Ascetic[246] "From early manhood, he exhibited piety, humility, and ascetic virtues. He had an exact acquaintance with the holy scriptures, the whole of which he had committed to memory. He enjoyed a reputation of a special sanctity and wonder-working power."[247] He wrote, "No one is as good and merciful as the Lord. But even he does not forgive the unrepentant." Despite everything, Christians rely on God's kindness.

Question: "Does God forgive the unrepentant or not? Are you relying on God's kindness?"

---

[245] (c360-c430 AD)
[246] of the Palestinian Desert in the fifth century AD.
[247] Strong Biblical Cyclopedia.

59

THREE FROG SPIRITS

16:12 "The sixth (angel) poured out his bowl on the great river, the Euphrates. Its water was dried up, that the way might be prepared for the kings that come from the sunrise. [13] I saw coming out of the mouth of the dragon, and out of the mouth of the beast, and **out of the mouth** of the false prophet, **three unclean spirits**, something like **frogs**; [14] for they are **spirits of demons**, performing signs; which go out to the kings of the whole inhabited earth, to gather them together for the war of that great day of God, the Almighty. [15] "Behold, I come like a thief. Blessed is he who watches, and keeps his clothes, so that he doesn't walk naked, and they see his shame." [16] **He gathered them** together into the place which is called in Hebrew, "**Megiddo**." [17] **The seventh** poured out his bowl into the air. A loud voice came out of the temple of heaven, from the throne, saying, "It is done!" [18] There were lightnings, sounds, and thunders; and there was a great earthquake, such as has not happened since there were men on the earth, so great an earthquake, and so mighty. [19] The great city was divided into three parts, and the cities of the nations fell. Babylon the great was remembered in the sight of God, to give to her the cup of the wine of the fierceness of his wrath. [20] Every island fled away, and the mountains were not found. [21] **Great hailstones**, about the weight of a talent, came down out of the sky on people. People blasphemed God because of the plague of the hail, for this plague is exceedingly severe." (Rev. 16:12-21 emphases added).

16:13 | Three unclean spirits emerge **out of the mouths** of the dragon, beast, and false prophet. John of Patmos describes them as "impure spirits." In Greek, there is a play on words in that the "three frog spirits" come from the evil forces' mouths. The voice is the speech organ and one of the most potent forces for good or evil. What we say and how we say it is tremendously important and can hurt or encourage others. The Greek word "spirit," as in "three frog spirits," is *pneuma,* which means "breath." We recognize this term in the phrase "pneumatic" as a "tire filled with air."

16:13 | Saying an **evil spirit** comes from a person's mouth is the same as admitting someone communicates with malicious intent. H. B. Swete wrote that the dragon, beast, and false prophet "breathed forth evil influences like three frogs, an unholy trinity." The three impure spirits are also often associated with plagues. One of Moses' ten plagues in Egypt was the frog plague. "He sent swarms of flies, which devoured them and frogs, which destroyed them" (Ps. 78:45).

16:13 | Frogs are considered **evil spirits** and impure creatures according to Jewish Law, and eating them is prohibited. "All that don't have fins and scales in the seas and rivers, all that move in the waters, and all the living creatures in the waters, are an abomination to you" (Lev. 11:10).

16:13 | Croaking **frogs** are also especially disliked for their annoying and continuous noise, like meaningless speech.[248] Some indigenous peoples consider their nocturnal vocalizations as spiritual outcries. However, male croaking serves to attract females to good breeding sites. Some species perceive only a narrow frequency range, hearing only their kind. They may also outline the male's breeding territory. There are little "peepers"[249] with a high-pitched squeak and the six-inch-long "bullfrog" with

---

[248] There are 31 frog species in the United States, of some 5000 species worldwide.
[249] Pseudacris crucifer small brown frogs up to ½" long.

a deep croak like a bull bellowing. The three frog spirits emerged from "the mouth of the dragon, the beast, and the false prophet," implying that their garbled words were unintelligible, impure, and harmful!

16:14 | The frog spirits are **spirits of demons** that perform signs. Their speech deceives people with cunning words and attempts to draw Christ's followers away from the faith. God warns faithful people in the Old and New Testaments to expect them. However impressive they may be at performing miraculous signs, even listening to one is forbidden.

16:14 | Deuteronomy warns of the **spirits of demons**. God tests Christians to discover whether they love him with all their hearts and souls. In the Law, a false prophet or dreamer of dreams "shall be put to death because he has spoken rebellion against Yahweh your God, to draw you aside out of the way which Yahweh your God commanded you to walk in." (Deut. 13.4—5).

16:14 | The Sanhedrin's specific duty in the Jerusalem Temple was to deal with **spirits of demons** and punish false prophets when they arose. H. B. Swete wrote that this covered "magic vendors, religious impostors, fanatics, deceivers or deceived persons who falsely interpret God's word." He asserts, "true religion has no worse enemies and Satan no better allies." They come like wolves in sheep's clothing and try to introduce alternative worship subtly. However, a wolf is no less a wolf because it's dressed in sheepskin, and the devil is no less the devil because it looks like an angel.

16:16 | The Lord **gathered** Gog and Magog to fight at Armageddon.[250] Ezekiel said, "Son of man, set your face toward Gog, of the land of Magog, the prince of Rosh, Meshech, and Tubal, and prophesy against him" (Ezek. 38:2). The image of them as fierce armies is etched deeply in Jewish thought. Everyone feared an invasion from the horseback riders of the European nomadic tribes,[251] which Gog would launch on Israel. However, the son of man will put hooks in the captives' jaws!

---

[250] The "Qur'an" mentions Gog and Magog as *Yakub and Majub*. Megiddo is in the Esdraelon Plain in Northern Israel.
[251] the "Khazars, Huns, Scythians, and Mongols."

16:16 | From ancient to Napoleonic times, **Megiddo** was one of the world's great battlegrounds. It was where Barak and Deborah overthrew Sisera's chariots, Ahaziah died by Jehu's arrows, and Judah's good King Josiah perished battling Pharaoh Necho the Second.[252] "Ahaziah's death was a tragedy to Jewish people and one they have never forgotten. It was "a battleground," says H. B. Swete, "familiar to any Hebrew history student."

16:16 | The last great battle will occur in the ancient city of **Megiddo**, otherwise known by its Greek name "Armageddon." Megiddo, like Jerusalem, was created as a "tell" by generations of people living together. Before the days of garbage removal or recycling, families dumped their rubbish outside, and the ground level built up over time. If a fire or earthquake destroyed a building, they simply rebuilt it on the rubble. Jericho is a fascinating example also. On a Holy Land visit to Jericho, I looked down upon layer on layer of household waste built up over the centuries and saw a tower beneath me in the city wall!

16:17 | The **seventh** angel poured out his bowl into the atmosphere, or as H. B. Swete said, "the air that all breathe." Air pollution threatens human beings as it is life at its source. The seventh bowl then caused a colossal earthquake. The first century was notable for earthquakes, but John of Patmos said that this one far surpassed previous horrors as it sank islands, leveled mountains, and brought huge hailstones. Rome thought she could do as she liked with impunity, but now God recalls her sin, and her fate is upon her. In the end, there is no escape from crimes committed. Henry Wadsworth Longfellow[253] wrote,

> "Though the mills of God grind slowly;
> Yet they grind exceeding small;
> Though with patience, he stands waiting,
> With exactness grinds he all."

---

[252] in BC 609

[253] (1807-1882) in "Retribution, Poetic Aphorisms, 1846" translated into English from the Greek philosopher Plutarch (46-119 AD).

16:21 | John of Patmos wrote about the Armageddon kings' battles and the **great hailstones** that rained upon them. Hail formed when drops of water froze together in the cold upper regions of thunderstorm clouds. The greatest ones in the United States have measured up to one and three-quarter inches in diameter, or golf ball size. The biggest recorded worldwide was eight inches in diameter, and the heaviest ever was over two pounds in Bangladesh. In Revelation, hailstones are enormous by comparison and weigh over sixty pounds, killing animals and people!

16:21 | **Great hailstones** were one of Egypt's plagues. "Yahweh rained hail on the land of Egypt, all that was in the field, both man and animal, and the hail struck every herb of the field and broke every tree of the field. Only in the land of Goshen, where the children of Israel were, there was no hail" (Ex. 9:23—26). The Lord spared Israel while the communities around them suffered.

16:21 | During the Middle Ages, Europeans rang church bells and fired cannons in an attempt to stop **hailstones** and crop damage. Cloud seeding after World War II eliminated the threat, particularly across Russia, and achieved a seventy percent reduction in crop damage. Governments induced rainfall in the clouds by shooting silver iodide up in rockets and artillery shells. Over fifteen countries have undertaken suppression programs between 1965 and today.

16:21 | In Israel's battle with the five Amorite kings at Beth-horon, enormous **hailstones** fell upon Israel's enemies. "Yahweh hurled down great stones from the sky on them to Azekah, and they died. There were more who died from the hailstones than those whom the children of Israel killed with the sword" (Joshua 10:11). Isaiah tells us, "Like a storm of hail, a destroying storm, and like a storm of mighty waters overflowing, he will cast them down to the earth with his hand" (Isa. 28:2). Ezekiel spoke about the time the Lord would judge. He will rain "an overflowing shower, with great hailstones, fire, and sulfur" (Ezek. 38:22).

Question: "Have you seen large hailstones. What do they mean?"

60

THE GREAT PROSTITUTE

17:1 "One of the seven angels who had the seven bowls came and spoke with me, saying, "Come here. I will show you the judgment of the **great prostitute** who sits **on many waters,** [2] with whom the kings of the earth committed sexual immorality. Those who dwell in the earth were made drunken with the wine of her sexual immorality." [3] He carried me away in the Spirit into a wilderness. I saw a woman sitting on a **scarlet-colored beast,** full of blasphemous names, having seven heads and ten horns. [4] The woman was dressed in **purple and scarlet**, and decked with gold and precious stones and pearls, having in her hand a **golden cup full of abominations** and the impurities of the sexual immorality of the earth.[5]And **on her forehead, a name** was written, "MYSTERY, BABYLON THE GREAT, THE MOTHER OF THE PROSTITUTES AND OF THE ABOMINATIONS OF THE EARTH."
(Rev. 17:1—5 emphases added).

17:1 | John of Patmos called the **great prostitute** "Babylon the Great," the "Mother of Prostitutes," and the "Abomination of the Earth." These names referred to the Roman empire's immorality. She encouraged godlessness and wickedness, but her greater sin was that she deliberately persuaded others. She deserved punishment for the worship of many gods and for shedding

Christian martyrs' blood. She used immoral means for her pleasure and prosperity.

17:2 | The great prostitute held a golden cup filled with terrible things. She sat **on many waters,** indicating oceans, seas, worldwide commerce, or a well-provisioned large city. Jeremiah commented, "You who dwell on many waters, abundant in treasures, your end has come, the measure of your covetousness" (Jer. 51:13).

17:2 | The Euphrates River may be the **"many waters"** Babylon sits on, for it was one of Western Asia's longest and most important rivers. It is also the center of an irrigation canal system in present-day Iraq, Turkey, and Syria, with lakes everywhere. John of Patmos wrote, "the waters which you saw, where the prostitute sits, are peoples, multitudes, nations, and languages" (Rev. 17:15). In contrast to the prostitute who exhibited terrible things that the Lord hated, the Bride of Christ, the church, was pure and obedient.

17:3 | The names of the **scarlet-colored beast** are the blasphemous titles of this seven-headed beast with ten horns, referring covertly to the ten Roman Emperors. It rises from the sea and appears as the great prostitute's accomplice. Blasphemous names cover the woman sitting on it, for it represents the Roman empire, with many heretical gods. Every one of its names insults Almighty God, defying his supreme authority. Nobody has the right to call himself God, save the one true deity.

17:3 | The **scarlet-colored beast's** blasphemous names may also refer to the many titles emperors claimed. One was *Augustus*, which meant "reverenced." Another was *theios*, Greek for "divine." Some called themselves *Soter* or "savior." A king often styled himself in Latin *dominus* or Greek *kurios*, meaning "Lord." The first commandment reminds us, "You shall have no other gods before me" (Ex. 20:3).

17:3 | The **scarlet-colored beast** possesses seven heads identified with the seven hills in Rome. It has ten horns with ten crowns on its horns, blasphemous names on its heads, and resembles a leopard with a bear's feet and a lion's mouth! Furthermore, one of its heads looked like it had been fatally wounded. The whole world was wonderstruck and followed this strange creature. People worshipped the dragon and the beast and asked, "who is like the beast? Who is able to make war with him?" (Rev. 13:4).

17:4 | The great prostitute's expensive and beautiful clothes are **purple and scarlet,** and she displays many gold and silver ornaments. She reveals herself in the lustful way that prostitutes do. It is a picture of a wealthy woman, decked out in her rich finery, determined to seduce men.

17:4 | She holds in her hand a **golden cup** full of abominations. This description is similar to Jeremiah's, where "Babylon has been a golden cup in Yahweh's hand which made all the earth drunk" (Jer. 51:7). Rome holds this golden chalice filled with abominations, which she pours out over the Roman empire.

17:4 | Society is still **full of abominations** today! Throughout history, oppressive governments have persecuted people for their beliefs. The great prostitute's drunkenness shows her pleasure in evil and her triumphal persecution of Christians. But every martyr who dies for their faith only serves to strengthen the church's resolve. Tertullian wrote in "Apologeticus" that "the blood of the martyrs is the seed of the church."[254] Alexander Souter translated this phrase "We spring up in greater numbers the more we are mown down by you: the blood of the Christians is the seed of a new life." A more faithful, if less poetic, rendering might be, "we multiply when you reap us. The blood of Christians is the seed."[255] Persecution's heirs take root and cause growth beyond all expectations!

17:5 | Interestingly, Babylon's great prostitute has **a name on her forehead**. In Rome's public brothels, prostitutes wore name signs upon their brows. These vivid details picture Rome as a tremendously corrupting influence.

Question: "If someone persecuted you for your beliefs, how would you feel about the Great Prostitute?"

---

[254] Tertullian "Apologeticus L. 13"
[255] the text of Oehler annotated, translation by Alex. Souter with introduction by John E B Mayor, Cambridge University Press, 1917

61

ROMAN CHRISTIAN PERSECUTION

17:6 "I saw the woman drunken with the **blood of the saints**, and with the blood of the **martyrs of Jesus**. When I saw her, I wondered with great amazement. [7] The angel said to me, "Why do you wonder? I will tell you the mystery of the woman, and of the beast that carries her, which has the **seven heads** and the ten horns. [8] The beast that you saw **was, and is not; and is about to come** up out of the abyss and to go into destruction. Those who dwell on the earth and whose names have not been written in the book of life from the foundation of the world will marvel when they see that the beast was, and is not, and shall be present." (Rev. 17:6—8 emphases added).

17:6 | The description by John of Patmos of Christian persecution was significant. Ancient Rome was drunk with the **blood of the saints.** The holy ones' oppression was a legal necessity because Christians disagreed with Emperor worship. The authority, pictured as a drunken woman, took great delight in mistreating and hounding Christians. She was the great persecutor who reveled in slaughter and enjoyed it as a drunk loved getting drunk. The blood of the saints intoxicated the woman.

17:6 | Emperor Nero was a brutal individual. At seventeen, he had his mother and later his wife[256] murdered. He was more than a little mad and very corrupt. William Hartston said, "In 67 AD, Nero competed in the Olympic Games and remarkably won events in chariot racing, singing, and acting, probably by bribing the judges."

17:6 | According to Tacitus,[257] Emperor Nero made a scapegoat of Christ's followers, and many became **martyrs**, the first documented evidence outside the Bible of the historical existence of Jesus and Christians. He wrote, "Christus, (or in some texts Chrestus) from whom the name Christian had its origin, suffered the extreme penalty during the reign of Emperor Tiberius[258] at the hands of one of our procurators, Pontius Pilatus.[259] Thus checked for the moment, a most mischievous superstition again broke out in Judaea, the first source of the evil, and even in Rome, where all things hideous and shameful from every part of the world find their center and become popular."

17:6 | According to Tacitus, the Neronic persecution and the **martyrs of Jesus** sprung from the great fire in Rome in 64 AD, which burned for six days and devastated the city. Roman citizens believed the outbreak was no accident, saw those who tried to extinguish it hindered, and the emperor's supporters deliberately rekindled the flames! People thought that the fire's instigator was Emperor Nero and that he had to invent a scapegoat to divert suspicion from himself. There was a myth that "Nero fiddled while Rome burned," but Hartston asserts this cannot be true because "fiddles or violin-like instruments did not exist until the eleventh century AD!"[260] The instrument could have been the stringed lyre that he played. He was passionate about impressive buildings and deliberately destroyed Rome's old, dilapidated wooden ones to replace them with grandiose marble. After

---

[256] Claudia Octavia (39-62 AD) was murdered in 62 AD.
[257] the Roman historian, senator, and observer in his "Annals 15.44." (54-117 AD).
[258] (BC 42-37 AD).
[259] (12 BC -?).
[260] according to the Daily Express writer William Hartston (1947-present).

the fire, he erected a large, landscaped villa called the *Domus Aurea* or "Golden House" in ancient Rome's heart. He falsely accused Christians of setting the fire, which became their earliest oppression and the most savage.

17:6 | Tacitus wrote of the **martyrs of Jesus.** "All who pleaded guilty were arrested. Upon their information, an immense multitude was convicted, not so much of the crime of firing the city as of hatred of humankind. They were covered with beasts' skins, torn by dogs, perished, or nailed to crosses. They were doomed to the flames and burned to serve as a nightly illumination when daylight had expired."

17:6 | In 250 AD, another Christian persecution took place under Emperor Decius[261] and produced many **martyrs of Jesus.** Decius issued a proclamation ordering that the empire's citizens, except for exempted Jewish people sacrifice to the Roman gods and the emperor's well-being. A signed and witnessed certificate called a *libellus* had to be completed as proof of one's agreement in a Roman magistrate's presence. Many certificates survive from Egypt, signed by witnesses. Here is one example of a "libellus."

> "To the commission chosen to superintend the sacrifices. From Aurelia Ammonous, daughter of Mystus, the Moeris quarter, priestess of the deity Petesouchos, the great, the mighty, the immortal. I have sacrificed to the gods all my life. Now again, I have sacrificed following the decree and in your presence. I have poured out a libation and partaken of the sacred victims. I request you to certify this below."

Decius reported that suspected Christians who cursed Christ were freed. Persecuting them was not Decius' mandate or intended goal. Nothing in these *libelli* inferred any need to deny being a Christian.

---

[261] (201-251 AD)

17:6 | Decius intended his proclamation as an empire-wide loyalty oath at his coming to power. Because he did not consider Christianity a religion, they were not exempt but forced to choose between religious beliefs and following the law. Their faith in one God did not allow them to worship others. Many Christians died as **martyrs** or were imprisoned for refusing to sacrifice. Some hid, while others performed the ceremonies regardless. The effects were long-lasting as they caused tensions between Christians who participated in the worship and those who did not.

17.7 | John of Patmos considered the concept of a resurrected Nero and how he connected with the Antichrist, described as the "scarlet beast." He wrote, "The seven heads are seven mountains on which the woman sits" (Rev. 17:9). The **seven-headed** beast pointed to ancient Rome's seven hills.

17.8 | The beast's mouth uttered blasphemous words. The beast is named as **"was, and is not, and is about to come**." This title is a strange imitation of God's eternal name. The beast's past, present, and future hint at the "Nero Redivivus legend," which was never far from John of Patmos' mind.

Question: "Could Christian persecution reoccur and where?"

62

SEVEN ROMAN EMPERORS

17:9 "Here is the **mind that has wisdom**. The **seven heads** are seven mountains on which the woman sits. [10] They are **seven kings**. Five have fallen, the one is, the other has not yet come. When he comes, he must continue **a little while**. [11] The **beast that was**, and is not, is himself also **an eighth**, and is of the seven; and he **goes to destruction**. [12] The ten horns that you saw are ten kings who have received no kingdom as yet, but they receive authority as kings with the beast for one hour. [13] These have one mind, and they give their power and authority to the beast. [14] These will war against the Lamb, and the **Lamb will overcome them**, for he is Lord of Lords, and King of kings, and those who are with him are called chosen and faithful."
(Rev. 17:9—14 emphases added).

17:9 | The angel told John of Patmos that understanding these images called for a **mind that has wisdom.** He meant, "Here is a clue. It's up to you to connect the dots and reach a conclusion." It's true for us today!

17:9 | John receives a hint about the **seven heads** or emperors who ruled Rome, the seven-hilled city. The hills[262] east of the River

---

[262] The names of the hills are Palatine, Capitoline, Aventine, Caelian, Esquiline, Quirinal, and Viminal.

Tiber enclose the geographical heart within the city walls. John of Patmos deliberately calls it "Babylon" to disguise it, but this concealment of Rome's name was well known to most Jewish and Christian people.

17:10 | There are **seven kings,** wrote John of Patmos. In Christianity's early centuries, many emperors were cruel to Christians, and thousands of them died at Domitian and Nero's hands. They were burned, sawn in half, skinned alive, impaled on stakes, crucified, thrown to wild animals, and killed by gladiators for sport in the arenas. The Colosseum, the oval amphitheater in Rome's center, was the largest and most prominent arena, but they built smaller ones in other places like Verona. Romans loved their sports like British and Italian people live for soccer, Americans cheer on baseball, and Canadians are mad about ice hockey! The games became the authorities' way of keeping order and entertaining citizens.

17:10 | John of Patmos had seen much cruelty towards Christians and believed God would eventually answer with equal ferocity. He described the Roman empire's punishment as a past event. The seven heads were the emperors, five of which have fallen, one exists, and the other, meaning Titus, has not yet come. When this last emperor does come, he will remain **a little while.** Titus was the first-ever emperor's son to inherit his father's position, but his reign lasted only two years.[263] In 70 AD, as a general, he successfully laid siege to Jerusalem, destroying it and the temple there. Today, the Arch of Titus stands in Rome, generously decorated with carvings of his battle successes. He completed Rome's massive Colosseum and showed incredible kindness to those who suffered from the Mount Vesuvius eruption and Rome's rebuilding after a terrible fire.

17:11 | The eighth emperor, Domitian, was described as the **beast that was.** The Roman empire was founded by Augustus, followed by Tiberius, Caligula, Claudius, and Nero. Domitian came after Titus. John of Patmos described him as "the beast that

---

[263] from 79-81 AD.

was and now is not and is on his way to destruction." Suetonius[264] called Domitian "Nero Redivivus" or "Nero Resurrected," but Christians believed he was "the Antichrist." A popular legend, surviving until the 5th century AD, claimed that Nero did not die but returned as Domitian.

17:11 | Can Domitian be identified with Nero Redivivus? He was undoubtedly as evil as the **beast that once was.** Suetonius, a Christian sympathizer, asserted that all hated him. A grim picture of him emerged at the beginning of his rule. "He spent hours in seclusion every day, doing nothing but catching flies and stabbing them with a keenly-sharpened stylus." Any psychologist would find this a curiously revealing picture of any man or woman. He was insanely jealous, suspicious, and cruel, reviving the old punishment of stripping his victims naked, hanging them by the neck in a wooden fork, and beating them with rods until dead.

17:11 | After Nero's death, there were two chaotic years in which several minor leaders came and went. These included Galba, Otho, and Vitellius, but no list of emperors included them. The seven Roman emperors concluded with Vespasian and his son Titus. The **eighth** was Domitian, who made Caesar worship compulsory and unleashed Christian persecution. Juvenal[265] said about Domitian that Rome was "enslaved to a bald Nero." For this remark, he was exiled and eventually murdered. Tertullian[266] described Domitian as "a man of Nero's type of cruelty" and a "sub-Nero." As we might say today, he was "a nasty piece of work!"

17:11 | Domitian claimed to be a god and insisted on being addressed as "Lord" and publicly worshipped. His fifteen-year reign was ruthless and eventually led **to destruction.** When the historian Hermogenes wrote unflattering things, he executed him and the scribe who copied his manuscript. He slaughtered

---

[264] (69-120 AD) According to "The Life of Domitian" by the Roman biographer.

[265] a Roman poet of the 1st and 2nd century AD, otherwise called Decimus Junius Juvenalis.

[266] a 3rd century North African Christian leader,

senators for no good reason. Suetonius[267] tells us that the governor of Britain, Sallustius Lucullus, was executed in 89 AD. He allowed a new lance design to be called a *Lucullan* after himself instead of Emperor Domitian. *Lucullan* later came to mean "extremely luxurious" and is the name of a beautiful marble type. Early in his reign, Domitian appeared wearing a golden crown with Jupiter, Juno, and Minerva figures. When he received his divorced wife, he announced: "she had returned to the divine couch." His official edicts began, "Our Lord and God bid this done," and this soon became the only permitted title. He was a fierce and ruthlessly efficient autocratic leader, and John of Patmos regarded him as the cruelest Roman Emperor. Domitian lived in his father Vespasian's[268] shadow until his death. After Vespasian died in 81 AD, his brother Titus,[269] a successful military leader, succeeded him.

17:11 | The day after the death of Titus, the Praetorian Guard declared Domitian the Emperor, but he was going **to his destruction**. Suetonius described him "as tall, with a modest expression and a high color. His eyes were large, but his sight was dim. He was handsome and graceful, especially when a young man, indeed in his whole body except for his feet, the toes of which were cramped. In later life, he became bald, with a protruding belly and spindling legs from a long illness." Though bald and wearing a wig, he was reputed to have written a book on hair care! He was so suspicious and fearful that he had his prisoners chained during hearings. He tiled the palace passages with reflective mica stone to see anyone creeping up behind him. When polished, they were like mirrors. He reigned for fifteen years, longer than anyone since Tiberius. Court officials murdered him,[270] despite all his precautions.

17:14 | In heaven, the beast and the Antichrist war with

---

[267] the Roman historian living in North Africa who wrote, "The Twelve Caesars" and the "Life of Domitian,"
[268] (9-79 AD).
[269] (39-81 AD),
[270] on the 18th of September, 96 AD.

the Lamb, but the Lamb destroys their power. In Domitian, the eighth emperor, John of Patmos saw Rome's supreme wickedness, defiance against God, and Nero's reincarnation, but the **Lamb will overcome them**. Therefore, he identified Domitian as the Antichrist who battled the Lamb. The ten horns refer to the ten kings who would unanimously agree to hand their power to the beast. They would rise with the harlot and war with the Lamb, who would finally defeat them.

17:14 | The chosen ones shared in the **Lamb's** victory in God's final triumph. Early apocryphal writings[271] encouraged persecuted followers, "Having borne a little chastening, they shall receive great good because God tried them and found them worthy of himself." "As gold in the furnace, he proved them, and as a whole burnt offering, he accepted them. They shall shine forth, and as sparks among the stubble, they shall run to and fro. They shall judge nations and have dominion over people." The Lamb will overcome because he is Lord of Lords and King of Kings.

Question: "What does John of Patmos say here to the mind with wisdom?"

---

[271] (Wisdom of Solomon 3:5-8)

63

GOD'S GREAT PURPOSE

17:15 "He said to me, "The waters which you saw, where the **prostitute** sits, are peoples, multitudes, nations, and languages. [16] The **ten horns which you saw, and the beast**, these will hate the prostitute, will make her desolate, will strip her naked, will **eat her flesh,** and will **burn her utterly with fire**. [17] For **God has put in their hearts to do** what he has in mind, to be of one mind, and to give their kingdom to the beast, until the words of God should be **accomplished**. [18] The woman whom you saw is the **great city**, which reigns over the kings of the earth." (Rev. 17:15-18 emphases added).

17:15 | Rome's wickedness was that she had come to hate good and love evil. The **prostitute's** lovers, representing Rome's vassal states, turned violently against her and destroyed her.

17:16 | **The beast** arose violently from the sea and received authority and power to devour the prostitute's flesh and burn her with fire. The prostitute was its mistress. "Beast" from the Greek *therion* means "wild animal" and refers to two such beasts, one from the sea and the other from the land.

17:16 | In the Old Testament, to **eat her flesh** and blood was the most savage action of a powerful and vengeful enemy. The Psalmist recalls, "When evildoers came at me to eat up my flesh, even my adversaries and my foes, they stumbled and fell" (Ps. 27:2).

17:16 | To **burn her utterly with fire** was another terrible punishment. The Law stated, "If a man takes a wife and her mother, it is wickedness. They shall be burned with fire" (Lev. 20:14). Later, we read, "The daughter of any priest if she profanes herself by playing the prostitute. She shall be burned with fire" (Lev. 21:9). These punishments were for the most terrible sins.

17:17 | The ten kings allied themselves with the beast. **God has put in their hearts to do what he has in mind** so that he might accomplish his goals and implement his words through the ten kings. Evil powers think they are working out their schemes, but unknowingly they fulfill God's great plan. R. H. Charles wrote that even anger creates praise for God, who never loses control of human affairs. Paul added, "We know that all things work together for good for those who love God, for those who are called according to his purpose" (Rom. 8:28). The phrase " those who love God" may equally mean "those who love him to bring about what is good."

17:17 | A lovely hymn was written by Arthur Campbell Ainger[272] to illustrate how God puts it into human hearts **to do what he has in mind,**

> "God is working his purpose out as year succeeds
> to year:
> God is working his purpose out, and the time is
> drawing near;
> nearer and nearer draws the time, the time that
> shall surely be;
> when the earth shall be filled with the glory of God
> as the waters cover the sea."

17:18 | Ten kings, Rome's subject nations, invaded and destroyed her. She fought Germanic "barbaric" tribes from the North for centuries, but after 300 AD, groups like the Goths encroached beyond her borders. She weathered a Germanic

---

[272] (1841-1919) Written as a tribute to the Archbishop of Canterbury in 1894. He based his words on Habakkuk 2:14.

uprising in the late fourth century. King Alaric,[273] who was once a Roman soldier and had grown up in "the most remote area in the vast world" sacked Rome. The empire was under constant threat for decades before a raid again in 455 AD by the Vandals. Finally, the Germanic races staged a revolt and deposed Emperor Romulus Augustulus.[274] His name meant "Little Augustus," but his soldiers turned his title into *Momyllusi,* or "little disgrace!"

Question: "What is God's great purpose for your life? Have you found it yet?"

---

[273] (c370-410 AD). In 410 AD, the first King of the Visigoths.
[274] (c465-c511 AD).

64

BABYLON'S DOOM SONG

18:1 "After these things, I saw another **angel** coming down out of the sky, having great authority. The earth was illuminated with his glory. ² He cried with a mighty voice, saying, "**Fallen, fallen is Babylon the great**, and she has become a **habitation of demons**, a prison of every unclean spirit, and a **prison of every unclean and hateful bird**! ³ For all the nations have drunk of the wine of the wrath of her sexual immorality, the kings of the earth committed sexual immorality with her, and the merchants of the earth grew rich from the abundance of her luxury."
(Rev. 18.1—3 emphases added).

18:1 | Over two thousand years ago, John of Patmos saw an **angel** come down from heaven from the presence of Almighty God, and the earth shone with his splendor. This luminous creature had "great authority" and carried a message of doom. Wikipedia tells us that the word *angel* arrived in modern English from the Old English *engel* and the Old French *angele*. Both of these derive from the Latin *angelus*, which in turn comes from the Greek *angelos* (literally "messenger.") According to the Dutch linguist R. S. P. Beekes,[275] *angelos* itself may be "an Oriental loan," like *angaros*, meaning "a Persian mounted courier."

---

[275] (1937-2017).

18:1 | A glowing **angel** no doubt reminded John of Patmos of the writings of Ezekiel. "Behold, the glory of the God of Israel came from the way of the east. His voice was like the sound of many waters; and the earth was illuminated with his glory" (Ezek. 43:2). H. B. Swete said of this radiant angel, "that he has so recently come from God's presence that in passing he brings a broad belt of light across the dark earth."

18:1 | In Revelation 18, an **angel** introduces "A Doom Song, " a standard form of Old Testament prophetic literature. Surprisingly, its concept has some similarities with "doom metal," or "an extreme subgenre of heavy metal music that typically uses slower tempos, low-tuned guitars, and a much "thicker" or "heavier" sound than other heavy metal genres. Both the music and the lyrics intend to evoke a sense of despair, dread, and impending doom."

18:1 | An **angel** introduces the doom song with the same sense of dread in heaven with a loud shout, "Fallen! Fallen is Babylon the Great." This announcement foretells Rome's destruction. Isaiah writes that Babylon "will be like Sodom and Gomorrah when God overthrew them" (Isa. 13:19). The Nineveh doom song explains that God will destroy Assyria, leaving Nineveh utterly desolate, like a desert, and occupied by evil.

18:2 | There are several unusual creatures mentioned in this **habitation of demons**. The *satyr* may indicate "a wild goat," and the *night hag* may refer to "night creatures." "The *night hag* or *old hag* is the name given to a supernatural creature, commonly associated with sleep paralysis, during which a person feels a presence of an evil being that immobilizes the person as if sitting on their chest or the foot of their bed. The phrase "nightmare" or "night terrors" describes this phenomenon."[276] People remain asleep during bad dreams, whereas nightmares can awaken them. However, remember that Jesus said, "Peace I leave with you. My peace I give to you; not as the world gives, I give to you. Don't let your heart be troubled, neither let it be fearful" (John 14:27).

---

[276] Wikipedia, the Free Encyclopedia for "night hag."

This sentiment calls to mind a beautiful and soothing Maranatha Singers composition,

> "My peace I give unto you,
> It's a peace that the world
> Cannot give,
> It's a peace that the world
> Cannot understand.
> Peace to know, peace to live
> My peace I give unto you."[277]

Take a moment to drink in this promise!

18:2 | John of Patmos tells us that Babylon will be utterly destroyed and become a **habitation of demons**. Like Isaiah's doom song, the Edom and Nineveh ones foretell their complete ruin to become haunts for every evil spirit. "Thorns will come up in its palaces, nettles, and thistles in its fortresses; and it will be a habitation of jackals, a court for ostriches" (Isa. 34:13). Other Isaiah and Zephaniah passages contain similarities and parallels to the Babylon Doom Song. They are all grim foretellings of the ruin of a mighty but corrupt city or nation. The pagan gods are banished from their reigns and inhabit the temple ruins where their power was once supreme.

18:2 | Babylon will become a domain of "**every unclean and hateful bird.**" The screech and desert owls will roost on the destroyed city's columns. Their hooting will echo through the windows, and rubble will fill the doorways. Isaiah says, "But the pelican and the porcupine will possess it. The owl and the raven will dwell in it" (Isa. 34:11). The precise identification of some of these creatures is difficult in Hebrew and Greek texts. Sometimes, rarely used words like these are challenging to identify as there are few parallels in other manuscripts to compare. The King James Version identifies the "desert owl" as a cormorant, the "screech owl" as a bittern, and the "great owl" simply as an owl.

---

[277] Source Musixmatch. Songwriter Keith Routledge.

Other Bible versions suggest various birds and animals, like the pelican, the hawk, and even the porcupine!

18:2 | Babylon's wicked city of **"every unclean and hateful bird,"** meaning Rome, contrasts with the heavenly city of the New Jerusalem. Babylon symbolizes any hostile system that is antagonistic to God today.

Question: "Have you experienced nightmares? How did you deal with them?"

65

SELF-CENTERED PEOPLE

18:4 "I heard another voice from heaven, saying, "**Come out of her, my people**, that **you have no participation in her sins**, and that you don't receive of her plagues, [5] for her sins have reached to the sky, and God has remembered her iniquities. [6] **Return to her just as she returned**, and repay her double as she did, and according to her works. In the cup which she mixed, mix to her double. [7] However much she **glorified herself, and grew wanton**, so much give her of torment and mourning. For she says in her heart, 'I sit a queen, and **am no widow**, and will in no way see mourning.' [8] Therefore **in one day her plagues will come:** death, mourning, and famine; and she will be utterly burned with fire; for the Lord God who has judged her is strong." (Rev. 18:4—8 emphases added).

18:4 | The cry **"Come out of her my people"** does not mean the city's evacuation but a call to Christians to separate themselves from sin. Christ's bride, the church, is to be pure and holy. Disciples have died for their beliefs because they lived consecrated lives. But every martyr punished because of their convictions only strengthens other faithful peoples' resolve.

18:4 | In the Roman empire, merchants were invariably self-centered and greedy people who grew rich by exploiting others.

Christians must **come out of her** and not have anything to do with this attitude and approach. It reminds me of some real estate investors who lie profusely to deceive a family into selling low and then turn around and flip the property for an exorbitant profit. They often seek out elderly sellers and those forced to move for other reasons like the need to be close to medical facilities, debt, increase in interest payments, a death, or to support their family. Investors try to intimidate their victims when they can, which is considered fair game. They often feel they are above the law, have no regard for truth, and have no desire to help others. My apologies to any honest real estate investors reading this, but that is my experience.

18:4 | Many business people today are greedy and self-absorbed, but God knows that **"her sins have reached to the skies."** I know, as an engineer, how easy it is to pad a quote or inflate an estimate. I admire the likes of Walmart, who charge for each item based on the purchase cost plus twelve percent for staff, benefits, overheads, and profits. That's why Walmart's prices often have trailing pennies like $6.23 rather than the $6.99 or $7.99 of other stores. Because they sell such large quantities, they can reduce their prices still further. God sees all we do and will one day bring everyone to account. Eric Fromm[278] wrote, "Greed is a bottomless pit which exhausts a person in an endless effort to satisfy their needs without ever reaching satisfaction." However, Christians should stay free from money's lure and status, which brings only eventual ruin. Jesus said, "No servant can serve two masters, for either he will hate the one, and love the other; or else he will hold to one, and despise the other. You aren't able to serve God and Mammon" (Luke 16:13). "Mammon" here refers to the Syrian god of riches and wealth whom people worshipped. The "Didascalia"[279] in 230 AD adds, "They think only of Mammon, whose God is the purse."

18:4 | On the other hand, Christians are called upon to **have no participation in** their sins and live according to Christ's

---

[278] (1900-1980) the German psychologist.
[279] A Christian legal treatise from Northern Syria from 230 AD.

values of service, self-sacrifice, obedience, holiness, and truth. It is an exacting standard to achieve. J. I. Packer[280] stated in his book "Knowing God," "There is nothing more irreligious than self-absorbed religion." Doctor Packer was a humble man who repudiated the success ethic. I remember meeting him at a conference in Ontario some years ago. He was tall and lean, had an encyclopedic mind, and opened up for questions at the end of each lecture. On one occasion, a Church Army officer asked him about Christian theology. Dr. Packer fired back an impressive six-point answer with all the Bible references and complete verses to go with it. I found him a kind, humble, and authentic Christian gentleman.

18:6 | Many financially comfortable people feel secure and do not need God. According to her works, **giving back to her as she has given** means returning just as she gave. God's judgment against those who see no need for him is harsh. Instead, Christians are encouraged not to become complacent and deluded by the myth of self-sufficiency if they are financially secure. Use your resources, be generous with others and advance God's kingdom by giving back as much as possible. I love the book "Die Broke"[281] by Stephen M. Pollan and Mark Levine. As a New York lawyer, he had worked out a plan he shared with his clients to free themselves of all their riches by the end of their lives. He planned that his last check for his funeral would bounce! His mantra was "Die broke, Live rich, Be happy." It is a book well worth a read!

18:6 | My wife and I were influenced by this philosophy when we decided to sell our large riverside property and buy a small condominium close to amenities in town. With the extra money we received, we gave away substantial packages to fifteen young people, children, and even babies so they would have something to start their college or university education. They greatly blessed us. In England and Canada, to a lesser degree, very few graduates have the opportunity to go to university without money behind them. In the US, young people expect it. Gifting these kids was one

---

[280] (1926-2020)
[281] Harper Business a division of Harper Colins ISBN 978-088730-942-7 1997.

of the most satisfying things we have ever done! The letters and calls with thanks were very uplifting. We now have the added joy of watching these young people go on to further education as they reach that age. I would recommend every Christian consider it.

18:7 | Wealth is always a temptation for Christians. We must avoid the attitude of Babylon, who **glorified herself and grew wanton**. Those tied to the world's system will lose everything when it falls, and it does periodically. It is akin to a stock market collapse when everybody's savings in stocks, mutual funds, bitcoins, or blue-chip stocks collapse. They can destroy in one fell swoop a lifetime's work. Those who labor only for material rewards will be left with nothing when they die, which is where everyone ends up. "For we brought nothing into the world, and we certainly can't carry anything out" (1 Tim. 6:7).

18:8 | John of Patmos writes that **her plagues will come in one day**. We live in an age of fake news and some corrupt politicians, business leaders, and even church officials tell half-truths and lies to achieve their ends. Babylon's people also lived self-centered luxuriant, and pleasure-filled lives. Influential, wealthy people today are prone to this same arrogance. John of Patmos writes that her plagues or consequences will descend one day. North America saw the Covid-19 plague come suddenly, an omicron variety, then a third variant followed by the monkeypox and now a worse seventh wave. They all seemed to arrive unexpectedly on the news one day. However, we will soon live in a place where there are no plagues nor sickness but only total health, peace, and happiness in the presence of our Lord.

Question: "Are you doing well with your resources? Do you plan to die broke?"

66

ANCIENT ROMAN LUXURY

18:9 "The kings of the earth who committed sexual
immorality and **lived wantonly** with her will **weep
and wail** over her, when they look at the smoke of her
burning, [10] standing far away for the fear of her torment,
saying, '**Woe, woe, the great city**, Babylon, the strong
city! For your judgment has come in one hour.'"
(Rev. 18:9—10 emphases added).

18:9 | The kings of the earth **lived wantonly** and poured
riches into Rome's lap. "Wantonly" means "in a deliberate and
unprovoked, lustful or sexually unrestrained or reckless way."
The kings of the earth lived in an undisciplined, carefree, and
immoral manner.

18:9 | Aristides[282] wrote about their **wanton** behavior. "The
long peace, the seas' safety, and trade freedom had made Rome the
entryway for every land's specialty products and delicacies from
the British Channel to the Ganges." "They brought merchandise
that every season and country produced, river and lake products,
Greek and Barbarian arts. If anyone wished to see these things,
he would have to visit the whole inhabited world or go to Ancient
Rome."

---

[282] (BC 530-468) an ancient Athenian statesman nicknamed "The Just."

18:9 | The elite **lived wantonly** and spent extravagantly in Rome. One of Nero's formerly enslaved people regarded a man with one million and a quarter dollars as a pauper compared to other Romans. Apicius[283] squandered two million dollars and committed suicide when he had only two hundred thousand left. He could not live on such a pittance! He did, however, compile a cookery book called "The Art of Cooking," which is still the oldest surviving collection of recipes in antiquity available in print today! Numerous covers in private collections date from 900 AD. However, many ingredients like flamingos' tongues or unusual herbs would be impossible to find in our modern supermarkets! Pliny the Elder, who died while attempting the rescue of a friend and his family by ship from the eruption of Mount Vesuvius, wrote that Apicius, the most gluttonous gorger of all spendthrifts, professed that the flamingo's tongue had a delicate flavor.

18:9 | The emperors **lived wantonly** and were renowned for their extravagance. In one day, Caligula[284] spent two hundred thousand dollars or three provinces' revenues. He was a horse lover and owned a stallion named "Incitatus."[285] which had a marble stall, an ivory manger, a jeweled collar, and even a house. In episode nine of the movie series "I, Claudius" with John Hurt, Caligula introduced his new senator, Incitatus, before Claudius' wedding. Incitatus invited dignitaries to dine with him!

18:9 | Emperor Nero later declared that money's only use was to **live wantonly** and squander it, and in a few years, wasted thirty-six million dollars! At one banquet, the Egyptian roses alone cost seventy thousand dollars! Our present-day excesses with fifty million dollar boats and houses are comparable with these excesses. Christians need to re-examine our luxurious Twenty-First Century lifestyles constantly. William Barclay asked, "How do our lives reflect the poor carpenter of Nazareth's holiness and righteousness?"

---

[283] (BC 25-37 AD) a Roman connoisseur and lover of good food and luxury in the first century AD.
[284] Emperor Caligula (12-41 AD).
[285] meaning "swift" or "at full gallop."

18:9 | The Roman Emperors' **wanton** living led to society's corruption and eventual collapse. The historian Suetonius, the director of the imperial libraries and Emperor Hadrian's private secretary, described the lavish ways of twelve successive emperors, from Julius Caesar[286] to Domitian. Suetonius wrote, "In reckless luxury, Caligula outdid the prodigals in ingenuity, inventing a new sort of bath and unnatural food varieties and feasts. He bathed in hot or cold perfumed oils, drank pearls of great price dissolved in vinegar, and set gold loaves and meats before his guests." He even built galleys with sterns studded with pearls.

18:9 | Nero **lived wantonly** and compelled nobles to set banquets before him, costing forty thousand dollars each. "He never wore the same garment twice and played dice for four thousand dollars a point. He fished with a golden net drawn by purple and scarlet threaded cords and did not journey with less than a thousand carriages and shod his mules with silver." Until this century, the royal family in England didn't wear the same clothing twice, and the press anxiously watched to announce the latest trends! The Town and Country magazine even listed the thirty times royals wore the same dress because they turned to the same elite designers. Only the Queen, when she was a driver/mechanic during the war, had to wear the same uniform every day. As a child, a young lad called Sidie Brown came to the front door and asked for hand-me-down clothes from my elder brother. Neighbors passed clothes around for growing children because they had nothing else.

18:9 | In Roman times, elites consumed dissolved pearl drinks just for fun worth thousands of dollars as part of **living wantonly**. Pliny tells us Cleopatra[287] drank a dissolved pearl[288] valued at one hundred and sixty thousand dollars to win a wager with

---

[286] (BC 100-44)

[287] (BC 69-30).

[288] Pearls consist of calcium carbonate deposited in concentric layers. When a pearl drops into white vinegar, its acetic acid reacts with the calcium carbonate, releasing carbon dioxide and dissolving it. Vinegar, in time, became the best way to authenticate a pearl as small drop of vinegar causes it to fizz, indicating a genuine pearl. Fake pearls didn't react to vinegar.

Mark Antony. Horace[289] claimed he had consumed Metalla's pearl earring to say that he had swallowed a million sesterces[290] or one point three million dollars!

18:9 | In a tremendously gluttonous age when people **lived wantonly**, hosts served dishes of peacock's brains and nightingale's tongues at many banquets. "Gluttony" from the Latin "gluttire" meant "to gulp down or to swallow." Gluttony resulted in over-indulgence in food, drink, or wealth items as status symbols. Vitellius,[291] Emperor for less than a year, succeeded in spending fourteen million dollars on food. Emperor Suetonius described his favorite dish. He mingled "pikes' livers, pheasants' and peacocks' brains, flamingos' tongues, and lampreys' milk, brought by his captains from Parthia to the Spanish strait." Such was the Emperor's and the ruling elite's extravagance and great gluttony!

18:9 | Gaius Petronius Arbiter[292] was a Roman courtier during Nero's reign. He devoted himself as a senator to a life of luxury, pleasure, and living **wantonly** and was considered by Pliny the Elder "the elegance judge" in his court. He wrote about Trimalchio's dinner, which has become shorthand for the ruling elite's worst excesses. "Each course represented one of the twelve zodiac signs." They included chickpeas, beefsteak, kidneys, crab, a sow's udder, different deserts, sea scorpion, fish, African fig, lobster, goose, and two fish mullets!" Another luxury dish was a large boar, with baskets of sweetmeats hanging from its tusks. A bearded hunter pierced its side with his hunting knife, and a ' thrush flight flew about the room from the wound. At the meal's end, strange sounds in the ceiling and the whole apartment's quaking startled the guests. The roof suddenly opened as they raised their eyes, and a large circular tray descended, with a "Priapus figure,"[293] bearing fruits and bonbons. When John of Patmos was writing, poverty was widespread.

---

[289] or "Quintus Horatius Flaccus" (BC 65-8), the Roman poet.
[290] worth $1.35 million today at a gulp."
[291] (15-69 AD).
[292] (927-66 AD).
[293] of a minor Greek fertility god.

18:9 | Kings from every land who once shared in ancient Rome's luxury will **weep and wail** over her collapse. A Talmud proverb proclaims, "ten wealth measures came down into the world, ancient Rome received nine and all the rest only one." One scholar added that we are babes in enjoyment in modern times compared with the ancient world. Our most extravagant modern luxury is poverty compared with ancient Rome's abundance and magnificence.

18:10 | Many great ships arrived from around the world every hour and season. Rome was a massive marketplace for luxurious Indian and Arabian cargoes, Babylonian clothing, and ornaments from far-flung lands. Merchandise, foreign products, precious metals, and every type of art arrived there. Everything produced and grown came to Rome, but the prophecy said, **Woe, woe the great city,** you mighty city of Babylon!" Rome's fall was inevitable.

Question: "Is there a modern equivalent to ancient Rome's exorbitance?"

67

ROMAN SILVER DISHES

18:11 "The **merchants of the earth** weep and mourn over her, for no one buys their merchandise any more: [12] merchandise of gold, **silver, precious stones, pearls**, fine linen, **purple, silk, scarlet**, all **expensive wood**, every vessel of **ivory**, every vessel made of most precious wood, and of **brass, and iron, and marble**; [13] and **cinnamon, incense**, perfume, frankincense, wine, olive oil, fine flour, wheat, sheep, horses, **chariots**, and **people's bodies and souls**. [14] The fruits which your soul lusted after have been lost to you. **All things that were dainty and sumptuous have perished** from you, and you will find them no more at all. [15] The merchants of these things, who were made rich by her, will stand far away for the fear of her torment, weeping and mourning, [16] saying, 'Woe, woe, the great city, she who was dressed in fine linen, purple, and scarlet, and decked with gold and precious stones and pearls! [17] For in an hour such great riches are made desolate.'"
(Rev. 18:11—17 emphases added).

18:11 | The **merchants of the earth** were not shopkeepers selling produce on street corners but wealthy traders of overseas goods. They were part of the upper-class elite and very influential in society. The Roman class system was similar to the eighteenth-century English model, with three classes and royalty at the top. The working class was at the bottom. Shopkeepers and all those in service of the elites were in the middle. The upper-class aristocracy ruled and controlled every aspect of society. A few royal families, from which the Caesars came, governed and received much of the wealth.

18:11 | My relatives were dramatically affected by this class system. My father's family were **merchants** and shopkeepers who owned a grocery store in Chester, providing goods for several stately homes. They were decidedly middle-class, so when my father wanted to marry my mother, his family refused and turned their back on him. The problem was that he had fallen in love with a chambermaid from a mansion house in Broughton, but she was from the working class and below my father's status. As a result, my father and mother moved away, and they didn't speak to his family again for forty years. He didn't see any of his eleven brothers and sisters until shortly before his death. My five brothers and sisters and I didn't meet our grandparents, uncles, and aunts. In John of Patmos' day, the same gulfs existed between the servants, the shopkeepers, the wealthy merchants, and the royals.

18:11 | The list of items imported by wealthy **merchants** emphasizes society's enormous materialism. Few of the goods were necessities and most luxuries. Roman civilization had become thoroughly indulgent. The traders' mourning was self-centered because their profits had disappeared.

18:12 | When John of Patmos was writing, there was a passion for **silver,** especially from Cartagena in Spain, where forty thousand men toiled in the mines. Wealthy Romans collected dishes, bowls, jugs, fruit baskets, figurines, and complete dinner services made of silver plate. Marcus Licinius Crassus,[294] called "the richest man in Rome," amassed an enormous fortune in silverware. Pompeius Paullinus,[295] the fighting general, carried dishes that weighed twelve thousand pounds on his campaigns.

---

[294] (BC 115-53) a general and politician.
[295] a fighting general and "Prefect of the Provisions."

Pliny[296] reported that women would only bathe in silver baths and that soldiers had swords with glistening silver hilts. Even poor women owned anklets of silver, and enslaved people carried silver mirrors. Pliny noted that in the first century AD, "looking glasses were so widespread that even maidservants used them." From six thousand BC, mirrors were of highly polished volcanic stones called obsidian. Later, they used polished brass, then silver and gold."[297] At the Saturnalia Festival every year, benefactors often gave out presents of little silver spoons.

18:12 | The elite passionately loved **precious stones** and pearls which came to the west through Alexander the Great's[298] conquests. At a betrothal feast, Lollia Paulina,[299] one of Emperor Caligula's wives, wore her wealth worth eight hundred thousand dollars of jewels and pearls in her hair around her neck, arms, fingers, and even on her shoes.

18:12 | Romans valued **precious stone** cures for their medicinal qualities and believed that amethyst[300] fixed drunkenness and helped intuition! Emerald was an indicator of love, compassion, and abundance, and jasper was called bloodstone and thought to stop bleeding, whereas green jasper was said to be an infertility cure. Diamonds indicated purpose, neutralized poison, and cured delirium. Amber worn around the neck was a treatment for fever. Beryl and opal appeared as women's ornaments, and sardonyx embellished men's signet rings. Pliny the Elder[301] wrote elegantly, "A gem's fascination was that the majestic might of nature presented itself in a limited space." This admiration still applies today!

18:12 | The Romans were as superstitious as some people are today. They believed opals caused the expansion of emotions beyond their true importance. **Pearls** were thought to create

---

[296] (61-113 AD).

[297] by A.D. Paul, Kerala in South India. "Mirrors in the Bible and in Jewish Tradition." Jewish Currents archive.

[298] (BC 356-323).

[299] (15-49 AD) wife of Emperor Caligula for six months in 38 AD. Source Wikipedia.

[300] The word *amethyst* means "not to make drunk."

[301] (23-79 AD).

self-care, nurturing, and emotional healing. The Romans loved pearls more than any gemstone and often dissolved them in wine vinegar and drank them![302] Emperor Julius Caesar[303] gave his mistress Servilia Caepionis[304] a pearl worth one hundred and thirty thousand dollars which she drank! Christians do not look upon the beauty of gemstones as cures but to the Lord Jesus as the great and only healer.

18:12 | Beautiful expensive purple cloth for priests and kings originated in Phoenicia. The Romans called the Phoenicians[305] "the **purple** men." Ancient purple was much redder than its modern equivalent.

18:12 | **Silk** may be run-of-the-mill today, but it was imported from China in Roman times and produced by mulberry silkworm caterpillars. The cloth's smooth, silky appearance was due to the fiber's prism-like structure, which refracted light. Silk was worth its weight in gold. Emperor Tiberius[306] legislated "against men disgracing themselves with silken garments" considered too showy outside the royal family! Purple silk's color came from the costly dye *Tekhelet* collected from a few drops of blood from a specific type of cuttlefish. The High Priest's clothing used the dye on the tassels and corners of their prayer garments. A pound of double-dyed purple cloth or a short purple coat could cost a fortune. Purple silk represented affluence and became the wealthy's color of choice. Pliny the Younger tells us of "a frantic purple passion in Rome."

18:12 | **Scarlet cloth**, like purple, was in great demand. "Scarlet" comes from *coccus,* meaning a "tiny grain." These tiny, scaled insects that produced the bright red color were so small that workers thought them to be a kind of "grain, seed, or berry." Strangely, *Coccus* has also become the name of a bacteria type with a similar spherical shape, from which we get the more familiar

---

[302] According to Pliny,
[303] (BC 100-44).
[304] (BC 104-42).
[305] The word "Phoenicia" comes from *phoinos,* meaning "blood-red."
[306] 258 (BC 530-468).

term, "streptococcus," for a severe throat infection. *Coccus* insects feed on oak trees in Turkey, Persia, Armenia, and other parts of the Middle East. The dead insect produced a permanent color giving rise to the phrase "died in the wool" for someone who held inflexible beliefs and wouldn't change!

18:12 | Romans sought tables of **expensive wood** like citronwood. The "hadar tree," called "costly wood" or "majestic trees," made the very best furniture. This most unusual wood of *citrus medica* was from the orange, lemon, lime, and grapefruit family. It originated in the North African Atlas region and was sweet-smelling, beautifully grained, and highly prized. Timber big enough for tabletops was scarce since it was seldom sufficiently large. Tables could cost up to thirty thousand dollars each. Nero's prime minister, Seneca the Elder,[307] owned three hundred such tops with marble legs.

18:12 | From ancient to medieval times, Romans used citrus or **expensive wood** to combat seasickness, breathing problems, intestinal treatments, scurvy, and other ailments. The Romans believed that the citrus tree juice mixed with wine was an effective antidote for poison.

18:12 | Even though citron tree wood was **expensive**, Jewish rituals required it during the Feast of Tabernacles. Leviticus required the "fruit of majestic trees, branches of palm trees, and boughs of thick trees, and willows of the brook" (Lev. 23:40). Some Bible translations describe citron trees as "majestic, beautiful or goodly."

18:12 | Roman Citizens also greatly valued **ivory**,[308] marble, and bronze articles for decorative purposes. Since ancient times, artisans have created sculptures, statues, sword hilts, furniture, ceremonial chairs, and doors from ivory. Juvenal[309] wrote, "Nowadays, a rich man takes no pleasure in his dinner. His venison has no taste. His roses smell rotten unless the broad slabs of his dinner table rest upon a ramping, gaping leopard of

---

[307] (BC 54-c39 AD).
[308] (BC 42-37 AD) Ivory articles from "carved animal teeth or tusks."
[309] (c50-c100 AD)

solid ivory." He comments sarcastically on this craze, "Generally, common sense is rare in the higher ranks."

18:12 | Roman **brass, iron, and marble** statues were world-famous. Iron from the Black Sea and Spain was in great demand. Babylon had used marble in buildings, but ancient Rome did not. Emperor Augustus boasted that he had found Rome of brick and left it of marble. The hunt for beautiful marble to decorate Rome's buildings was so crucial that the government employed an official with the sole task of looking for it. As a site engineer on a 20-story building project in Birmingham, I was surprised to discover that the bank in the atrium displayed five different types of marble on its walls and floors shipped from all over the world. The Romans would have been proud!

18:13 | In ancient times, **cinnamon**,[310] fine wine, incense, and perfumes from the spice trade brought great wealth to merchants. They transported cinnamon from Northern India, China, and Arabia, from tree bark as a luxury spice for sweet and savory foods.

18:13 | **Cinnamon** was so valuable that merchants tried to conceal its source from others and concocted a tale that it came from cinnamon birds' nests, which didn't exist! Sweet-smelling cinnamon balsam provided Romans with oil for hairdressing and funeral rites. According to Pliny the Younger, one pound of cinnamon cost four hundred denarii, a working man's yearly wage. Usually, it was too expensive for funeral rites, but Emperor Nero burned Rome's yearly supply at his wife's funeral in 65 AD![311] Cinnamon perfume greeted guests at banquets and scented rooms after meals. Another similar spice called *cassia* from the Hebrew "to strip off the bark" came from Arabia and Ethiopia. "Spice and the spice trade" also included other substances like cardamom, ginger, pepper, and turmeric. Cinnamon, myrrh, cassia, spikenard, saffron, and other ingredients accompanied the incense in the Temple.

---

[310] "Cinnamon" from the Greek *kinnamomon* which referred to its mid-brown color. The English word appeared in the 15th century.

[311] Toussaint-Samat 2009, p. 437f.

18:13 | The merchants also traded **carriage**s. The "wagons" described are not racing or military chariots but four-wheeled private carriages for wealthy aristocrats to ride around Rome in style. They were the equivalent of the Camaro and Mustang muscle cars without the big engines and just two or four horsepower! Carriages were showy and often silver-plated!

18:13 | **Wine** was drunk by everyone in the ancient world, although drunkenness was frowned upon as it was considered a grave disgrace. Servants diluted two parts of wine with five of water, and even enslaved people received an ample daily ration.

18:13 | Revelation's list of merchants' business items close with the sad mention of **people's bodies and souls** or "human beings sold as enslaved persons." The Greek word for "enslaved person" is *soma* and means "a body." People were valuable commodities in the Roman world, and men, women, and children were routinely bought and sold. Civilization depended on serfs, and the merchants met this demand. Some scholars think there were sixty million enslaved people in the Roman empire, but others consider this too low. It was not unusual for one gentleman to own four hundred bondservants himself. One writer said, "Use your slaves like your body's limbs, each for its end." When Rome fell, the merchants wept and mourned over their lost profits.

18:13 | The slave market was "where merchants sell **people's bodies.**" Traders followed the Roman armies and bought the rights to take fit and healthy captives, which they auctioned off. Signs listing their qualities hung around their necks in the marketplace. Those considered "secondary goods" were offered separately and forced to wear a cap to indicate it! Traders were essential in providing serfs with various functions in Roman society. They were property, and their families had no rights. Over time, however, some were allowed to earn money, save, buy their freedom, and even own property. Many masters treated them kindly, like their own children.

18:13 | Merchants sold **people's bodies** for a variety of functions. Some whispered in their owner's ear and reminded them of their clients' names! The wealthy were sometimes too weary even to know they were hungry and needed someone to remind them. Enslaved people walked before their masters to return others' greetings when they were too tired or disdainful to answer. Traders sold men, women, and children for mainly menial work but sometimes more sophisticated tasks like writing, reading, or teaching children. Accountants and physicians were often enslaved persons. Lantern-bearers, sedan-chair carriers, street attendants, and outdoor garment keepers each had a particular service.

18:13 | Some secretaries read letters aloud or researched a treatise for a man writing a book. One servant memorized Homer[312] and another the lyrical poets and recited them back to their masters. Many stood behind their owner as he dined and prompted him with suitable quotations and helpful things to say to his neighbor. The merchants also sold **people's bodies** as oddities like dwarfs or giants. There was a demand for "men with short arms, three eyes or pointed heads." Merchants would artificially produce dwarfs for sale! It was a grim picture of salespeople manipulating human beings for profit and others' entertainment. Others called "Flowers of Asia" were handsome youths who, like the uniformed footmen on TV's "Downton Abbey," stood around at banquets to delight the eye of those attending! There were many cupbearers, but the guests often chose to wipe their greasy hands on their hair!

18:13 | Wiping one's hands on **people's** hair throws new light on the biblical account of a woman who poured perfume on the feet of Jesus and wiped them with her hair. "A woman in the city who was a sinner brought an alabaster jar of ointment. Standing behind at his feet weeping, she began to wet his feet with her tears, and she wiped them with the hair of her head, kissed his feet, and anointed them with the ointment" (Luke 7:37—38). She dried his feet with her hair just like an enslaved person. This touching gesture is very illuminating!

18:14 | The merchant's wealth failed with the empire's

---

[312] (c700 BC).

economic motor, and they lost their lucrative trade. John of Patmos writes that **all things that were dainty and sumptuous have perished** forever.

18:14 l The **merchants** probably counted their losses on a hand "abacus," the first portable calculating device for merchants, engineers, and tax collectors, which significantly reduced the time performing basic arithmetic. These counting boards were called *calculi*, no doubt the source of our modern word "calculator." The Latin word *calx*, meaning little stone, comes from the string of pebbles counted on an abacus. The market's collapse was the end that John of Patmos anticipated, for a society built on wealth, wantonness, pride, and callousness to human life is necessarily doomed, even from the human point of view.

Question: "Was the slavery system essential or not for Rome's success?"

68

ROMAN SHIP CAPTAINS

18:17 "For in an hour such great riches are made desolate. Every **ship master**, and everyone who sails anywhere, and mariners, and as many as gain their living by sea, stood far away, [18] and cried out as they looked at the smoke of her **burning**, saying, 'What is like the great city?' [19] They cast dust on their heads, and cried, **weeping and mourning** saying, 'Woe, woe, the great city, in which all who had their ships in the sea were made rich by reason of her great wealth!' For she is made desolate in one hour. [20] "Rejoice over her, O heaven, you saints, apostles, and prophets; for God has **judged** your judgment on her." (Rev. 18:17-20 emphases added).

18:17 | Kings, merchants, and every Roman **ship master** wept over Rome. John of Patmos undoubtedly recalled Tyre's fall when the mariners stood on the shore. They "will cause their voice to be heard over you and cry bitterly. They will cast up dust on their heads. They will wallow in the ashes" (Ezek. 27:30).

18:17 | Although Rome received copious goods from the sea, it was not situated on the coast but fifteen miles inland on an inlet. Its port, Ostia Antica, was at the mouth of its principal river, the Tiber, which was close enough to Rome to see it **burning**. At its founding around 620 B.C., Ostia began using the salt gleaned from nearby flats as a valuable meat and fish preservative. The world's merchandise flowed from ocean-going ships to Rome. Today, some beautiful floor mosaics exist in Ostia, advertising merchants' goods like fish or wheat. The ship's captains and sailors lamented that the trade, which brought so much wealth to them, was now gone.

18:19 | The merchants **weeping and mourning** were not for the city of Rome but themselves. The joyful sound belonged to those glad to see God's revenge on his enemies and persecutors. "Rejoice, you nations, with his people, for he will avenge the blood of his servants. He will take vengeance on his adversaries, and will make atonement for his land and his people" (Deut. 32:43).

18:19 l Abraham Lincoln's friends told him he was too lenient on his opponents and must destroy his adversaries. He answered, "Do I not destroy my enemies when I make them my friends?" The people here are not praying for those who despitefully use them, for whatever we may feel about this voice of vengeance, it is the voice of faith. These men and women are confident that no one on God's side can lose in the end. There is no personal bitterness, for people are not our enemies so much as God's. At the same time, this is not the most excellent way. Jesus encourages us to make our enemies into our friends. The best Christian attitude is to destroy hostility, not by force, but by the power of the love of Calvary's cross.

Question: "Why are the ship captains so upset?"

69

BABYLON'S DESTRUCTION

18:21 "A mighty angel took up a stone like a great millstone and cast it into the sea, saying, "Thus with violence will **Babylon**, the great city, be thrown down, and will be found no more at all. ²² The **voice** of harpists, minstrels, flute players, and trumpeters will be heard no more at all in you. No craftsman, of whatever craft, will be found any more at all in you. The **sound of a mill** will be heard no more at all in you. ²³ The **light of a lamp** will shine no more at all in you. The voice of the bridegroom and of the bride will be heard no more at all in you; for your merchants were the princes of the earth; for with your sorcery all the nations were deceived. ²⁴ In her was found the **blood of prophets** and of saints, and of all who have been slain on the earth." (Rev. 18:21—24 emphases added).

18:21 | Ancient Rome and her final devastation begin with a symbolic action. A mighty angel takes a massive millstone and hurls it into the sea. He symbolically obliterates Rome. John may be remembering the stories of the earlier destruction of ancient **Babylon**. Jeremiah tied a stone to the scroll he had read and cast it into the middle of the Euphrates River. The Lord says, "Thus will Babylon sink, and will not rise again because of the evil that I will bring on her" (Jer. 51:64).

18:21 | Strabo, whose name meant "squinty"[313] because of his poor eyesight, constructed a map called "Geographica" in seventeen volumes of the known world between BC 7 and 18 AD. Interestingly, Columbus probably used a 1469 translation of it when he set out to discover the new world. Strabo noted in his original that the obliteration of ancient **Babylon** was so complete that no one dared to say that the desert where it stood was once a great city. It was abandoned and empty.

18:22 | The Lord's doom song against Tyre was, "I will cause the noise of your songs to cease. The sound of your harps won't be heard anymore" (Ezek. 26:13). The **voice** of your songs will end. The festival and funeral flute, the games trumpet, concerts, and all music are now to be silent. Even the love of a bride and groom and the strains of a happy occasion will disappear. Never again in Babylon would anyone hear the noise of a craftsman plying his trade.

18:22 | The **sound of a mill** grinding grain or even laughter at a wedding will cease. The clatter of course wheat ground into fine flour with two circular millstones, one revolving on the other, will end.

18:23 | John of Patmos continues that you will never again see the light of a lamp in your streets or houses. Christianity saw the light as a symbol of eternal life and God's wisdom. It was symbolic of a source of spiritual or intellectual inspiration. Oil lamps lit homes in Roman times, and the earliest form was a bowl filled with olive oil and a wick laid on the rim. Later they developed a pinched vessel and a clay lamp with a nozzle for one or more wicks.

18:23 | World Archeology magazine[314] writes that **the light of a lamp** "was used in temples, churches, synagogues, and mosques but was also an essential household appliance. A husband was obliged to supply an oil lamp for his wife, even if he separated

---

[313] "Squinty" was a Roman term for anyone with distorted or deformed eyes! In later years, Strabo struggled with the mysterious question of why seashells could be found so many miles from the sea and often embedded in rock!

[314] © 2022 Current Publishing. All rights reserved.

from her. An individual who lacked a lamp was in desperate straits: to be 'in want of all things' meant 'in want of lamp, knife, and table." Unique motifs often decorated clay lamps. Jewish lamps showed the Temple facade, while Christians illustrated theirs with different types of crosses, and Pagan lights invariably pictured scenes of harbors with ships. But here, John of Patmos says the lamp light will be no more.

18:24 | Jeremiah issues a similar prophecy, "Moreover I will take from them the voice of mirth and the voice of gladness, the voice of the bridegroom and the voice of the bride, the sound of the millstones, and the light of the lamp" (Jer. 25:10). Rome was to become a silent, desolate city. This punishment was because she worshiped affluence and found no pleasure except in material things. Rome flirted with evil powers and magic spells, and she was guilty of spilling the **blood of prophets,** for, within Rome, martyrs died, and persecution spread over the whole earth.

Question: "What would life be like without essentials like an oil lamp, a wedding celebration, or fresh flour for bread? What are their parallels today?

70

HALLELUJAH PRAISE SHOUT

19:1 "After these things I heard something like a loud voice of a **great multitude in heaven,** saying, "**Hallelujah! Salvation, power, and glory** belong to our God; [2] for his judgments are true and righteous. For he has judged the great prostitute, who corrupted the earth with her sexual immorality, and he has avenged the blood of his servants at her hand." [3] A second said, "Hallelujah! Her smoke goes up forever and ever." [4] The twenty-four elders and the four living creatures fell down and worshiped God who sits on the throne, saying, "Amen! Hallelujah!" [5] A voice came from the throne, saying, "Give praise to our God, all you his servants, you who fear him, the small and the great!" [6] I heard something like the voice of a great multitude, and like the voice of many waters, and the voice of mighty thunders, saying, "**Hallelujah! For the Lord our God, the Almighty, reigns!**" (Rev. 19:1—6 emphases added).

19:1 | The hallelujah praise shout rises from a **great multitude in heaven.** We have already come across two vast holy choirs, the "ten thousands of ten thousands, and thousands of thousands angels" (Rev. 5:11) and the great multitude "of every nation and of all tribes, peoples, and languages" (Rev. 7:9). John of Patmos says that he hears something like the sound of a great crowd, the rush of many waters, and the claps of mighty thunders. They bring a combined cheer of "praise God."

19:1 | The religious leader Ezra also wrote about a praise cheer from **a great multitude** when they laid the foundation of the Lord's house. All the people shouted with a loud cry "because the foundation of Yahweh's house had been laid" (Ezra 3:11). Many priests, Levites, and family heads, who had seen the first temple, sobbed aloud when they laid the new stones, and many others screamed uncontrollably. They could not discern the cry of delight from the sound of weeping. Some "wept with a loud voice." Others "shouted aloud for joy" (Ezra 3:12).

19:1 | The heavenly praise shout begins with **hallelujah.** This word meaning "God be praised," "praise God," or "praise the Lord" occurs as "halleluyah," "alleluia," or "halleluiah." *Hallelujah* comes from two Hebrew words, *Hallel,* meaning "a joyous praise in song," and *Jah,* "the name of God." Today, it is a popular religious word, but it only appears four times in the scriptures and on every occasion in this Revelation chapter. It is one of only a few Hebrew words established in the English religious language. *Hallelujah* and "Praise the Lord" have become acceptable spontaneous expressions of joy, thanksgiving, and praise towards God in many Christian denominations.

19:1 | **Hallelujah** became a praise response in the early church's Easter worship. Although it appears only in Revelation, it occurs elsewhere in a different translated form as "Praise God."[315] Psalms 113-118 are called the "Hallel Psalms" and are part of every Jewish boy's essential education. Psalms 113 and 117 begin with "Praise Yah." *Hallelujah* is similar to *hosanna* or the Hebrew *Hoshana* used at the Palm Sunday entrance into Jerusalem. *Hosanna* means "help" or "save I pray," as in "Save us now, we beg you, Yahweh!" (Ps. 118:25).

19:1 | The performer Leonard Cohen[316] immortalized the word

---

[315] This phrase begins Psalms 106, 111-113, 117, 135, and 146-150.

[316] Words and music Leonard Norman Cohen (1934-2016) Selected verses. Source: Musixmatch. Songwriter: Leonard Cohen. Hallelujah lyrics © Sony/atv Songs Llc, Leo Robin Music Co. Columbia Records Release date December 11, 1984

"**Hallelujah**" in his songs. His lyrics caught some of the sense of worship that sprang from this beautiful word. Some interpreters believe he was in a heated conversation with God." He wrote, "But you don't really care for music, do you?" He struggled to find the right chords, "the fourth, the fifth, the minor falls, the major shifts," to express his faltering praise. He was encouraged that David played "and it pleased the Lord." Cohen wrote eighty draft verses for "Hallelujah" over seven years, yet the studio version used only seven of them. The verses were envelopes for the chorus itself. He concluded each one with a gasp of exhaustion that there was "nothing on my tongue but hallelujah." Artists have recorded this song again and again because they felt its lilting praise power.

> "Now I've heard there was a sacred chord,
> That David played, and it pleased the Lord.
> It goes like this, the fourth, the fifth
> The minor falls, the major lifts
> The baffled king composing Hallelujah.
> I'll stand right here before the lord of song
> With nothing on my tongue
> But hallelujah. Hallelujah."

19:1 | After hallelujah, we read of God's three great attributes of **salvation, power, and glory** to awaken our hearts,

- "Salvation" releases our gratitude for the sacrifice of the crucified Jesus.
- "Power" revives our trust in him alone.
- "Glory" evokes our reverence for creation's greatness all around us.

These are constituent elements of praise.

19:6 | The multitude in heaven raises a tumultuous cry, **hallelujah, for the Lord our God, the Almighty, reigns.** Praise is the heartfelt response of those who love God. The more you get to know him and realize what he has done for you, the more you will respond in this way. Acclamation is at the center of true worship, though it may sometimes be more of a whisper than a bellow. It emanates from a heart crammed full of praise. There is a lovely chorus,

> "Let the power of your presence, Lord Jesus
> From the center of my life shine through.
> Oh, let everybody know it,
> I really want to show it,
> That the center of my life is you."[317]

Let your applause flow from realizing who the Lord is and how much he loves you.

Question: "Is your hallelujah praise shout more of a whisper than a bellow? Can you learn how to praise?"

---

[317] Copyright Alan Price © Daybreak Music 1990

71

LAMB'S MARRIAGE SUPPER

19:7 "Let's **rejoice and be exceedingly glad,** and let's give the glory to him. For the **wedding of the Lamb** has come, and his wife has made herself ready." ⁸ It was given to her that she would array herself in bright, pure, **fine linen:** the fine linen is the righteous acts of the saints. ⁹ He said to me, "Write, 'Blessed are those who are invited to the **wedding supper** of the Lamb.'" He told me, "These are true words of God." ¹⁰ I fell down before his feet to worship him. He said to me, "Look! Don't do it! I am a fellow bondservant with you and with your brothers who hold the testimony of Jesus. **Worship God,** for the testimony of Jesus is the **Spirit of Prophecy.**" (Rev. 19:7—10 emphases added).

19:7 | The redeemed hosts shout, **"rejoice and be exceedingly glad."** The verbs "rejoice" and "be glad" are combined in other places. The Psalmist writes, "let the earth rejoice! Let the multitude of islands be glad!" (Ps. 97:1). Later, he says, "we will rejoice and be glad!" (Ps. 118:24). Then, Jesus announces, "Rejoice and be exceedingly glad" (Matt. 5:12). The multitudes rejoice and are thrilled to be redeemed.

19:8 | God's holy people receive **fine linen** garments indicating their saintliness. The church, the bride of Jesus, is clothed in shining whiteness in startling contrast to the great harlot's scarlet and gold. Their glowing white garments represent God's purity and holiness. John of Patmos is told, "The fine linen is the righteous acts of the saints." Radiant or brilliant robes are indicators that the wearer comes from God's presence.

19:9 | Next comes the **wedding supper** for the Lamb's bride. This banquet cements the union between Jesus and his church. Marriage symbolism denotes the intimate and indissoluble relationship of Christ with the community he has purchased with his blood.

19:9 | The **wedding of the Lamb** is a metaphor for Christian marriage. Again and again, the prophets in the Old Testament thought of Israel as "God's chosen bride." Isaiah wrote, "for your maker is your husband" (Isa. 54:5). Many Jewish people believed God would welcome his people into a magnificent banquet when the Messiah eventually came.

19:9 | Marriage symbolism and the **wedding supper of the Lamb** appear throughout the Gospels. Jesus describes the marriage banquet as "a certain king who made a wedding feast for his son" (Matt. 22:2). He also speaks of "groomsmen," saying, "Can the groomsmen fast while the bridegroom is with them? (Mark 2:19). The term "bridegroom" here indicates Christ himself. The first mention of *bridegroom* dates to 1604, from the Old English *brydguma*, a compound of *bryd* (bride) and *guma* (man).

19:9 | For Paul, Christ's relationship to his church at the **wedding supper** is the ideal model for the union of a husband and wife. The concept of Christian marriage and the Lamb's wedding supper contains certain great mutual truths. In any Christian marriage, love must be central, for a loveless marriage is a contradiction in terms. There may be intimate communion when a man and his wife become one, but the union of Jesus with us must be the closest relationship ever, for there is nothing like the joy of loving and being cared for by Jesus. Paul writes to the Corinthian church, "I married you to one husband, that I might present you as a pure virgin to Christ" (2 Cor. 11:2). Christians must be as faithful to Jesus as he is to them.

19:10 | In this passage, John of Patmos calls The Father by the unique name, **God Almighty.** The word used here is *Pantokrator* which means "the one who controls all things," "The Almighty," or "The All-powerful." The significant thing about *Pantokrator* is that it occurs only ten times in the New Testament, with nine in Revelation. Paul writes, "says the Lord Almighty" (2 Cor. 6:18).

19:10 | Some Eastern Orthodox Churches paint their central domes with the "Jesus Christ Pantokrator" image. They deliberately show different facial expressions on either side of the face of Jesus, which may represent Christ's two natures as fully divine and fully human. In other words, "Lord **Almighty**" is the typical title for God the Father in Revelation but may also indicate God the Son as in "the Lord God, 'who is and who was and who is to come, the Almighty'" (Rev. 1:8). The references to God the Father and God the Son are at times interchangeable. The use of "Lord Almighty" as "the one who controls all things" is remarkable when hostile forces stand against the church, and Christians endure great suffering and the prospect of a cruel death. Yet, John calls God "the Lord Almighty!"

19:10 | John of Patmos faints and falls over at the appearance of the angel messenger, who responds, "Don't do that! Worship God, for the testimony of Jesus is the **Spirit of Prophecy.**" All Scripture points to Jesus, whose word is the focal point of all prophecy. It reminds me of the excellent advice given to novice preachers, "Start anywhere but finish with Jesus."

Question: "Are you looking forward to attending the Lamb's marriage supper?"

72

JESUS KING OF KINGS

19:11 "I saw the **heaven opened,** and behold, a **white horse**, and he who sat on it is called **Faithful and True.** In righteousness he judges and makes war. [12] His eyes are a flame of fire, and on his head are many crowns. He has names written and a name written which no one knows but he himself. [13] He is clothed in a garment sprinkled with blood. His name is called "The **Word of God.**" [14] The armies which are in heaven followed him on white horses, clothed in white, pure, fine linen. [15] Out of his mouth proceeds a sharp, double-edged sword, that with it he should strike the nations. He will rule them with an iron rod. He treads the wine press of the fierceness of the wrath of God, the Almighty. [16] He has on his garment and on his thigh a name written, "**KING OF KINGS,** AND LORD OF LORDS." (Rev. 19:11—16 emphases added).

19:11 | John of Patmos sees one of the most dramatic moments after **heaven opened,** the conquering king's emergence. H. B. Swete wrote of Jesus as "a royal commander followed by a dazzling retinue." Jewish dreams are full of this warrior Messiah, who will lead God's people to victory and destroy their enemies. The wonderfully named "Targums of Onkelos and Jonathan ben

Uzziel"[318] describe the Rabbinic Messiah, "How beauteous is the King Messiah, who shall rise from the house of Jehudah.[319] He has bound his loins and gone to war against those who hate him, kings and princes, whom he will slay."

19:11 | Next, the **white horse** or war horse shows Jesus like a victorious general riding into Rome in a triumphal parade to celebrate his battle victories. Romans were familiar with successful leaders on white mounts entering the city with captives and booty to the crowd's cheers. King Jesus on a snowy stallion contrasts with riding on a donkey through Jerusalem's Golden Gate, but he is a king on both occasions!

19:11 | Jesus Christ is then called the **Faithful and True** and comes to bring justice to the nations in line with Jewish expectations. Rabbi Dovid Zaklikowski[320] writes, "For thousands of years, Jewish people have been evoking 'Blessed is the true judge' at funerals in response to death and tragedy." The Greek for "true" is *alethinos*, meaning "the one who never has any falsehood in anything he says." *Alethinos* also means "genuine," "honest," and "not fake." The Greek for "Faithful" is *pistos*, meaning "reliable and trustworthy."

19:11 | Genuine truth is sometimes hard to find. Harvard University's motto in Cambridge, Massachusetts, is *Veritas*, meaning **truth,** and the engraving on Harvard's statue reads, "John Harvard, Founder, 1638." However, the Puritan clergyman wasn't the university's founder but its benefactor. Also, the date is incorrect, as the university was founded in 1636, not 1638. Furthermore, the statue is not of John Harvard either because there are no known accurate representations of him. Daniel Chester French[321] sculpted the famous statue in 1884, and Sherman Hoar[322] modeled it as a young man for him. Hoar later became a member of Congress and US District Attorney for Massachusetts. The

[318] on the Pentateuch Volume 1"
[319] (Judah).
[320] in the "Jewish Blessing on Death,"
[321] (1850-1931).
[322] (1860-1898).

university motto is "Devoted to excellence in teaching, learning, and research, and to developing leaders who make a difference globally." Being devoted to truth is something else!

19:11 | John of Patmos understood the problem of determining what is **true**, describing Jesus Christ as "Faithful and True." He knew all about the perversion of justice, for no one could expect it from a tyrant emperor and his apparatus, for even the proconsul's tribunal in Asia Minor was subject to bribery. Wars were matters of ambition, tyranny, and oppression rather than justice. But when Jesus Christ, the supreme judge, comes, he will exercise his power righteously and truthfully.

19:13 | Jesus, with the new name, the **Word of God**, rides out of heaven with an angelic army on white horses to destroy the godless nations and shatter unrighteous rulers. This new title conveys the reality that from the beginning, "The Word was with God, and the Word was God" (John 1:1).

19:16 | The entrance of Jesus reveals him as the **King of Kings**. The first monarch to have called himself "King of Kings" was Tukulti-Ninurta I.[323] He used it as a city-state emperor with other sovereigns in submission to him. With his empire's formation, Assyrian kings became rulers over city-states. The title was adopted later by the Babylonian ruler Nebuchadnezzar.[324] Ezekiel writes, "Nebuchadnezzar, king of Babylon, king of kings, from the north." (Ezek. 26:7). Daniel calls him, "You, O king, are the king of kings" (Dan. 2:37). His full name was "Great King, King of Kings, King in Fars, King of the Countries."

19:16 | In Judaism, the **King of Kings** is taken up a notch above the Babylonian and Persian rulers' royal titles as the new King of Kings of Kings. Being a monarch was not an honorary position in ancient days, for it required brutality to put down one's enemies.

19:16 | Although Jesus is called the "**King of Kings** and Lord of Lords," this verse implies that no name can do him justice, for he has absolute sovereignty. Most of the world worships the beast

---

[323] of Assyria (BC c1243-c1207).
[324] (BC 643-562).

and the Antichrist, but suddenly, Jesus rides out of heaven with an angelic army and his name written on his robes and thigh. A chorus to a traditional Israeli tune swirls around in my mind.

"King of Kings and Lord of Lords, Glory Hallelujah.
Jesus, Prince of Peace, Glory Hallelujah."[325]

19:16 | The **King of Kings'** entrance signals the end of false powers, for when a king conquers another nation, the defeated sovereign bows to the more powerful one and casts his crown symbolically before him. The word used for "cast," meaning "to cause to move or send forth by throwing," is also employed in the phrases "cast a fishing lure" and "cast dice." When we meet Jesus in heaven, we will willingly and joyfully throw down our crowns and kneel before him!

Question: "How would you visualize the grand entry of the King of Kings today?"

[325] Writers "Naomi Batya and Sophie Conty" Publisher/Copyright "1980 Universal Music – Brentwood Benson Publishing."

73

BEAST NERO RESURRECTED

19:17 "I saw an angel standing in the sun. He cried with a loud voice, saying to all the birds that fly in the sky, "Come! Be gathered together to the great supper of God, [18] that you may eat the flesh of kings, the flesh of captains, the flesh of mighty men, and the flesh of horses and of those who sit on them, and the flesh of all men, both free and slave, small and great." [19] I saw the **beast**, and the kings of the earth, and their armies, gathered together to make war against him who sat on the horse, and against his army. [20] The beast was taken, and with him the **false prophet** who worked the signs in his sight, with which he deceived those who had received the beast's mark and **those who worshiped his image**. These two were thrown alive into the lake of fire that burns with sulfur. [21] The rest were killed with the sword of him who sat on **the horse**, the sword which came out of his mouth. So all the birds were filled with their flesh." (Rev. 19:17—21 emphases added).

19:19 | The early church called the **beast** by the Latin name *Nero Redivivus*, which meant "Resurrected Nero." During the early centuries AD, there was a widespread notion that somehow he would return after his death.

19:20 | Nero[326] was the fifth and last emperor of Augustus' dynasty. Christians came to believe he was the **false prophet** meaning "anyone who, without having it, claims a special connection to the deity and sets him or herself up as a source of spirituality, as an authority, preacher, or teacher."[327] Jesus warns, "Beware of false prophets, who come to you in sheep's clothing, but inwardly are ravening wolves" (Matt. 7:15). He tells them, "Be careful that no one leads you astray. For many will come in my name, saying, 'I am he!'" (Mark 13:5-6).

19:20 | Several variations of the **false prophet** legend existed, playing on the hopes and fears of Nero's return. The earliest written version[328] claimed that he did not die but fled to Parthia, where he assembled a large army to return to destroy Rome. This legend pivoted later to a belief that he was the Antichrist.

19:20 | At least three Nero imposters emerged to lead rebellions and were all considered **false prophets**. The first appeared in 69 AD. He sang and played the *kithara*[329] or *lyre*[330] and even looked like the dead emperor. The Greek word *kithara* is the source of the modern word "guitar." Another impostor, who also looked like him, appeared in Asia but was exposed. Twenty years after his death, during Domitian's reign, a third pretender arose supported by the Parthians.

19:20 | Nero, who became the **false prophet,** was born Lucius Domitius Ahenobarbus in 37 AD. His mother was Agrippina, the sister of Emperor Caligula. Growing up in Rome as part of a powerful elite family, he probably knew of the new Christian "sect" among the Jews that had migrated from Jerusalem and Judea. When he was seventeen years old, his mother married Emperor Claudius after his father's mysterious death. As he was then known, Lucius became emperor after the poisoning of Claudius by his mother that very same year. He took the ancestral

---

[326] Nero ruled from 54 to 68 AD.
[327] Wikipedia for "False Prophet."
[328] in the Sibylline Oracles.
[329] an ancient Greek and Roman stringed musical instrument similar to the *lyre*."
[330] a small U-shaped harp with strings fixed to a crossbar

name of Nero Claudius Caesar Augustus Germanicus, claiming descent from his step-father Claudius and Augustus, his great grandfather. Nero was part of an elite family with great power. He was popular with the members of his Praetorian Guard and lower-class commoners in Rome and its provinces, but the Roman aristocracy deeply resented him.

19:20 | In his fifth year as emperor in 59 AD, Nero, the **false prophet,** appointed Festus as procurator in Judea. Paul had been imprisoned for two years by his predecessor Felix before they charged him with crimes against the Jewish people. Festus attempted to send him to Jerusalem for trial in a religious court, but Paul insisted on being tried before the emperor himself as a Roman citizen.

19:20 | Though Paul had asked for an audience with Nero, believed to be the **false prophet,** political considerations at that time kept this from happening. Claudius had once exiled Jews from Rome, but circumstances had improved by the time Paul arrived. He met with many believers in the house where he was confined and preached there for two years within the capital of the world's most powerful government. He reached many for Christ "in Caesar's household."

19:20 | Nero released Paul in 63 AD but became paranoid, living up to his title of the "**false prophet.**" Both Peter and Paul testified that Rome was persecuting the church and warned of these coming harsh conditions. In a late edition of Paul's second letter to Timothy, a postscript identified Nero as Caesar during Paul's final imprisonment. When the Jewish people revolted in 67 AD, Nero put down the rebellion. He died young, committing suicide at the age of thirty after being declared a "public enemy" by the Roman Senate. Civil war broke out in Rome, and three contenders for emperor arose during the year until Vespasian returned and began his reign.[331]

19:20 | In Nero's fifteen years as emperor, most contemporary sources described him as authoritarian, indulgent, and lustful,

---

[331] Vespasian ruled 70-79 AD.

supporting his title as the **false prophet.** The general persecution subsided as John dictated his gospel. Nero had to be on his mind when he warned of fresh persecution.

19:20 | Nero, the **false prophet,** seemed to be the "man of sin" or the "man of lawlessness" to which Paul had referred. "Let no one deceive you in any way. For it will not be unless the rebellion comes first. The man of sin is revealed, the son of destruction who opposes and exalts himself against all that is called God" (2 Thess. 2:3—4). "Son of destruction" is equated with the "Antichrist" in Christian thought. Peter and Paul's martyrdoms were the acts of an "anti-Christ," and many in the following centuries considered Nero the "coming Antichrist."

19:20 | Some Christians also considered Nero to represent in a general sense the provincial organization administering Caesar worship, controlling the beast's mark and **"those who worshiped his image."** Christians believed Nero would lead the dreaded "Parthian hosts" from Iraq and Iran against Rome. The horse rider here is Christ, defeating all evil powers, including the resurrected Nero. Forces hostile to God assembled, but the warrior Christ conquered them. God cast the Antichrist's followers into the fiery lake of burning sulfur, and all their slain supporters waited in Sheol for the final judgment. With these events, the cosmic drama was drawing to a close.

Question: "Can you imagine Nero playing a guitar-like instrument and singing?"

74

DEVIL ABYSS

20:1 "I saw an angel coming down out of heaven, having the
key of the **abyss** and a great chain in his hand. ²He seized
the dragon, the old serpent, which is the devil and Satan,
who deceives the whole inhabited earth, and bound him for a
thousand years, ³and cast him into the abyss, and shut it, and
sealed it over him, that he should deceive the nations no more,
until the thousand years were finished. After this, he must be
freed for a short time. ⁴I saw thrones, and they sat on them, and
judgment was given to them. I saw the souls of those who had
been beheaded for the testimony of Jesus, and for the word of
God, and such as didn't worship the beast nor his image, and
didn't receive the mark on their forehead and on their hand.
They lived and reigned with Christ for a thousand years."
(Rev. 20:1—4 emphases added.)

20:1 The general resurrection will occur after Satan is bound
and cast into the **abyss,** which is then shut and sealed for a
thousand years. The abyss[332] may be either a "subterranean cavern,
bottomless pit, desolate place, gorge or chasm connected to the
surface by a shaft." It reminds me of the 1959 movie "Journey to

---

[332] Abyss dates back to the 14th century from the middle English *abissus*, the Latin
abyssus, and the Greek *abyssos*, meaning "bottomless." It is equivalent to *byssos*,
meaning the "bottom of the sea."

the Center of the Earth" based on a book by Jules Verne. My dad and I saw it at the Regent cinema in Birkenhead, showing James Mason, Pat Boone, and a group of explorers descending into a dormant volcano and emerging in a light-filled cave beside an underground ocean. We both enjoyed the film. It was a great movie! Maybe the Abyss is like this inactive volcano reaching the earth's center; who knows? In Revelation, the angel locks the shaft with a key to keep the Devil in prison.

20.1 | The word **abyss** has found its way into everyday usage, like "Abyssinia" for Ethiopia. The Queen of Sheba originated there, according to the historian Josephus.[333] King Halle Selassie[334] ruled until a military coup overthrew him in 1974. Many Rastafarians claim descent from the Queen of Sheba and King Solomon and, therefore, to be distant relatives of Jesus! In June 2020, King Halle Selassie was in the news again when his statue in Cannizaaro Park, London, was destroyed by protesters.

20:1 | Devils seem to fear the **abyss** more than anything else. In the story of Legion, many evil spirits possessed a demoniac man from the eastern Gadarene shore of the Sea of Galilee. They begged Jesus not to force them into the Abyss but to go into a herd of pigs, and Jesus allowed them. "The herd rushed down the steep bank into the lake and drowned" (Luke 8:33). The demons feared the pain and punishment of the Abyss. It is locked, and Satan was tied up there for a thousand years.

20:4 | The twelve apostles and Israel's twelve leaders will sit on their thrones as **judges.** The word "martyr" from the Greek word *martys* means "witness," like the protomartyr Stephen. They gave their lives, whereas confessors suffered but did not die.[335] Edward the Confessor ruled England for twenty-four years and was one of the last Anglo-Saxon kings. His name reflects the traditional view of confessors as "unworldly and

---

[333] Josephus in Antiquities 2.5-2.10.

[334] (1892-1975)

[335] H. B. Swete defines "confessors" as "those who, although they did not die, willingly bore suffering, reproach, imprisonment, loss of goods, disruption of their homes and personal relationships for the sake of Christ."

pious." He had an uncle named King Edward the Martyr[336] who died for his faith.

20:4 | Those who died for Christ and those who live for him will receive an appropriate reward. Jesus also allows a chosen group of disciples the privilege of being part of the final **judgment**. This concept appears more than once in the New Testament, where Jesus says, "when the Son of Man will sit on the throne of his glory, you also will sit on twelve thrones, judging the twelve tribes of Israel" (Matt. 19:28).

20:4 | In the sheep and goats parable, **judge** Jesus receives glory when he comes with his angels and sits on his throne. All the nations will gather, "and he will separate them one from another, as a shepherd separates the sheep from the goats" (Matt. 25:32).

20:4 | Paul reminds us that the destiny of the saints is to **judge**. He asks, "Don't you know that the saints will judge the world?" (1 Cor. 6:2). The coming world will redress the balance of this one. A Christian may be under judgment but in the life to come, the judges will be "the judged!" Paul's speech in Athens adds, "God has appointed a day in which he will judge the world in righteousness by the man whom he has ordained" (Acts 17:31). Jesus is the one who is to judge the living and the dead, and this he will do through his apostles!

Question: "What is the Abyss like, do you think?"

---

[336] (962-978)

75

JESUS CHRIST'S MARTYRS

20:5 "The rest of the dead didn't live until the **thousand years** were finished. This is the **first resurrection**. ⁶ Blessed and holy is he who has part in the first resurrection. Over these, the second death has no power, but they will be **priests of God** and of Christ, and will reign with him one thousand years. ⁷ And after the thousand years, Satan will be released from his prison, ⁸ and he will come out to deceive the nations which are in the four corners of the earth, **Gog and Magog**, to gather them together to the war; the number of whom is as the sand of the sea. ⁹ They went up over the width of the earth, and surrounded the camp of the saints, and the beloved city. Fire came down out of heaven from God and devoured them. ¹⁰ The devil who deceived them was thrown into the lake of fire and sulfur, where the beast and the false prophet are also. They will be tormented day and night forever and ever." (Rev. 20:5—10 emphases added).

20:5 | Judge Jesus reigns for a **thousand** years and rules the earth, the Devil, and the Abyss. God releases the devil's bonds in the end, but he has not learned his lesson, for he continues where he left off. He assembles the nations for one final attack before the judgment. Jesus, on his great white throne, symbolizes purity and integrity. He announces, "the Father judges no one, but he has given all judgment to the Son" (John 5:22).

20:5 | The **first resurrection** describes those who die and rise from death. God raises the martyrs, confessors, and those who have suffered and shown loyalty to Christ in the first resurrection. One way the authorities cruelly executed martyrs was to behead them with an ax. Two of King Henry the Eighth's wives and cousins were beheaded this way, which was more humane than hanging! "Confessors," on the other hand, resisted worship of the beast and did not receive his mark on their hands or foreheads. Historians debate the exact date and place where Paul died. Still, they universally accept that he would have been beheaded as a Roman citizen and therefore entitled to be spared a brutal crucifixion or other death.

20:6 | By his demise on the cross, Jesus became a bridge between God and human beings. The Latin for "priest" is *pontifex*, which has been used since 1579, comes from *pont* for bridge and *facere* to equal "a bridge-builder" or bridge maker. Christians can be bridge-builders and **priests of God** as they point people to Jesus.

20:6 | One summer evening, I remember talking to a man outside a bingo hall in Blackpool. He shared how his prison had released him after three years. He had heard our group singing and wondered what he would do with his life now. A team member had sung, "The old rugged cross," and had moved him. On the corner, in the dark, he committed his life to Christ. I happened to be the intermediary, but Jesus made his new life possible by dying on the cross. The great bridge-builder is the only one who can make that connection complete by bringing God and human beings together. The human **priest** is a pale shadow of Jesus, not capable of bringing God and mortals together but can introduce Jesus, the perfect bridge-builder.

20:8 | In Jewish thought, **Gog and Magog** stood for everything evil against God. The titles came from the Hebrew, *Gog u-Magog*, where Gog was an individual and Magog was his land. So we read, "Son of man, set your face toward Gog, of the land of Magog" (Ezek. 38:2). These hostile armies under Gog from Magog advanced against God's people and Jerusalem. Fire from heaven consumed them and cast the devil, the beast, and the false prophet into the lake of fire and brimstone.

Question: "Are you a bridge-builder, and have you built any bridges lately?"

76

GREAT WHITE THRONE

20:11 "I saw a **great white throne**, and him who sat on it, from whose face the **earth and the heaven fled** away. There was found no place for them. [12] I saw **the dead,** the great and the small, standing before the throne, and they **opened books.** Another book was opened, which is the **book of life.** The dead were **judged** out of the things which were written in the books, according to their works. [13] The sea **gave up the dead** who were in it. Death and Hades gave up the dead who were in them. They were judged, each one according to his works. [14] Death and Hades were thrown into the **lake of fire.** This is the second death, the lake of fire. [15] If anyone was not found written in the book of life, he was cast into the lake of fire." (Rev. 20:11—15 emphases added).

20:11 | In chapter twenty, we hear the final announcements and see the judge on his **great white throne.** Its gleaming fine porcelain whiteness reminds us of God's holiness and purity. The throne concept comes from the "place of judgment" at the Olympics in ancient Athens, where an official sat on the *Bema* or "Judgment Seat" at the finish line of the races. It was where he decided what position the runners finished, whether first, second, or third, and then presented the appropriate awards.

20:11 | Judgement seats like the **great white throne** are mentioned elsewhere in the New Testament. At Jesus' trial, Pilate sat on "the judgment seat" (Matt. 27:19). Paul advises, "For we will all stand before the judgment seat of Christ" (Rom. 14:10). He also said, "I am standing before Caesar's judgment seat" (Acts 25:10).

20:11 | In Jewish synagogues, a *bema* is where an official reads the Torah during the services and, like the **great white throne,** is the equivalent of a Christian pulpit today. A judgment seat is an elevated platform or a church's raised sanctuary area. I recall visiting a church in Streatham in South London, England, and seeing an unusual pulpit arrangement. It was once the church of abolitionist William Wilberforce[337] who became a powerful force for good in his generation. After the sermon, the preacher in Wilberforce's day stepped through a door and preached his message to the crowds outside! Madame de Stael[338] described Wilberforce as the "wittiest man in England." The Prince of Wales said he would go anywhere to hear him sing!

20:11 | The **earth and the heaven** fled from the Lord's face because he had appeared. When the Lord came in his glory and majesty, the sky vanished, and the earth passed away. "The earth and the heaven fled away" may mean that both the sky and the world disappeared utterly. The Psalmist said they "will wear out like a garment" (Ps. 102:26), though this concept is hard to conceive. Peter confirms, "But the day of the Lord will come as a thief in the night; in which the heavens will pass away with a great noise, and the elements will be dissolved with fervent heat, and the earth and the works that are in it will be burned up" (2 Pet. 3:10). It sounds like a cataclysmic event! The old world must be lost, and the heavens must vanish because Christ's people must have everything new, even a pristine planet and sky!

20:12 | John of Patmos writes, "**I saw the dead both great and small**" stand before heaven's throne, with the great books open before them. God records every person's deeds in the "Book of Life" and all his judgments. Do you know what God has written about you in his Book of Life? I believe we can, for we are all

---

[337] (1759-1833).

[338] the writer, and socialite.

writing our destinies throughout our life. It is not so much that God judges people, but people incur judgments on themselves by what they do or don't do. It depends on what they are and what they are not! Doing does not save us but counts as clear evidence of our relationship with God in Christ. The beast's followers are those whose names were not written "from the foundation of the world in the book of life of the Lamb" (Rev. 13:8). No one, whether wealthy or poor, is too important or insignificant to escape God's judgment or merit his rewards. But here's the kicker. The Lord God removes every reference to misdeeds from the Book of Life for those who have received Christ's forgiveness. It's as if Jesus steps forward, erases all the references to our sins from the volume, and says, "See, Ron Meacock's sins are wiped away, OK!" This is a wondrous thing!

20:12 | The review begins at "Christ's judgment seat," where **they opened books** containing records of every person's deeds. Daniel tells of a dream, "the judgment was set, the books were opened" (Dan. 7:10). Each review reveals a person's work and worth. Paul argues, "But if anyone builds on the foundation with gold, silver, costly stones, wood, hay, or stubble, each man's work will be revealed. For the Day will declare it because it is revealed in fire" (1 Cor. 3:12—13).

20:12 | The **book of life** is then opened. In Exodus, Moses pleads with God for his people, "if you will forgive their sin—and if not, please blot me out of your book which you have written" (Ex. 32:32). Moses is willing to be erased from the Book of Life to save his people. The Psalmist adds of his enemies, "Let them be blotted out of the book of life" (Ps. 69:28). Paul speaks about Clement and the rest of his fellow workers, "whose names are in the book of life" (Phil. 4:3). The risen Christ promises the Sardis church to reward those who overcome. Still, he will destroy those whose names the book of life does not contain.

20:12 | An interesting side note is that many rulers in those days controlled a "living citizens' register," also called a **book of life**. When a person died, the ruler erased their name. Colin

J Hemer[339] refers to another custom in ancient times whereby civic registers removed condemned criminals' listings at their execution.

20:12 | The glorified Christ **judges** the dead. Jesus said, "when the Son of Man comes in his glory, and all the holy angels with him, then he will sit on the throne of his glory. Before him, all the nations will be gathered, and he will separate them one from another" (Matt. 25:31—32). In Paul's Athens speech, he announces that God has appointed a day when the Lord Jesus Christ "will judge the living and the dead at his appearing and his Kingdom" (2 Tim. 4:1).

20:12 | Some people have questioned whether it is the Father or Jesus who **judges**. In the Trinity, the Father and Son's unity is such that there is no difficulty ascribing one's action as a judge to the other. Paul can therefore write that "we will all stand before the judgment seat of God" (Rom. 14:10) and later added, "before the judgment seat of Christ" (2 Cor. 5:10). Here, "Christ" and "God" are interchangeable.

20:12 | Only those who place their faith in Jesus Christ have their names recorded in the "book of life" and avoid the lake of fire. The vision of John of Patmos does not permit any gray areas in God's **judgment**. If we have not identified with Christ on earth, confessing him as our Lord, there is no hope, second chance, or other appeal. Finally, God hurls Death and Hades into the lake of fire. As H. B. Swete wrote, "These voracious monsters who have themselves devoured so many are themselves destroyed in the end."

20:13 | On Judgment Day, the sea gave up **the dead.** Loved ones cannot bury those who drown at sea, but God will raise them on the last day when the sea gives up those who drowned in it. Then, he judges each one when the ocean, death, and Hades surrender them. H. B. Swete comments, "The accidents of death will not prevent any from appearing before the judge." No matter how a person dies, God judges them, and they will not escape

[339] (1930-1987)

their punishment or lose their reward. Jesus considers each one according to their relationship with him.

20:13 | Some people believe that **a dead** person's spirit wanders for three days after death based on the time between Jesus' crucifixion and resurrection. An Irish wake lasts this long, and the mourners open a window to allow the deceased person's spirit to leave. The early church felt that Christian burial and graves were so essential that they purchased plots for those members who could not afford them. These cemetery places were the church's only possessions! The word *cemetery* from the Greek for "sleeping place" means "an area of ground to bury bodies." It originally applied to the Roman catacombs.

20:13 | There was a hierarchy in burial places in cemeteries. Initially, officials placed **the dead** bodies in mass graves until they decomposed, removing the bones to ossuary boxes along the graveyard's walls. Important people were often laid to rest within the church, even under the holy table with stone inscriptions or plaques on the floors or walls. If you go to Westminster Abbey today and down the side aisle, you will see the tombs of princes and princesses, and as you get closer to the communion table, you will observe the names of kings and queens.

20:13 | In the cemetery, the real estate axiom, "Location, Location, Location," remains true. The better plots for **the dead** were on the church's east side, facing the rising sun. The next best were in the South, while the North contained unknown travelers, undesirables, and stillborn babies. Wealthier families usually could afford a headstone. The more extensive the inscription or artistic value demonstrates their importance. Those who could not afford a monument placed a metal or wooden cross at the burial site.

20:13 | Occasionally, a cemetery **gave up the dead**. A flood was often disastrous, emptying layers of floating coffins and cadavers into the surrounding neighborhood. One such incident occurred in Monrovia Cemetery in Charleston in 2018. Ten caskets floated out of the ground, and many headstones were displaced. In 1774 AD, in Paris, France, skeletons were exhumed from graveyards out of fear of exposure and moved into the catacombs under the city to be stacked into walls and around supports up to five stories underground. They contained the bones of more than six million people in part of the former ancient stone quarries.

20:13 | We would be wise to compare today's churches' belongings to those of the early ones. Burial sites for **the dead** were their sole possession. Do we, like them, own burial plots for those of our number who cannot afford them? Most Christian denominations possess huge buildings and substantial bank accounts with stocks, bonds, and valuable silver and gold items, yet do not care in this way for the members of their fellowship!

20:13 | As well as the act of burial, which is called "inhumation," today's Protestant and Catholic churches also allow cremation of **the dead**, although the Orthodox Church still insists on burial. Interestingly, funeral directors have recently begun offering jewelry from your loved one's ashes. I was stunned to be told that my brother's ashes, who died in 2021, had been turned into a necklace and then given a tea-bag-like sachet of his ashes. What are you supposed to do with these? For the very wealthy, several companies will now produce a diamond for you from your loved ones' remains. Depending on the size, it costs between fourteen hundred and twenty-eight thousand dollars to create one of these under extremely high temperatures and intense pressure. Several colors are available, from natural amber, greenish-yellow, red, pink, black, and blue, to pure colorless.

20:13 | Interestingly, Desmond Tutu, former Archbishop of Cape Town,[340] chose "aquamation" as an alternative to cremation or burial of **the dead**. Treating the cadaver with chemicals takes only four to six hours. The remains are then dried, turned to ash, and returned to the family for interment. Aquamation is currently only legal in South Africa, nineteen states in the US, Saskatchewan, Quebec, and Ontario in Canada. It is not presently allowed in the United Kingdom due to problems with wastewater disposal.

---

[340] a onetime president of the Church Army in the UK.

20.14 | "The **lake of fire**" is related to the Jewish *Gehenna*, a valley outside Jerusalem where garbage continuously burned, and the fires never went out. But death is forever vanquished for those whose names are in the book of life.

Question: "Do you plan to be buried, cremated, aquamated, or turned into a diamond? Does it matter which?"

77

RENEWED HEAVEN AND EARTH

21:1 "I saw a **new heaven and a new earth**: for the **first heaven and the first earth have passed away**, and the **sea is no more.** ² I saw the **holy city, New Jerusalem**, coming down out of heaven from God, prepared like a bride adorned for her husband. ³ I heard a loud voice out of heaven saying, "Behold, God's dwelling is with people, and **he will dwell with them**, and they will be his people, and God himself will be with them as their God. ⁴ He will wipe away every tear from their eyes. Death will be no more; neither will there be mourning, nor crying, nor pain, any more. The first things have passed away." (Rev. 21:1—4 emphases added.)

21:1 | Jewish and Christian people have always dreamed of a **new heaven and a new earth.** The Lord says, "I create new heavens and a new earth" (Isa. 65:17). Peter agrees, "According to his promise, we look for new heavens and a new earth, in which righteousness dwells" (2 Pet. 3:13). God will wipe away every tear from every eye, and everything will be brand new there. Death, mourning, crying, or pain will no longer exist, for it will be a paradise with God.

21:1 | People everywhere have wanted to replace what we

have now with a **new heaven and a new earth.** No one likes climate change, flooding, forest fires, intense heat, melting ice caps, global warming, or carbon emissions. We all look for a change for the good. There is a fascinating story of an elderly sailor weary of battling the sea. He placed an oar on his shoulder and set out to journey inland until he reached a people who knew so little of the ocean that they would ask him what this strange thing was. In Jewish dreams, the end of the sea was the end of a force hostile to God and human beings.

21:1 | Gone will be sorrow, sin, and darkness, for the **first heaven and the first earth have passed away,** and time will turn into an everlasting eternity. Our beliefs today encompass our immortal longings, our inherent sense of wrong, and our abiding faith that, in the end, God will resolve all injustices with a new heaven and earth. No matter what you are going through, whether it's the death of a loved one, a struggle with addiction, depression, illness, or a family member that has gone astray, it's not the last word, for God writes the final chapter. It is about fulfillment and eternal joy for those who love him. What a beautiful truth!

21:1 | Dr. Billy Graham[341] was once asked by a reporter what he planned to do in **heaven.** He replied that he expected God would send him off to evangelize a new world elsewhere in the Universe! He wrote, "my home is in heaven, I'm just traveling through this world," and "I've read the last page of the Bible. It's all going to turn out right."

21:1 | Everlasting life with God will not be boring but more wonderful than we can imagine. It's not like the town of "Boring," Oregon, which has twinned with two others called "Dull" in Scotland and "Bland" in Australia. "The League of Extraordinary Communities," or the "Trinity of Tedium," was inaugurated in 2014. Two were named after founders, William H. Boring and William Bland, whereas Dull may be from the old Gaelic word meaning "meadow." William Bland was anything but dull in reality as he had been a trained surgeon who killed a man in

---

[341] (1918—2018)

a duel in Bombay, India, and as a convict, was shipped off to Australia to begin a new life! Heaven will not be dull, bland, or boring like any of these!

21:1 | In this futuristic vision, we encounter one of Revelation's most intriguing phrases, "The **sea is no more**." This concept has a much more significant meaning than we might realize. It is not that there will be dry land instead of water bodies around the earth but something more remarkable. In John of Patmos' day, Jewish people believed the seas were home to demons. They were afraid of evil spirits who killed those who fell into the water and drowned. The prospect that there would no longer be this threat would have been a great comfort to many.

21:1 | Israelis feared the **sea** so much that they employed other nations like the Phoenicians to ship supplies from different Mediterranean ports. Phoenicia[342] was unusual because it was a *thalassocratic* state operating "with primarily maritime realms, a seaborne empire." Instead of one land mass like most countries, it occupied the coastal areas of today's Lebanon, Northern Israel, and Arwad in Syria. It controlled the coastal city of Ashkelon in Israel's south, Cadiz in Spain, and Carthage in North Africa. The Phoenicians were spread all over but were great friends of Israel.

21:2 | The **holy city, New Jerusalem,** also called the "Heavenly Jerusalem" or "Zion," is where God will erase all pain and sorrow. "Zion" or "Sion" is also the name in the Hebrew Bible for the Temple Mount and also describes the "Land of Israel" and the future "World to Come." Thinking about "beautiful Zion" takes my mind back to the singing at the Keswick Convention meetings under the big tent in the Lake District,

> "Come ye that love the Lord, And let our joys be known.
> Join in a song with sweet accord, And thus surround the throne.

---

[342] This ancient Semitic-speaking Mediterranean civilization originated in the Fertile Crescent's west. Phoenicia spread across the Mediterranean Sea between BC 1500 and 300.

We're Marching to Zion. Beautiful, beautiful Zion.
We're Marching upwards to Zion, The beautiful
city of God."

Then let our songs abound, And every tear be dry;
We're marching through Immanuel's ground,
To fairer worlds on high."[343]

21:2 | The one seated on heaven's throne promises an
eternal experience in the **New Jerusalem** for those who love
him. "Eternity," derived from the Latin *Aeternus*, is an infinite,
everlasting place prepared for us, where physical limitations do
not hinder contact, and everything is unique. We will have new
bodies like Jesus in this future existence in God's presence. Most
of the descriptions of eternal bliss fall short as they are only hints
using terms and ideas from our present experiences to describe
the unknown.

21:3 | Christians who persevere will receive God's promised
blessings, for **he will dwell with them**. One of God's most
significant promises in the Bible is that he will be with us. It is
the one thing generations of faithful people have longed for and
requested. Christians will be given a unique name and authority
over the nations, be included in the book of life, and sit near Christ
on his throne. What a magnificent eternal prospect that will be!

Question: "What will your renewed heaven and earth be like?"

---

[343] Written by Isaac Watts (1674—1748). Sung to the tune "Zionwards." Listen on
YouTube.

78

JESUS ALPHA AND OMEGA

21:5 "He who sits on the throne said, "Behold, I am **making all things new."** He said, "Write, for these words of God are faithful and true." [6] He said to me, "I am the **Alpha and the Omega**, the **Beginning and the End.** I will give **freely** to him who is thirsty from the spring of the water of life. [7] **He who overcomes, I will give him these things.** I will be his God, and he will be my son. [8] But for the **cowardly, unbelieving, sinners, abominable, murderers, sexually immoral, sorcerers, idolaters, and all liars**, their part is in the lake that burns with fire and sulfur, which is the **second death.**" [9] One of the seven angels who had the seven bowls, who were loaded with the seven last plagues came, and he spoke with me, saying, "Come here. I will show you the wife, the Lamb's bride." [10] He **carried me away in the Spirit** to a great and high mountain, and showed me the coming down out of heaven from God, [11] having the **glory** of God. Her light was like a most precious stone, as if it were a jasper stone, clear as crystal; [12] having a **great and high wall**; having twelve gates, and at the gates twelve angels; and names written on them, which are the names of the **twelve tribes of the children of Israel.** [13] On the east were three gates; and on the north three gates; and on the south three gates; and on the west three gates. [14] The wall of the city had twelve foundations, and on them twelve names of the twelve Apostles of the Lamb." (Rev. 21:5—14 emphases added.)

21:5 | Almighty God speaks from his throne and says he is **making all things new.** Centuries before, Isaiah heard, "Don't remember the former things, and don't consider the things of old. Behold, I will do a new thing" (Isa. 43:18—19). Paul agrees, "Therefore if anyone is in Christ, he is a new creation. The old things have passed away. Behold, all things have become new" (2 Cor. 5:17). Jesus deletes the old human failures, renews people's lives, and transforms them wonderfully! God re-creates a brand new universe for the brand new saints.

21:6 | Jesus of Nazareth is called the **Alpha, the Omega,** and the initiator of this new creation. He was there before the beginning and will be there at the end of time after all earthly things have passed away. John's Gospel reflects this truth, "In the beginning was the Word, and the Word was with God, and the Word was God. The same was in the beginning with God" (John 1:3). The "Alpha and the Omega" or the "Beginning and the End" covers everything and asserts that Jesus is everlasting.

21:6 | These statements point to the perpetual nature of Jesus, for early Christians drew the **Alpha and Omega** symbols on the walls of the Roman catacombs to encourage one another. Their graffiti reassured them that Jesus would be with them forever when everything seemed dismal. John of Patmos hears Israel's King and Redeemer, the Lord Almighty say, "I am the first, and I am the last, and besides me, there is no God." (Isa. 44:6).

21:6 | In Jewish Rabbinic literature, "truth" is *emet* and comprises the Hebrew alphabet's initial, middle, and final letters into one of God's names. The **alpha, and the omega,** encompass all time. The Oxford Dictionary defines "time" as "the indefinite continued progress of existence and events in the past, present, and future regarded as a whole." Baltasar Gracian[344] agrees, "All that belongs to us is time; even he who has nothing else has that." Jesus is the *emet,* the Lord of all time, from the beginning to the end, and everything in between.

21:6 | Interestingly, "time" is the most widely used noun in

---

[344] Also known as Baltasar Gracian (1601—1658) a Spanish writer and philosopher.

the English language and more popular even than "year," "man," or "woman." Time has a **beginning and an end**. In Islam, the Qur'an gives us the words *al'Awwal,* meaning "the beginning," and *al 'Akhir,* meaning "the end," as two of God's names.

21:6 | The Greek word for "**beginning**" is *arche* and does not simply mean "first in point of time but first in the sense of the source of all things." Jesus, being at the beginning, was the source, the architect, or the archetype of all things. "Archetype" from *arche* means a "pattern copied by others." The Greek word for "end" is *telos* which does not mean "end in time" but the "goal of time." These words point us to Jesus as the source and the culmination of all things.

21:6 | Jesus **freely** offers the living water spring to the spiritually thirsty. The water of life is abundant, accessible, and stimulating in heaven. Refreshing pure water is a wonderful gift for someone living in an arid region with few wells. A living spring containing all God's blessings for human beings is even more welcome and will completely satisfy their longing hearts. Life's goal is to receive God's living water.

21:7 | To those faithful to Jesus Christ, God makes the most fantastic promise, "**He who overcomes, I will give him these things**." The phrase "who overcomes" occurs seven times in Revelation, and each contains a promise of faithfulness. Here are the special rewards for overcomers

- "To him who overcomes I will give to eat from the tree of life, which is in the Paradise of my God" (Rev. 2:7).
- "He who overcomes won't be harmed by the second death" (Rev. 2:11).
- "To him who overcomes, to him I will give of the hidden manna, and I will give him a white stone, and on the stone a new name written, which no one knows but he who receives it" (Rev. 2:17).
- "He who overcomes, and he who keeps my works to the end, to him I will give authority over the nations." (Rev. 2:26).

- "He who overcomes will be arrayed in white garments, and I will in no way blot his name out of the book of life, and I will confess his name before my Father, and before his angels" (Rev. 3:5).
- "He who overcomes, I will make him a pillar in the temple of my God, and he will go out from there no more. I will write on him the name of my God and the name of the city of my God, the New Jerusalem, which comes down out of heaven from my God, and my own new name" (Rev. 3:12).
- "He who overcomes, I will give to him to sit down with me on my throne, as I also overcame, and sat down with my Father on his throne" (Rev 3:21).

There is no more incredible honor than God's blessing on those faithful to him. The Almighty will bless those who overcome in a wonderful new way.

21:8 | A list of those who will suffer in the second death begins with the **cowardly**. Timidity or cowardice is to deny Christ for safety's sake and is the opposite of bravery and courage in those who stand firm.

21:8 | **Murderers** mean those who illegally and intentionally kill another person. The word "murdered" comes from the 1300–1350 AD middle English *mortherer,* or *morderer*.[345] The word *mord* means "death." It may also refer to persecutors and killers of martyred Christians.

21:8 | **Fornicators** are men and women who have sex with someone to whom they are not married. This word comes from the sixteenth-century Latin *formicari* and *fornix,* meaning "basement vaulted brothel." To fornicate meant to consort with prostitutes in vaulted basements!

21:8 | Ephesus was full of **sorcerers** who practiced magic. As a result of preaching Christ's name, Luke recounts that some magicians turned from their evil ways, "those who practiced magical arts brought their books together and burned them."

---

[345] Random House Kernerman Webster's College Dictionary, © 2010 K Dictionaries Ltd. Copyright 2005, 1997, 1991 by Random House, Inc. All rights reserved.

"They counted their price, and found it to be fifty thousand pieces of silver" (Acts 19:19). This was a lifetime's wages for an agricultural laborer or a million dollars today!

21:8 | Idolaters are those who worship false gods and idols of any sort. These could be carved images in John of Patmos' day and probably would today include expensive cars, motorcycles, luxurious houses, cottages, and large boats. Then there are high-priced clothes, shoes, and extensive investment accounts. Christians, however, need to live more simply. William Barclay expressed it well, "How do our lives reflect the poor carpenter of Nazareth's holiness and righteousness?"

21:8 | Liars are guilty of purposely speaking falsehoods. They cover up for someone else and deceive using "white lies," untruths, half-truths, and fake news in our modern terminology. Lying is a significant problem in today's society, and people are so used to it that they do not think about it. On a recent bus trip to Quebec, our group visited an interesting cheese-making facility. The tour director who spoke with the group seemed to have intimate knowledge of the process as if he had grown up in it. Later we learned that he had quietly told the bus driver that he had only been hired three years ago and was told to pretend to be the founder's grandson! Some people lie all the time, even about their name, and give a false address to conceal their true identity!

21:8 | The **second death** is a Jewish and Christian concept related to punishment after natural death. The phrase occurs four times in Revelation[346] as the ultimate destination for immoral and unrepentant sinners. The Jewish scholar Harry Sysling[347] regards it as "the judgment, following the resurrection, on the Last Day."

21:10 | John of Patmos says, "God **carried me away in the Spirit** to a great and high mountain, and showed me the coming down out of heaven from God." Ezekiel was also transported to a high point, "In the visions of God he brought me into the land of Israel, and set me down on a very high mountain" (Ezek. 40:2).

---

[346] In Revelation 2:11, 20:6, 20:14, and 21:8

[347] Harry Sysling (1922—2014) *Teḥiyyat ha-metim: the resurrection of the dead in the Palestinian Targums* p222 1996

21:11 | The "**glory** of the holy city" describes its light and radiance. The word "glory" translates from the Greek *phoster*, meaning "that which gives light." The term "light" usually is *phos*, but the creation story uses *phoster*. God said, "Let there be lights in the expanse of the sky to divide the day from the night" (Gen. 1:14). Later in Revelation, it is noted, "the city has no need for the sun or moon to shine, for the very glory of God illuminated it, and its lamp is the Lamb" (Rev. 21:23). The New Jerusalem needs no sun or moon to give it light for God himself and the Lamb are its glories and the source of all illumination!

21:12 | The New Jerusalem's gates are part of a **great and high wall**. An angel guards each of the twelve gates, named after one of the twelve tribes. When God drove humans out of the Garden of Eden after the Fall, we read, "he placed cherubim at the east of the garden of Eden, and a flaming sword which turned every way, to guard the way to the tree of life" (Gen. 3:24). There were three north, south, east and western gates. The word "gate" is interesting. The standard term for "gate" is *pule*, but not here. Instead, it uses *pulon*, meaning "a large house by a magnificent gate in the outer wall leading into a spacious vestibule." Jerusalem's Golden Gate, though blocked up, is one such gate, similar to a gatehouse in that it has an entrance building as part of the wall. Each gate in New Jerusalem is a single glistening pearl.

21:12 | There are twelve gates in the New Jerusalem. The names of the **tribes of the children of Israel** are inscribed over the gates. To understand this significance, we must look to Abraham's grandson, Jacob, whom God later called Israel.[348] His twelve sons became Israel's tribal names, and God chose those twelve groups to inherit the promised land, receive the Law, and become his covenant people. The northern gates are Reuben, Judah, and Levi, and the east side will have three gates named after Joseph, Benjamin, and Dan. The south side gates will be called Simeon, Issachar, and Zebulun. The west side will be the gates of Gad, Asher, and Naphtali.[349] God had previously specified a similar

---

[348] Gen. 32:28.
[349] Ezek. 48:31–34.

arrangement around the wilderness tent of meeting, probably for defense, with three tribes camping on each side (Num. 2:1). The New Jerusalem sits on twelve foundations, representing the apostles who will reign over Israel's tribes.

21:12 | Someone has said, "**Names** determine our destiny," possibly from the Roman saying *nomen est omen*, or "name is destiny." While there is no scientific evidence to prove names affect our destiny, psychologists assert this phenomenon determines how we react to our names. Children who like their names often turn out to be more confident and self-assertive than those who don't!

Question: "Consider the seven Revelation promises to those who overcome. Are there any that stand out for you?"

79

JERUSALEM CITY CUBE

21:15 "He who spoke with me had for a measure a golden reed to **measure the city**, its gates, and its walls. [16] The city is **square**, and its length is as great as its width. He measured the city with the reed, twelve thousand twelve stadia. Its **length, width, and height** are equal. [17] Its wall is **one hundred forty-four cubits**, by the measure of a man, that is, of an angel. [18] The construction of its wall was jasper. The city was pure gold, like pure glass. [19] The foundations of the city's wall were adorned with all kinds of **precious stones**. The first foundation was jasper; the second, sapphire; the third, chalcedony; the fourth, emerald; [20] the fifth, sardonyx; the sixth, sardius; the seventh, chrysolite; the eighth, beryl; the ninth, topaz; the tenth, chrysoprase; the eleventh, jacinth; and the twelfth, amethyst. [21] The twelve gates were **twelve pearls**. Each one of the gates was made of one pearl. The street of the city was pure gold, like transparent glass." (Rev. 21:15—21 emphases added.)

21:15 | John of Patmos looks on as the angel **measures the city** and tells us that the New Jerusalem is to be an exact cube.[350] It is unique because only five such solids have the same number

---

[350] named after the Greek philosopher Plato (c428-c348 BC). It has six faces, twelve edges, and eight vertices and symbolizes perfection like a Platonic solid

of faces meeting at each vertex. Interestingly, many viruses, such as the herpes virus, have a similar configuration but with twenty triangular faces! Nature exhibits many such unusual and extraordinary structures.

21:16 | The footprint of the New Jerusalem is described as **square**. Aristotle[351] was a classical Greek philosopher who wrote that a man considered perfect was called "foursquare." New Jerusalem is perfect.

21:16 | It is interesting in our modern context because **"foursquare"** also describes "the location-based social networking website for mobile devices such as smartphones." It is a local search-and-discovery mobile application providing personalized recommendations of places to go close to the user's current location. I am sure many of us have used this feature on a sat-nav or mobile phone in our cars to find a restaurant or address.

21:16 | **Square** city plans were pretty typical in ancient times. Babylon, the Tower of Babel, and Nineveh were all built in a geometrically square form. The New Jerusalem city cube is not only square but of the same height. More importantly, the Holy of Holies in Solomon's Temple was also a perfect cube. The Lord God intended us to understand that the whole of the New Jerusalem's city cube is one great Holy of Holies and God's future dwelling-place for devout and holy followers of Christ.

21:16 | The New Jerusalem city cube's **length, width, and height** are all fourteen hundred miles, creating an unimaginably vast building. The angel measured the city with a "reed" or a "golden measuring rod." Ezekiel also described such a measuring stick when in a vision, God took him to a very high mountain in Israel, on whose south side was a city. "A man, whose appearance was like the appearance of bronze, with a line of flax in his hand, and a measuring reed; and he stood in the gate" (Ezek. 40:2—3). The line of flax (or "linen cord") was probably a plumb line or chalk line. Egyptian measuring rods had marks for the Remen measurement of approximately fifteen inches, as was used in the

[351] (384-322 BC).

construction of the Pyramids. The Roman measuring rod was ten Roman feet long and hence called a *decempeda,* Latin for 'ten feet.' It was usually of a square section capped at both ends by a metal shoe and painted in alternating colors.

21:17 | The angel measured the width of the city wall as **one hundred and forty-four cubits** or about two hundred and sixteen feet thick![352] Each side was one thousand three hundred and eighty miles. William Barclay states, "the city's total area is two and a quarter million square miles. This vast area illustrates that God is more eager to bring people into the New Jerusalem than to shut them out, and his church must be the same! In the holy city, there is room for everyone!" By comparison, the Old City of Jerusalem's walls[353] were twelve thousand feet long or two and a half miles, their height was thirty-nine feet, and they were over eight feet thick. Even this is very impressive! Rabbis may dream of the re-created Jerusalem, but the New Jerusalem covering such a vast area far exceeds their greatest expectations! A city with the New Jerusalem's area and dimensions would stretch from London to New York!

21:17 | Some scholars have suggested that the **one hundred and forty-five cubits** or two hundred feet wall should read "high" rather than "thick." However, a wall this high is not very tall by modern standards or even the building standards of the period. The world's tallest modern building, "Burj Khalifa" [354] in Dubai, is two thousand seven hundred and seventeen feet high. Ancient Babylon's wall, by comparison, was three hundred feet tall, and the walls of the porch of Solomon's temple built in 832 BC were one hundred and eighty feet high. However, a two hundred and sixteen-foot thick wall in the New Jerusalem cannot be for defense, for all spiritual and human hostilities have been

---

[352] or 65.8 meters.

[353] rebuilt by Sultan Suleiman 1 between 1537 and 1541 AD.

[354] (828-metre) built in the United Arab Emirates in 2010. It was designed by Skidmore, Owings & Merrill (SOM), an American architectural, urban planning and engineering firm.

obliterated or cast into the Lake of Fire. Therefore, it must be for the wall's structural integrity and appearance.

21:19 | The New Jerusalem's **precious stones** in the foundation walls display incredible beauty and purity that will last forever. Some of the precious stones' precise identification is uncertain, but the sparkling colors must have been stunning to John of Patmos. The New Jerusalem will be the only worship place, sparkling with the beauty and excellence of gold and precious stones as the centerpiece of God's earthly presence.

21:21 | The city's measurements describe a place that will hold all God's people and be perfect. There are twelve gates, like **twelve pearls**. The precious stones' variety and measurements are multiples of twelve, symbolizing God's people. Twelve foundations support the walls, and twelve gates open into the city. God names these after Israel's twelve tribes and the twelve apostles.

Question: "Could any modern engineer or architect design a structure like the Jerusalem city cube?"

80

JERUSALEM CITY TEMPLE

21:22 "I saw no temple in it, for the Lord God, the Almighty, and the Lamb, are its **temple**. [23] The city has no need for the sun or moon to shine, for the very glory of God illuminated it, and its **lamp** is the Lamb. [24] **The nations** will walk in its light. The kings of the earth bring the glory and honor of the nations into it. [25] Its gates will in no way be shut by day (for there will be **no night** there), [26] and they shall bring the glory and the honor of the nations into it so that they may enter. [27] There will in no way enter into it **anything profane**, or one who causes an abomination or a lie, but only those who are written in the Lamb's book of life." (Revelation 21:22—27 emphases added).

21:22 | John of Patmos describes the New Jerusalem's unique features as the city of God. There is no **temple** or sanctuary, and it will need no holy place because God and the Lamb's presence will be everywhere. Nothing will hinder Christians from worshipping or being with him. Almighty God and the Lamb's presence continuously sanctify the city.

21:22 | Buildings do not make a church or a **temple.** Four essential elements turn a place into a Christian worship center. There can be no church or assembly without all of these.

- Jesus Christ (the Lord God).
- The Holy Spirit.
- Christian believers.
- The Bible.

21:23 | This new city needs no lighting system! William Barclay reminds us, "God's city needed no created **light** because God the uncreated light was in her midst." Only when we see things in his light, do we see them as they are. Some things that seem vital to us are unimportant in his light and others that appear insignificant turn out to be otherwise. The psalmist tells us, "For with you is the spring of life. In your light we will see light" (Ps. 36:9).

21:24 | The Lord's glory is the New Jerusalem city light, and the Lamb is its **lamp**. The prophet Isaiah writes, "The sun will be no more your light by day; nor will the brightness of the moon give light to you, but Yahweh will be your everlasting light, and your God will be your glory" (Isa. 60:19).

21:24 | On this day, **the nations** will walk by his light and go up to Mount Zion to be taught the law and learn the Lord's ways. "Behold, you shall call a nation that you don't know; and a nation that didn't know you shall run to you, because of Yahweh your God, and for the Holy One of Israel; for he has glorified you" (Isa. 55:5). A new Christian nation will come to the Lord, and people who didn't know God will run to him.

21:25 | The Lord God and the Lamb will cast out all darkness, for there will be **no night** in the New Jerusalem. Some ancient peoples were afraid of the dark. This extreme fear of darkness, called "nyctophobia," causes intense anxiety and depression. It often begins in childhood and may become excessive and irrational, impacting daily life. In the new world, frightening darkness will be no more, for God's presence will bring a special light. The psalmist reminds us, "even the darkness doesn't hide from you, but the night shines as the day" (Ps. 139:12). Again and again, in history, a dark age has followed a period of brilliance.

Still, in the new era, the darkness will be gone forever, and there will never again be anything but light.

21:27 | There is a warning here that nothing impure or **anything profane** will ever enter the New Jerusalem. God will allow in a sinner who has sinned, repented, and been forgiven but will deny another who deliberately sins. No one whose name does not appear in the Lamb's book of life will enter the New Jerusalem.

Question: "What will our lives be like without any darkness?"

81

THE TREE OF LIFE

22:1 "He showed me a river of **water of life**, clear as crystal, **proceeding out of the throne of God** and of the Lamb, ² in the middle of its street. On this side of the river and on that was the **tree of life**, bearing twelve kinds of **fruits**, yielding its fruit every month. The **leaves of the tree** were for the healing of the nations." (Rev. 22:1—2 emphases added).

22:1 | The ever-flowing **water of life** symbolizes eternal spiritual and physical refreshment, and this crystal clear fluid floods continuously from God's throne down the New Jerusalem high street. Some translations read "pure water of life," indicating the absolute purity of this fluid. "Purified water" is mechanically filtered or processed to remove impurities using processes such as "capacitive deionization, reverse osmosis, carbon filtering, microfiltration, ultrafiltration, ultraviolet oxidation, or electrode ionization."[355] The liquid flowing from God's throne needs none of these processes, for it is absolutely pure already! There is nothing that refreshes better than a clean, delicious drink. I remember being at a neighbor's house in the country and watching a specialist company drilling a well. The machine pounded away

---

[355] "Spring Water vs. Purified Water: Which is the Better Choice?". *SpringWell Water Filtration Systems*. 2021-01-27.

for an entire week in the rock, then water appeared, at first muddy, dirty brown, and then crystal clear. It reminded me of Jesus offering another kind of spiritual refreshment to the woman of Samaria, telling her the drink he will give "will become a well of water springing up to eternal life" (John 4:14).

22:1 | John of Patmos emphasizes that water flowing **from the throne of God** produces health and strength wherever it goes. God's throne seems to be the source of the precious living fluid.

22:2 | The **tree of life** reminds us of the "Garden of Eden."[356] "God made every tree to grow that is pleasant to the sight, and good for food, including the tree of life in the middle of the garden" (Gen. 2:9). The ancient symbol of the Tree of Life represented emotional, relational, physical, spiritual nourishment, transformation, and liberation.[357] After Adam and Eve ate from the tree of the knowledge of good and evil, God prohibited them from the tree of life, which grew alongside it. He denied Adam and Eve eternal life because they disobeyed his command. In some places, the African baobab tree is called the tree of life. It resists the earth's warming and grows in hot, arid climates. It is also known as the bottle tree for its ability to store up to 1,200 gallons of water in its trunk.

22:2 | The New Jerusalem residents eat freely from the **tree of life** and live forever. It may be related to an ancient belief in a mythical "World Tree," portrayed as a gigantic trunk, branches, and roots supporting the heavens and connecting the earth and sky.

22:2 | Paradise is a perfect place. Its gardens delight the eye, and the **tree of life** nourishes God's people. It is an idealized Garden of Eden[358] re-created in heaven's New Jerusalem. "Eden" is associated with the Hebrew word for "pleasure" and is closely related to an Aramaic root meaning "fruitful and well-watered." The Latin Vulgate translates "garden in Eden" as "paradise of pleasure" (Gen. 2:8).[359]

---

[356] Eden was called "God's Garden" or the "Terrestrial Paradise."
[357] Google information under "tree."
[358] The name Eden derives from the Akkadian *edinnu*, meaning "plain" or "steppe."
[359] Douay-Rheims 1899 American Edition (DRA).

22:2 | Fruit **trees** of all kinds will grow on both river banks. The prophet Ezekiel tells us, "By the river on its bank, on this side and on that side, will grow every tree for food, whose leaf won't wither, neither will its fruit fail. It will produce new fruit every month because its waters issue out of the sanctuary. Its fruit will be for food, and its leaf for healing" (Ezek. 47:12). The garden's produce is for nutrition, and the tree of life's leaves are for healing.

22:2 | Some people ask why the nations need the healing **leaves of the tree** of life in heaven if all sickness and disease are gone? The scriptures clearly say that the tree's leaves are for the healing of the nations, but that was before the Resurrection. Ezekiel could not have imagined a people without any ailments or diseases, for the new bodies we receive will be perfect without any blemishes.

22:2 | Revelation closes human history in Paradise,[360] a "timeless harmonic place," as Genesis opened it there. Heaven is a picture of perfect agreement, which God will restore in the coming world. Genesis describes Adam and Eve walking and talking with God, but Revelation speaks of believers worshiping him face-to-face. What a fantastic experience that will be!

Question: "What excites you about the new Garden of God in heaven?"

---

[360] *Paradise*, from the Persian word for "Paradise garden," is a "timeless harmonic place."

82

PROMISED BLESSINGS

22:3 "There will be **no curse any more**. The throne of God and of the Lamb will be in it, and his servants will serve him. ⁴ They will see **his face**, and his name will be on their foreheads. ⁵ There will be no night, and they need no lamp light or sun light; for the Lord God will illuminate them. They will reign **forever and ever**. ⁶ He said to me, "These words are faithful and true. The Lord God of the spirits of the prophets sent his angel to show to his bondservants **the things which must happen soon**." ⁷ "Behold, I come quickly. **Blessed** is he who keeps the words of the prophecy of this book." ⁸ Now I, John, am **the one who heard and saw these things.** When I heard and saw, I fell down to worship before the feet of the angel who had shown me these things. ⁹ He said to me, "See you **don't do it**! I am a fellow bondservant with you and with your brothers, the prophets, and with those who keep the words of this book. Worship God." ¹⁰ He said to me, "Don't seal up the words of the prophecy of this book, for the **time is at hand**. ¹¹ He who acts unjustly, let him act unjustly still. He who is filthy, let him be filthy still. He who is righteous, let him do righteousness still. He who is holy, let him be holy still." ¹² "Behold, **I come quickly**. My reward is with me, to repay to each man according to his work. ¹³ I am

the Alpha and the Omega, the First and the Last, the
Beginning and the End. [14] Blessed are those who do his
commandments, that they may have the right to the tree
of life, and may enter in by the gates into the city."
(Rev. 22:3—14 emphases added).

22:3 | The final part of the description of life in "God's City"
tells us there will be **no curse** there. There will be no swearing,
but also, there will be none of the pressures on us to do wrong.
When I was eighteen years old, I was on my way to work on
a building site in Birmingham. Before that time, I swore like
everyone else on the site as it was a part of our daily Monday to
Saturday conversation. I am very thankful that when I committed
my life to Christ, I suddenly found that I couldn't use foul or
vulgar language anymore. When the Lord Jesus took away my
sins, he also removed the desire or the ability to curse. The other
precious gift at that moment was that previously I had thought
of the bible as a book of stories, but suddenly the Gideon's bible
at my bedside became real as if someone was speaking to me
directly from its pages. The Word of God burst into life, and that
fire has never gone out!

22:4 | In the New Jerusalem, God will fulfill the promise that
we will see **his face.** Jesus said, "Blessed are the pure in heart, for
they shall see God" (Matt. 5:8). The Lord offers something denied
even to Moses, for he said, "You cannot see my face, for man may
not see me and live" (Ex. 33:20). Men, women, boys, and girls can
not only see God but know him as a friend.

22:4 | Seeing **his face,** produces a perfect worship scenario,
and all life becomes an act of praise. God has consecrated the
city's inhabitants, for they have his mark on their foreheads and
belong exclusively to him.

22:5 | This vision ends with the promise that "the people
of God will **reign forever and ever.**" They will find absolute
freedom as part of his royal family.

22:5 | "The **God who inspired** the prophets" may equally
mean "the God who breathed into the prophets." "Breathed"

reminds us of the Hebrew word *ruach,* meaning "spirit," which occurs in Genesis in the "spirit that moves over the waters" at the creation. When spoken, the word "sounds like a deep breath" and engages one's breath and lungs"[361] The Latin equivalent to *ruach* is *spiritus* or *spirare,* meaning "God's breath."

22:5 | I still remember a special night in Blackpool on a Beach Mission there. The team was on the church hall stage, praying together about what had occurred that day and what we planned for the next day's ministry. Though heavy curtains surrounded us from floor to ceiling and no doors or windows were open, the Holy Spirit's wind blew through that room and against my face, and I heard its sound. It was a very wonderful and, at the same time, an extremely frightening experience. I felt goosebumps on my face and arms. It was as if God, the Holy Spirit, was telling me, "Don't worry, I am the God with all the power you need." This incident reminds me of a similar experience in the early church on the day of Pentecost. "They were all with one accord in one place. Suddenly there came from the sky a sound like the rushing of a mighty wind, and it filled all the house where they were sitting" (Acts 2:1—2). A lovely lilting song expresses these same sentiments,

> "Jesus told us all about you,
> How we could not live without You,
> With His blood, the power bought,
> To help us live the life He taught.
>
> Wind, wind, blow on me,
> Wind, wind, set me free,
> Wind, wind,
> The Father sent the blessed Holy Spirit."[362]

22:6 | John of Patmos was a devout student who saw, heard, and faithfully recorded **the things which must happen soon.**

---

[361] Fellowship of Israel Related Ministries.(FIRM).
[362] Composer: Jane and Betsy Clowe. Arranger: David Peacock. © 1974, 1975 Celebration/Kingsway's Thankyou Music

Jesus himself emphasized how short his delay would be. He blessed every devout student who read and kept these prophetic words. The faithful scholar is the best of all pupils. Too many are devoted to service, pious, and sincere, but not students, for they will not accept the learning discipline. Some even look suspiciously upon further knowledge. Too many learners are not devout and interested only in intellectual understanding but not in prayer and the service of their fellow human beings. Devout students must read, mark, learn, and inwardly digest God's word, for it deserves devoted attention.

22:8 | John of Patmos identified himself as **the one who heard and saw these things.** He named himself responsible for ensuring the accurate copying down of Revelation's message.

22:9 | Then, strangely enough, John again fell at the angel's feet, and the angel told him abruptly, **"See you don't do it!"** He reminds us again how wrong it is to worship any other than God. We must reverence the Lord God Almighty and the Lamb alone.

22:10 | This passage indicates that Christ's coming is close, saying that **the time is at hand**. "Look, I am coming soon!"

Question: "Have you ever experienced the wind of the Holy Spirit blowing on you? What does it mean?"

83

REJECT MAGIC ARTS

22:15 "Outside are **the dogs,** the sorcerers, the **sexually immoral**, the murderers, the idolaters, and everyone who loves and **practices falsehood.** [16] I, Jesus, have sent my angel to **testify these things to you** for the assemblies. I am the **root and the offspring of David,** the **Bright and Morning Star."** (Rev. 22:15—16 emphases added).

22.15 | A new Hebrew phrase here is "the dog" or *kelev.* While dogs are mentioned multiple times in the Bible, only one breed is specifically featured, the greyhound. Proverbs states, "There are three things which are stately in their march, four which are stately in going: "The lion, which is mightiest among animals and doesn't turn away for any; the greyhound; the male goat; and the king against whom there is no rising up" (Prov. 30:29-31). There are thirty-two general mentions of dogs in the Old Testament and nine in the New Testament. Domesticated dogs served as companions, hunting dogs, sheep dogs, and guard dogs in Bible times. Most others seemed to have been wild. The story of Lazarus and Dives tells us more, "A certain beggar, named Lazarus, was taken to his gate, full of sores, and desiring to be fed with the crumbs that fell from the rich man's table. Yes, even the dogs came and licked his sores"

(Luke 16:20—21). Some commentators[363] have noted the benefits of a dog licking a person's sores. It knows to lick its wounds to ensure they remain clean and heal quicker.

22.15 | Palestine's wild **dogs**, called "pariah dogs," were not docile pets but the symbol of everything savage and unclean. "They return at evening, howling like dogs, and prowl around the city" (Psa. 59:6). People feared them, especially in packs. H. B. Swete wrote from his experience, "No one who has watched the dogs prowling in an eastern city will wonder at the contempt and disgust the word suggests to the oriental mind."

22.15 | Jewish people focused this contempt on Gentiles by calling them "**dogs**." A rabbinic saying warned, "Whoever eats with an idolater is the same as he who would eat with a dog. Who is a dog? He is not circumcised." Later, "dogs" came to refer to Christians who had abandoned their faith after their baptism. In pagan temples, female and male prostitutes were also commonly called "temple dogs" and regarded as thoroughly immoral persons.

22:15 | There follows a list of people barred from God's city. A similar record appears of those cast into the lake of fire. It includes the cowardly, unbelieving, vile, murderers, and **sexually immoral**. The "sexually immoral" are those not conforming to biblical moral standards. Practicing magic arts means engaging in spiritualism and the occult.

22:15 | Those who **practice falsehood** employ lies, half-truths, and false news to sell products and gain power through social media, television, advertising, and daily contact with others. There are consequences to these acts. When we sold our Norwood home, the prospective buyers spun us a tale that they wanted to give their two girls the experience of country life in a family cottage. We thought they would become ideal community members. After signing the contracts, we discovered that they were real estate investors keen to make a lot of money on the sale and rent the house for a thousand dollars a day! They had already

---

[363] Justin David Strong's article "From Pets to Physicians: Dogs in the Biblical World" published in the May/June 2019 issue of *Biblical Archaeology Review*.

perpetrated the same crime with other cottagers in this area. We discovered the two girls in their photos were probably not their children but borrowed for the photographs. Even their address on the sale documents proved to be false. Their lies, unfortunately, fooled everyone, including the lawyers, two sets of real estate agents, and ourselves!

22:15 | Those who **practice falsehood** in this way are sowing destructive weeds in their lives with harmful consequences for themselves and their descendants. Lies corrode people's characters, and children learn to lie by listening to and copying their parents. A small falsehood leads to a larger one and a bigger fabrication to cover the earlier ones. The Psalms speak against liars, saying, "He who practices deceit won't dwell within my house. He who speaks falsehood won't be established before my eyes" (Ps. 101:7). Unfortunately, truth to many people means "saying what they need to say to get what they want!" Our society has even developed a new vocabulary to make lying acceptable, such as "half-truth," "white lie," "fake news," or even a "fib" as a bit of a lie! Putin and his cronies in Russia tell bare-faced lies to impress the Russian people or to cover some of his failures. Everybody sees that they are untrue.

22:16 | In the verse, "I have sent my angel to **testify these things to you**," the first-person plural of "you" indicates "many people." In the Liverpool area, working people would pronounce the plural of *"you"* as "yous." So my "Liverpudlian Version" of this text might be, "I have sent my angel to testify these things to yous!" This news is for everyone.

22:16 | Jesus calls himself the **root and the offspring of David**. He is the eternal source from which Jesse, David, and his promised descendants come. The Greek word for "root" is *rhiza*. John the Baptist says, "even now, the ax is laid to the tree's root" (Matt 3:10). Isaiah prophesied, "A shoot will come out of the stock of Jesse, and a branch out of his roots will bear fruit" (Isa. 11:1). These examples refer to Jesus, who will "bear much fruit." In the Garden of Gethsemane, three olive trees, which are almost a thousand years old, are of the same lineage. "Gethsemane" is from the Aramaic word for "olive press," The trees can grow back from the roots if the trunk is cut down. These Olive trees are native to the land of Israel and the city of Jerusalem and could be the same ones amongst which Jesus walked.

22:16 | Jesus is also the "**offspring of David**." The Greek word translating "offspring" is *genos* for "a social group claiming common descent" and gives us the word "generation," referring to one's descendants, kin, lineage, or family. Matthew and Luke's Gospels both have genealogies, showing the ancestors of Jesus either from Abraham forward or from Jesus back to Adam. The Genesis[364] genealogies give us the lineal male descendants from Adam to Abraham, including the years each person lived.

22:16 | Jesus is the **Bright and Morning Star** and dispels the night of sin and death. The word "bright" uses the word *phosphorus*, which is also a chemical element with the symbol "P,"[365] which emits a faint glow when exposed to oxygen, hence the description "light-bearer." Phosphorous is highly reactive, glows in the dark, and "phosphoresces" after illumination. It was an essential component in the early production of matches. When the risen Christ claims this title, he means that he is the world's light and the vanquisher of darkness.

Question: "Why is it important that Jesus has not one but two genealogies in the Gospels?"

---

[364] Genesis 4, 5, and 11

[365] The Greek god "Phosphorus" reputedly shone brightly The first phosphorous was produced in Hamburg, Germany, by Hennig Brandt in 1669.

84

COME SPIRIT BRIDE

22:17 "The **Spirit and the bride say, "Come!"** He who hears, let him say, "Come!" He who is thirsty, let him come. He who desires, let him take the water of life freely. [18] I **testify** to everyone who hears the **words of the prophecy of this book, if anyone adds to them**, may God add to him the plagues which are written in this book." (Rev. 22:17—18 emphases added).

22:17 | The risen Christ speaks to the seven churches. The Spirit and the bride appeal to him to fulfill his promise to appear quickly, followed by an invitation to those who are thirsty. John of Patmos writes several times that the **Spirit and the bride say, "Come."** Jesus may appear at any moment. He warns us to keep a lookout, for he will arrive soon!

22:17 | The Holy Spirit and the bride invite everyone **who is thirsty** to receive the gift of the water of life. We can all satisfy our deepest spiritual needs, for Jesus said, "Whoever believes in me will never be thirsty" (John 6:35). In him alone, the soul's longing for the water of life is satisfied.

22:18 | John of Patmos then says, "I **testify** to everyone who hears the words," which is his warning against changing the actual wording and meaning of the text and that it is a severe offense. This ancient book's end warning is not unique, for many other early writers finished their manuscripts similarly.

22:18 | Irenaeus[366] ended one of his writings, "I **testify** to anyone who copies this book, by our Lord Jesus Christ, and by his glorious advent, when he comes to judge the quick and the dead. Compare what you write, correct it carefully by this manuscript, write this earnest solemn appeal, and place it on your copy!" As a writer, I also feel the weight of this warning when presenting the book of Revelation so that ordinary people may better understand God's Word.

22:18 | At one time, all **books** were hand-copied by scribes, but a worker was not allowed a single mistake. If a Medieval clerk found even one error in a manuscript that may have taken months to copy, they destroyed it. Such was the importance of adhering precisely to the original text.

22:18 | Revelation issues a stern warning to anyone adding to the **words of the prophecy of this book**. God will inflict a plague on him as a punishment and take away his part in the tree of life and the holy city. Changing the meaning, distorting the text, or removing scripture will place that person under a curse. Paul writes, "but even though we, or an angel from heaven, should preach to you any "good news" other than that which we preached to you, let him be cursed" (Gal. 1:8).

22:18 | John of Patmos warns against **anyone adding to** the scriptures. It is relatively easy to change the scripture's text, even without knowing it, to suit our ideas, be politically correct, or leave out a few phrases that do not sit right with us. I would question the modern practice of the New International Version and other similar translations, adding paragraph headings that are not in the original. "Every word of God is flawless, and we must not add to them, lest he reproves us and make us liars" (Prov. 30.5—6). I would, however, applaud the same publishers for adding the Psalm introductions from the original manuscripts and the term *selah*, which in the original was probably a chorister's instruction to pause between verses.

---

[366] the second-century Christian scholar. (130-202 AD).

22:18 | The World English Bible (WEB), which you have been reading, has a similar warning at the end to not change or **add to** the text. Even though it is in the public domain, it explains, "You may copy, publish, proclaim, distribute, redistribute, sell, give away, quote, memorize, read publicly, broadcast, transmit, share, back up, post on the Internet, print, reproduce, preach, teach from, and use the World English Bible as much as you want, and others may also do so."

22:18 | The World English Bible then **adds** the compelling rider, "All we ask is that if you CHANGE the actual text of the World English Bible in any way, other than changing from American to British spelling or vice versa, you not call the result the World English Bible any more." It explains, "This is to avoid confusion, not to limit your freedom. The Holy Bible is God's Word. It belongs to God. He gave it to us freely, and we who have worked on this translation freely give it to you by dedicating it to the Public Domain." I would question any publisher who charges a writer to use a particular translation. The bible is God's word and belongs to God. However, publishers sell the ink, paper, and bindings and all the work involved to the public, and profits from these should pay to preserve each version of God's word.

22:18 | In the second century BC, seventy Jewish scholars translated the Hebrew Bible into Greek.[367] On completion, they pronounced a curse **if anyone added to them** allowed an omission or changed the written words!

22:18 | Tyrannius Rufinus,[368] in his book "On Origins," **added** a similar appeal, "In the sight of God the Father, Jesus the Son, and the Holy Spirit, anyone who read or copied this book is not to add, take away, insert, or alter anything!"

Question: "Do you believe that every Word of God is flawless, as Proverbs thirty verse five indicates?"

---

[367] The Greek version of the *Septuagint*, at the King of Egypt's order. As recorded in the Letter of Aristeas 310, 311.

[368] a monk, historian, and theologian. In his book's preface "On Origins." (340-410 AD).

85

LORD JESUS COME

22:19 "If anyone **takes away from the words** of the book of this prophecy, may God take away his part from the tree of life, and out of the holy city, which are written in this book. [20] He who testifies these things says, "**Yes, I come quickly.**" Amen! Yes, come, Lord Jesus. [21] **The grace of the Lord Jesus Christ be with all the saints. Amen.**" (Rev.22:19—21 emphases added).

22:19 | Revelation is a book of hope which comes with a warning. It alerts readers not to **take away** or tamper with its text. Some translations read "book of life" rather than the "tree of life," indicating that God will remove anyone from the Book of Life if they take something away from these words.

22:19 | In 1631 AD, the royal printer in London produced an edition of the Bible **taking away** the word "not" in verse fourteen of the seventh commandment, "You shall not commit adultery" (Ex. 20:14). The printed version read, "You shall commit adultery." The bible came to be known as the "Wicked Bible," the "Adulterers' Bible," or the "Sinners' Bible." It was produced on a press run of a thousand copies by the London Royal Printers. Omitting this single three-letter word caused an explosion in society. The Archbishop of Canterbury wrote, "experts carefully produced the printing, the Bibles especially. Grave and learned men worked with good compositors and the best correctors. The paper and fine letters are in every way the best, but now the paper is of nothing, the composers' boys and the correctors unlearned." King Charles 1[369] furiously ordered the burning of every "Wicked Bible," only a few copies escaped, and only nine are known to exist today. In 2015, Bonhams auctioned one such wicked bible in London for ninety-nine thousand dollars.

22:19 | This error in **taking away** a single word resulted in a fine in 1631 of sixty thousand dollars on Robert Barker and Martin Lewis, who had their publishers' licenses canceled. Charles and the Archbishop of Canterbury made a joint statement condemning the wicked Bible's omission. "His Majesties printers, at or about this time, had committed a scandalous mistake in our English Bibles by leaving out the word "not" in the Seventh Commandment." Being made acquainted with it by the Bishop of London, Charles gave an order calling the Printers to report to the High Commission. After hearing the evidence, the whole printing was recalled. To prevent misunderstandings in the future, should the word "not" be omitted by mistake again, the Associated Press today advises reporters to use the phrase "innocent" instead of "not guilty" in court proceedings.

22:20 | John of Patmos repeats the Spirit and the bride's call, **"Come, Lord Jesus."** This refrain is similar to the ancient Aramaic phrase *Marana tha*[370] traditionally translated as "O Lord, come," which urges his urgent return.

22:20 | **"Amen"** is Christ's final word in the book of Revelation, but how do you say "Amen?" The British pronunciation is different from the American one. The British say "aamen" and Americans pronounce it "aymen." However you say it, amen embodies wholeness and completeness. "Amen" means "so be it!" or "let it be!" It "expresses solemn ratification, makes an expression of faith, hearty approval, or an assertion."[371] Jewish, Christian, and Muslim worship use it to close off a prayer.

---

[369] (1600-1649)

[370] First recorded in 1350–1400; from Late Latin *Marana tha*, from Greek *marána thá*.

[371] *Merriam-Webster.com Dictionary*, Merriam-Webster, https://www.merriam-webster.com/dictionary/amen. Accessed 30 May. 2022

22:20 | Like **"Amen,"** at a prayer's end, the "Alpha and Omega" are the Greek alphabet's beginning and last letters, indicating that Jesus is the first in line and the last word. Jewish people use the phrase *aleph* to *tau,* meaning "start to finish completeness." For instance, they might say, "Abraham kept the whole Law from *aleph* to *tau.*" As the Amen, Jesus embraces in himself all time, for he is the "first and the last." He is the author of all things and the eternal one. An old saying states, "Since God is the beginning, he receives his power from no one. Since he is the middle, he shares his power with no one. Since he is the end, he hands over his power to no one."

22:20 | **"Yes, I am coming quickly,"** says the Lord. "Come, Lord Jesus," is the final appeal of Jesus and John of Patmos' last statement. The word "soon" indicates "at any moment." We must be ready for Jesus and always prepared for his return. As we close our studies, I am drawn back to the lovely words of the song, "I have fixed my mind,"

> "When shall the son of man appear. The trumpet sounds its blast.
> And Christ descends in glorious fire. With all the saints amassed."
> We'll rise with those. Who sleep no more. To meet Him in the air.
> When shall the son of man appear? The son of man appears."[372]

Question: "Can you say "Amen" to what you have read in this book?"

---

[372] Credits Writer(s): David Huntsinger Lyrics powered by www.musixmatch.com. sung by Reggie Smith.

FINAL WORDS

The Lord Jesus urges us, "Be faithful unto death, and I will give you the crown of life" (Rev. 2:10).

At the end of this book, I hope that you have glimpsed something of the glory that is Jesus himself. I would encourage you to make him the Lord of your life. Augustine spoke of a void in every person's heart that only God can fill. He wrote, "Thou hast made us for thyself, O Lord, and our heart is restless until it finds its rest in thee." Becoming a Christian means finding fulfillment, life, peace, and happiness in Jesus Christ.

Please pray in the quietness of your own heart or out loud,

"Dear Lord Jesus, I am sorry for my sins, and I turn from them. I ask you to come into my heart, to be my Lord and Savior. I want to become a Christian and follow in your footsteps. I will serve you, Lord Jesus, no matter what, until you come again. Amen."

If you prayed this simple prayer, I would encourage you to attend a good Bible-based church, study the Bible, begin with John's Gospel, and pray daily. Find a Christian community for worship and tell others about your Christian faith. Keep God in first place in your life."

I would love to hear from you about your walk with Jesus. Don't hesitate to contact me at Ron Meacock, 211-1111 Water Street,

Peterborough, Ontario, Canada K9H 3P7, or online at www. tellout.com.

I offer you a short prayer from Ruth Fazel to use each day alongside the Lord's Prayer,

"Send us out in the power of Your Spirit, Lord.
May our lives bring Jesus to the world,
May each thought and word, Bring glory to Your name,
Send us out in Your spirit, Lord, we pray." Amen.[373]

[373] Words and Music by Ruth Fazal Copyright 1993 Ruth Fazal, Breathe New Life In Us, 296 Glebemount Ave., Toronto, Ontario CANADA. All rights reserved. International copyright secured by CCLI and SOCAN.

ABOUT THE AUTHOR

God has blessed me over the years with the opportunity to enjoy four quite different professions. First as a civil and structural engineer, second as a Church Army Evangelist in England, third as an ordained Anglican Clergyman in Canada, and fourth as a digital internet evangelist.

The term "digital evangelist" is not new in internet terminology. It means "a person who builds a critical mass of support for a given technology." The words "evangelism and evangelist" are widely used in business circles and are borrowed from religion due to the similarity of "relaying information about a particular set of beliefs to convert the recipient." Some argue it's more about "showcasing technology's potential to lead someone to adopt it for themselves." It sounds a little like Paul telling Philemon, "I pray that as you share your faith with others, it will grip their lives too, as they see the wealth of good things in you that come from Christ Jesus" (Philem. 6).[374]

I am a Christian who uses the computer to share the Good News about Jesus Christ. One minister explained that he had evolved a new approach to witnessing. When someone asked him what he did for a living, he replied, "I answer peoples' questions." The enquirer then naturally asked, "what kind of questions?" and answered, "about the meaning of life." The questioner then

---

[374] The Living Bible. The Living Bible copyright © 1971 by Tyndale House Foundation. Used by permission of Tyndale House Publishers Inc., Carol Stream, Illinois 60188. All rights reserved.

replied, "What is the meaning of life?" So a spiritual discussion ensued.

As an engineer, I set out to bring precision and order to this task. Working on building sites and in design offices helped me understand ordinary working people and their various philosophies in life. I always encourage Christian people to devote their lives to Christ, read the Bible, and share their faith with others. This book attempts to provide a resource to do that.

Tellout has communicated the Good News to many people every day since it launched in 2000. Inquiries have come from about two hundred countries worldwide. More than half of those who visit this website use mobile devices in the US and Canada.

As people engage with God's Word, he transforms their lives through their relationship with Jesus. "There are two great days in a person's life," wrote William Barclay, "the day we were born, and the day we discover why." Paul explains this discovery, "Therefore if anyone is in Christ, he is a new creation. The old things have passed away. Behold, all things have become new." (2 Cor. 5:17).

The Rev. Cpt. Ron Meacock P. Eng.

AN EVANGELIST'S STORY

Conviction, energy, joy, and curiosity are some words that come to mind as I reflect on how I have heard the voice of The Rev. Cpt. Ron Meacock on these pages. I hope and believe that the reader also will encounter these excellent attributes in abundance. Ron does not write primarily as a biblical scholar, although at times, his recognition of the scriptural context of passages he is considering is impressive. He does not present as a historian, although those interested in the fascinating historical contexts of the seven churches of Asia Minor say, or the Roman empire in the third century will find much that Ron has to say very illuminating. He does not write as a systematic theologian, although strong themes run through his work that you will not miss. The chief is the call to faith in Christ as the accomplisher of human salvation, the way to complete eternal life, and the Lordship of Christ over all time and space. Ron writes as what he is, an evangelist.

I see this mainly because, as the CEO of Church Army U.K. and Ireland, we are in the business of calling, developing, and sending evangelists, and Ron is a Church Army evangelist. My experience of evangelists is that they are often people of conviction, energy, joy, and curiosity. They speak of what they have received and experienced, of those things they have found that bring light and fulfillment in life. Sometimes one has questions that it would be good to pursue. Some details may seem important to the reader or hearer to which the evangelist does not directly attend. That is not because the evangelist does not think they are essential, but because they are not the things that have fired his imagination and faith.

To read "Glimpse of Glory" is then something of an encounter with Ron, or more accurately, with life and ministry.

Revelation has been, for many people, as Ron observes early on, a matter of mystery, a confusing text that one normally steps around. When a passage from Revelation appears as a Sunday reading, I guess that most preachers will decide to focus on the Gospel instead.

"Glimpse of Glory" offers much that will help locate the complex imagery of Revelation in the life and experience of the early church and its broader historical and narrative context, making its complexities more accessible without diminishing their power. Moreover, it will help the reader understand how this biblical text has shaped, challenged, and envisioned the life of one who is an evangelist at heart.

The Ven. Dr. Peter B. Rouch, M.A. (Oxon) M.A. (Cantab) Ph.D.
CEO of the Church Army U.K. and Ireland,
Sheffield, ENGLAND

GOSPEL AT THE FOREFRONT

Ron has a heart for evangelism; therefore, throughout, the reader will discover the author's desire that the church of Jesus Christ acts as the church and constantly reaches out to people with the truth of the gospel. This book is a continuous reminder that the gospel must continue to be at the forefront of the thoughts and actions of every believer. He has dedicated many years of research and study to provide this detailed commentary on one of the most under-read biblical books, "The Revelation of Jesus Christ." Reading "Glimpse of Glory" will encourage greater interest in this all-important biblical book.

In the introduction, the author states, "The biblical Revelation is a rich treasure trove for those who wish to explore it." This statement is true, but the book is also a treasure trove of information for the serious Bible student and reader. I am deeply impressed with the detailed information provided. Excellent references to Christian and secular history interest the reader to dig deeper for their knowledge and understanding.

Pay special attention to the author's introduction on "Revelation's Symbolic Colors" and "Revelation's Devotional Numbers." This book is well worth reading. His unique perspective provides an excellent basis for study, discussion, and internalization.

The Rev. Dr. Lionel A. Pye, B.Sc., M.A.R., D.D.
Pastor, Campbellford Baptist Church,
Ontario, CANADA

ADDITIONAL RESOURCES

Books

"The Evangelism Handbook" Welch Publishing Company Inc. Burlington, Ontario, Canada ISBN 0 919649 84 X by Ron Meacock © 1983.

"Jesus Nine to Five" Welch Publishing Company Inc. Burlington, Ontario, Canada ISBN 1-55011-101-9 by Richard Tanner © 1989.

"The Daily Study Bible" Welch Publishing Company Inc. Burlington, Ontario, Canada ISBN 0 919532 18 7 by William Barclay © 1956.

"Free to Fail" Triangle SPCK London, England ISBN 0-281-04527-2 by Russ Parker © 1992.

"A Shepherd Looks at Psalm 23" Harper Collins Publishers New York by Philip Keller © 1970.

"Angels: God's Secret Agents" Word Publishing Denver Colorado ISBN 0849905427 by Billy Graham © 1987.

"Pilgrim's Progress" Nath Ponder Cornhill London, England by John Bunyan © 1678.

"Everyman a Bible Student" Zondervan ISBN 0310356512 by J. E. Church © 1977.

"On Genesis" New City Press ISBN 978-1-56548-175-6 by Augustine of Hippo © 1982 (c388-418)

"Matthew Henry Commentary On the Whole Bible" Hendrickson Publishers ISBN-10 1598564366 by Matthew Henry © 1706

"Systematic Theology" Banner of Truth Denver Colorado ISBN-10 9780851510569 by Louis Berkhof © 1959.

"The Works of John Owen – Volume 3" Banner of Truth Denver Colorado ISBN 9780851513928 by John Owen © 1826 (1689).

"Cruden's Complete Concordance." Alexander Cruden ISBN-10 0917006313 by Alexander Cruden © 1990

"Systematic Theology" - Augustus Hopkins Strong. Banner of Truth Denver Colorado ISBN: 9781312065833 by Augustus Hopkins Strong. © 2014

"A First Index to Early Church History" The Johnson Head ASIN B00ILAL6FE by Donald Jones. © 1911

"In Understanding be Men" InterVarsity Press ISBN 085110567X by T. C. Hammond © 1936

"Evangelism in the Early Church" William B. Eerdmans Publishing Company Grand Rapids, Michigan/ Cambridge U.K. ISBN 0-8028-2768-3 by Michael Green © 1970, 2003

Website

tellout.com
https:// tellout.com
https://www.tellout.com
https://www.tellout.com/revelation/nowindex.htm

Videos

https://www.tellout.com/book/handbook4AC.htm
youtube.com/user/telloutonline/videos

Ron's Blog

ronmeacock.blogspot.com

Printed in the United States
by Baker & Taylor Publisher Services